P9-DHK-439

 **Latin American Studies Series**

Series Editors Michael C. Meyer John D. Martz Miguel León-Portilla

The question that still engages the attention of Latin American historians is the amount of real change that occurred with the achievement of political independence from Spain in the early nineteenth century. In this collection, historians examine the social, political, and economic history of Argentina from the onset of the Bourbon Imperial reforms of 1776 through formal independence, social disorder, and dictatorship until the foundation of the modern bourgeois democratic state in 1860. Argentina in this period was particularly influential in shaping broader Latin American political and intellectual currents, so that an examination of Argentina's situation has important implications for the Latin American republics.

LIBRARY

VIRGINIA
POLYTECHNIC
INSTITUTE
AND
STATE
UNIVERSITY

Revolution and Restoration:

The Rearrangement of Power

in Argentina, 1776–1860

WITHDRAWN FROM THE VPI & SU LIBRARY COLLECTION

Edited by Mark D. Szuchman and
Jonathan C. Brown

University of Nebraska Press
Lincoln and London

Copyright © 1994 by the
University of Nebraska Press
All rights reserved
Manufactured in the United
States of America

☺ The paper in this book meets the
minimum requirements of
American National Standard for
Information Sciences—
Permanence of Paper for Printed
Library Materials,
ANSI Z39.48-1984.

Library of Congress Cataloging
in Publication Data

Revolution and restoration :
the rearrangement of power in
Argentina, 1776–1860 / edited by
Mark D. Szuchman and Jonathan C. Brown.
    p   cm. — (Latin American studies series)
Includes bibliographical references and index.
ISBN 0-8032-4228-X (alk. paper)
1. Argentina—History—1776–1810.
2. Argentina—History—War of
Independence, 1810–1817.
3. Argentina—History—1817–1860
I. Szuchman, Mark D., 1948–   .
II. Brown, Jonathan C.
(Jonathan Charles), 1942–   .
III. Series.
F2841.R48   1995
982—dc20
94–4381
CIP

Contents

Illustrations

Preface

This work originated from our desire to bring together some of the best scholars in Argentine history for a project that would examine, from a variety of perspectives, the transitional era from colony to nation. We were also interested in bringing to the fore the research of Argentines whose work does not come easily or promptly to the attention of the wider reading public of students and scholars in the United States. Four of the ten chapters are written by Argentines, some of whom work in this country, others abroad. We believe that their familiarity with a wide variety of research collections and archives in the United States, Argentina, and Europe significantly enhances the range of perspectives and informs the findings more richly.

This volume represents the patient efforts and support of many people and institutional resources. Florida International University's Latin American and Caribbean Center, Graduate Program in International Studies, and College of Arts and Sciences provided funding for manuscript preparation and translation. Patricia Jepsen worked patiently on the translations, and Elena Maubrey diligently transcribed some of the contributions. David Hall, of FIU's University Computer Center, was instrumental in disk format conversion, thereby saving us a considerable amount of effort. And to the contributors, all of whom have shown a remarkable degree of patience throughout a lengthy period of preparation, we are greatly indebted.

MDS

JCB

Revolution and Restoration

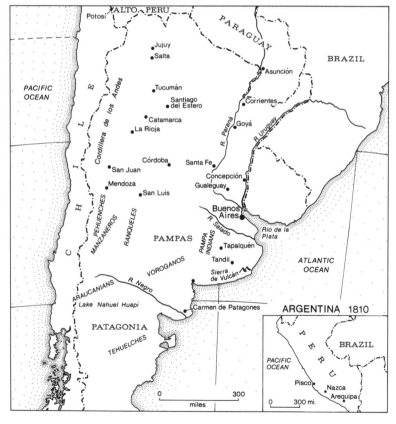

Map 1. Argentina in 1810.

Mark D. Szuchman

From Imperial Hinterland to Growth Pole: Revolution, Change, and Restoration in the Río de la Plata

Contradictions and Conflicts

It is a basic tenet of Spanish American history that the relative importance of any area during the early colonial period did not accurately predict that region's standing in the eighteenth century. In a similar fashion, a region's marginal standing in the seventeenth century failed to determine its political or economic status in the early 1800s. Argentina represents the case of a hinterland that bolted to administrative prominence and economic growth in the late colonial period. In addition, this area—which could be characterized as politically inert, where political turbulence had been virtually unknown, and where political and financial spoils had proved insufficient incentives to spawn military chieftains—stirred from its somnolence to experience a vast mobilization of men and resources in the process of liberating itself, along with half of Spanish South America, from colonial domination.

Observers of the initial stages of nationhood in Spanish America have begun to note that the apparent political peace and social stability of the colonial era represented only the thin façade of a society that underwent significant erosion in the process of achieving independence. Freedom from Spain provided the peoples of Spanish America with the opportunity to uncover long-simmering differences that would transform the hinterlands—where time had not altered the lackluster existence of a people anchored in their routinized habits—into battlegrounds. The cities, where only the bustle of market fair days had stirred normally quiet streets and plazas, became sites of popular demonstrations, parades by armed men, and scenes of military occupation. Whether or not this turmoil altered the fundamental nature of Spanish American society remains a subject for debate among historians.[1] Some point out the clear continuities in political conduct and social values: they argue that despite the change from a royal to a republican form of government, and notwithstanding the altered civic discourse, significant modifications in the substance of political transactions are not easily discerned.[2] Others have emphasized that a liberal ethos existed in the more dynamic and cosmopolitan urban centers while the conservative hinterlands were bent on retaining traditions that reflected a medieval worldview.[3]

Historians continue to be called upon to unravel the evidence and probe these contradictions, which became increasingly apparent in the transition from colony to nation. The contributors to this volume address some of the most important social, political, and economic issues that emanated from this change in political status. Moreover, they carry out their inquiries with an unusually inclusionary territorial perspective; that is, the case studies deal with widely different regions of the Río de la Plata, a rare feature in English-language treatments of a history that is usually viewed through the lens of urban Buenos Aires, the richest and most cosmopolitan zone. The traditional narrowness of the historical perspective on the Argentine experience is remarkable, since the struggles that defined much of the nineteenth century dealt with the establishment of a balance of rights and obligations between Buenos Aires and the rest of the country.[4]

This collection has four general objectives: to provide an overview both of changes and of the resistance to changes, beginning in the 1770s with the Bourbons' administrative reforms and ending with the beginnings of state consolidation in the 1860s; to analyze this historic period by emphasizing its intellectual, political, and economic contexts; to address issues from the perspectives of regions well beyond the city of Buenos Aires; and to suggest a periodization of Argentine history that offers an alternative to the conventional division, which, more simply, distinguishes the colonial from the republican eras. Some of the essays point to the continuities that underlay the region's political styles. These are seen in the forms of political patronage; in the ambivalence of the intellectual class; in the structure of landownership and production; in the attitudes toward and policies concerning Indians on the frontier; and, finally, in the political chieftains and their strategies for obtaining support both from and for their military machines.

These studies center on the period that opens with the Bourbon era of the late eighteenth century and ends with the beginning of the structuring of the state apparatus around the 1860s. Within that century, notions derived from European liberalism struggled with existing hierarchical traditions for supremacy. This contest, always discordant, often militarized, was reflected in ideas, social relations, economic organization, and political styles. The independence movement thus may appear to have been less of a radical break with the past than a manifestation of the unresolved battle between the forces of change and continuity.

Colonial Background

The territory covered by the Argentine Republic in the 1860s differed considerably from the area that in 1776 was the responsibility of the newly created Viceroyalty of the Río de la Plata. The viceroyalty spanned areas now filled by the republics of Argentina, Uruguay, Paraguay, and Bolivia. This proliferation of independent nations from a single colonial unit reflects one of the clearest consequences of the conflicts that plagued the region in the first part of the nineteenth century.

The creation of the Viceroyalty of the Río de la Plata represented the new, enlightened administrative style of the Bourbon Crown. Designed to overcome the traditionally inefficient management characteristic of the fiscal and administrative styles of the Hapsburg monarchs dating back to the early sixteenth century, the viceroyalty was planned with the aspirations and rationality of the late 1700s. Systematic in its design, utilitarian in its objectives, the viceroyalty was not merely a cosmetic act limited to reapportioning peoples from older to newer administrative domains. In the 1760s, the Spanish Bourbons had begun to export the reforms that much of western Europe had been experiencing since the start of the century. The Indies would now join this shift by undergoing a similar administrative revolution, motivated by the Crown's need for a fiscal reconquest that would fix its possessions in a closer, more dependent relationship with Spain. In sum, the colonies were to become more responsive to Spanish needs.

Lands that had been part of the Viceroyalty of Perú since the sixteenth century were carved out to form the new viceroyalty. The administrative subdivisions of the Viceroyalty of the Río de la Plata (including *audiencias*, intendancies, and subintendancies) were to provide a more rational and efficient outlet of goods to the southern Atlantic.[5] The fabulous yields from the silver mines of Potosí, located in the highlands of present-day Bolivia, would be shipped directly to Spain from the port city of Buenos Aires, designated as the viceregal capital.[6]

By the eighteenth century, the cattle ranch (the estancia) and the export of hides had become increasingly vital features of the regional economy. Ranching not only entailed differences in the forms of production relative to the silver mining found in Upper Perú; it also presented significant variations in the racial composition of laborers, in the "rhythms" or seasonal aspects of production, and in the destination of production. Significant differences also appeared in the spatial and demographic aspects related to pastoral and mining activities. Cattle ranching concentrated on the central and eastern regions of the Argentine and Uruguayan plains, the pampas. The principal demographic features of this area were sparseness and dispersal: a very small population was spread out unevenly in small pockets of settlement along the streams and tributaries of the Paraná and Uruguay Rivers northwest of the city of Buenos Aires. The same population arrangement was found along the streams that dotted the pampas due west. To the south, colonization and growth were limited by the periodic threat of raids from the Indian settlements that lay beyond the pockets of "Christians," as contemporaries defined anyone who was not Indian. The frontier stretched westward from the Atlantic some fifty to seventy miles south of Buenos Aires. This was a tenuous border, held by a threadbare line of distantly spaced forts and outposts, where both manpower and morale were questionable. Indian raids periodically sounded the alarm among a dispersed population of settlers, ranch hands, vagrants, and petty merchants (*pulperos*), who combined such tasks as dispensing cheap liquor and dry goods with trading in contraband items at their rustic stores, or *pulperías*. This was, then, a rural society characterized by simple divisions: extreme wealth was rare, and an easy subsistence lifestyle was assured by a cheap and plentiful supply of food, principally in the form of meat. Freedom of movement, facilitated by easily available horses, accounted for the limited success of social control mechanisms.

In contrast to the rural population in the northern regions of the viceroyalty, located in the higher elevations of Salta, Jujuy, and, finally, Upper Perú, workers engaged in the pastoral production of the eastern plains were not bound by the traditions of Indian communal life. Nor did workers on the pampas suffer from the rigorous labor obligations that whites had imposed on people of color since the conquest era of the sixteenth century. In fact, the racial composition of the ranch hands and rural workers, the gauchos, reflected generations of mixture among whites, Indians, and Africans. These people were imbued with a highly developed sense of individualism: even kinship ties and social solidarities were ephemeral. The busiest season, the *faena*, when cattle were slaughtered and hides were prepared for processing, signaled the gathering of gauchos, swelling the number of ranch hands well beyond the skeleton crews charged with the routine maintenance of the estancia.[7] The forging of new friendships and the renewal of old ones were conditioned by factors having little to do with affective relations: the duration of the season, the lure of higher wages on another estancia, the rumor of a posse coming to arrest a gaucho on the run, and other circumstantial events easily dissolved the bonds created in the workplace. Thus, bonds of community were largely missing from the cattle-ranching regions of the pampas; loyalty to outsiders and adherence to universal concepts of government were even more difficult to establish.

Although administrative measures were enlightened, based on rational approaches to problem solving, they were applied by bureaucrats who naively thought that they were dealing with a single people.[8] Bourbon administrators thus ignored the racial, economic, and cultural distinctions among the regions that comprised the new Viceroyalty of the Río de la Plata. The coherence of the viceroyalty was only apparent, since its territorial boundaries had been determined by calculations that were external to the conditions of the area. For example, the royal treasury was motivated by the economic benefits obtained from shipping silver from distant Upper Perú through Buenos Aires more speedily and at lower costs. In addition, the geopolitical calculation was based on concern about the Portuguese forces that occupied the contested areas between southern Brazil and the Uruguayan plains. Thus, imperial authorities tended to underestimate the heterogeneity of peoples who, sparsely spread across the Viceroyalty of the Río de la Plata, represented a patchwork of races, production techniques, vested interests, and values. Such distinctions would account for the bloody clashes that were generated by fundamentally antagonistic value systems soon after the start of the independence efforts, pitting traditionalists against innovators, regionalists against centralists, and conservatives against liberals. The colonial administration did not foresee the dilemmas: the philosophical motivations of enlightened royal officials—some of which were later reconstituted by postemancipation authorities—were transformed into attempts to impose an unrealistic commonwealth. Such attempts sacrificed the vital interests of a heterogeneous people and diverse regions for the sake of distant abstractions, such as centralized authority and standardized economic and political policies. In the Río de la Plata, these antagonisms spilled over to the field of battle when the only ingredient of unity, the Crown itself, fell victim to the Napoleonic wars.[9]

The Río de la Plata was not the region where the seeds for polarization subsequently developed in the nineteenth century. Spain itself had been undergoing similar experiences. During the Enlightenment, the mother country had to deal with ideas of renewal that had largely been imported from other regions of Europe. Such notions were absorbed into, and propagated by, only a modest portion of the Spanish population, primarily the uppermost levels of society. That is, to the extent that reforms took place, they did so from the top—indeed, from the Crown—in bureaucratic fashion and not as the result of popular or revolutionary stimuli. Thus, Spain became as divided in her people's habits of mind and value systems as did her possessions: a vocal minority of reformers, intent on refashioning society and changing fundamental attitudes, tried to be heard by a majority who resisted reformist currents.

In Spain, the majority's disposition to resist changes brought in from the outside and to maintain traditions were characteristic of a people who were rooted to the land and who abided by simple, broadly acknowledged social regulations. On the eve of the nineteenth century, the Spanish population numbered between ten and eleven million people. Of every one hundred Spaniards in the late eighteenth century, eight were nobles, six were members of the clergy, two served in the military, ten earned their livelihoods primarily in the cities as merchants and artisans, and one served as a public official. Finally, 7 percent of the Spanish population worked as servants, and fully 60 percent were peasants, who lived in virtually feudal conditions of servitude. Thus, Spain's social hierarchy was unusually top-heavy, with approximately 800,000 people claiming noble title.[10] This group, which formed a sort of social cartel, hoped to shape an aristocratic habit of mind among people beyond its own membership. But because of its determination to maintain its privileges, it became increasingly removed from an awareness of the majority's material conditions and requirements. Therefore, it is not surprising that the Spanish Crown was unable to register the very different needs of a patchwork of regions and acted instead by joining them together, under an administratively convenient construct, as the Viceroyalty of the Río de la Plata. To be sure, the society of the Río de la Plata was not weighed down by a nobility that was richer in titles than in wealth and was thus kept busy trying to maintain an untenable lifestyle. Such a combination of title and dependency was a feature of Spain's society. And yet, the political leadership that resided in the commercial metropole of Buenos Aires proved to be as ignorant and detached from the needs of the majority of Argentines as the Spanish aristocracy was to the needs of the peninsula's commoners.

Diversity in the viceroyalty's characteristics, production, racial composition, and the underpinnings of regional elites led to competition for political and economic supremacy, as the engine of wealth turned away from the silver production of the highlands of Upper Perú toward the commercial transactions of the coastal zones of the Atlantic around Buenos Aires. In the end, the city of Buenos Aires became the principal beneficiary of the Bourbon economic measures, that which reformed and liberated trade regulation while encouraging certain forms of production, especially in pastoral activities. Thus, growth in the ranching and export sectors contributed significantly to sharp increases in revenues. In only one decade, from 1791 to 1802, revenues at the port of Buenos Aires more than doubled while pastoral production—now undergoing diversification with the entry of merino sheep—increased to the point that wool became one of the most important factors in the region's output. The shipping statistics of the era reflect the expansion of trade: between 1772 and 1776—the years just prior to the implementation of the free trade policies—only thirty-five ships called at the port of

Buenos Aires while during the 1790s over sixty vessels came annually to trade. In 1802, with the expanded war in Europe and the freedom to trade with ships flying flags of neutral countries, a total of 188 ships entered the port of Buenos Aires.

The positive picture of increased revenues and trade, however, was limited in geographic reach. The wider opening afforded by free trade policies meant greater competition for those interior regions of the viceroyalty that produced cheap cloth, including areas of the center and center-north. Textile production had long been the prevalent form of artisanry in Tucumán, Catamarca, and northern Córdoba. Because the labor force in these regions was overwhelmingly female, there was virtually no other alternative for those women who contributed fundamentally to their household incomes by working with their rustic looms. The few exceptions to the general downturn in the economy of the interior, such as saddlemaking, were insufficient to counteract the new balance in favor of the coastal regions, the littoral, and, particularly, the city and hinterland of Buenos Aires.

Traditional historiography holds that the wine production of Mendoza, a region located in the western confines of the viceroyalty at the foot of the Andean range, was also adversely affected by the new policies of free trade. However, in his essay in this volume, Samuel Amaral argues that the traditional view of an economic downturn in the Andean wine-growing area is grounded on contemporary views that had little basis in reality. The wine economy enjoyed a golden age until it fell victim to the civil wars after the process of independence. Amaral argues that the grievances that were repeatedly registered after the enactment of the free trade policies and tax revisions of the Bourbon era represented the institutionalized reactions of players in an economy based on the doctrine of privileges. Competition was seen as signaling the end of assured profits; the response took the traditional form of the formal complaint and the petition seeking special dispensation, in other words, the restoration of special privileges. Yet, the empirical evidence Amaral presents indicates that the Andean area successfully adapted to greater competition. The demise of the regional economy, he argues, had little to do with the Bourbon reforms; instead, it represented the consequences of Argentine's failure to achieve a lasting political compact as well as the resultant militarization that underlay the first half of the nineteenth century. In the littoral, the central economic feature was its significant turn toward pastoral production. Cattle products—including the output of leather tanneries, meat-salting plants, and tallow processing—found a dramatically expanded market. In Buenos Aires and in the riverine areas upstream along the Paraguay and Paraná Rivers, ship works that produced small and medium-sized vessels also experienced significant growth in the late eighteenth and early nineteenth centuries.

The invigoration of the coastal economy was echoed in the region's demographic growth, especially that of the city of Buenos Aires, where the population grew from approximately 20,000 inhabitants in 1776 to over 40,000 in 1810.[11] This population increase helped to diversify the region's "human capital." The flow of immigrants, primarily from Spain, included a significant number of government bureaucrats and military officers in addition to a considerable contingent of young entrepreneurs. These merchants crossed the Atlantic Ocean in search of opportunities to capitalize on the growing importance of the Río de la Plata as a commercial entrepôt and bureaucratic center. This fresh wave of immigrants, in turn, provided local patriarchs with renewed opportunities for their daughters to marry influential peninsular (Spanish) officials, thereby reinforcing their local dominance in an age when local fortunes were put at risk by decisions made in Spain.[12] Indeed, virtually all reforms had been fashioned in Europe, and their application to the Río de la Plata environment took place within the Crown's Eurocentric concerns. Thus, the economic boom, which was driven primarily by increases in trade and services, had a detrimental effect on local artisanal and industrial production. The notion of a self-subsistent colonial possession was now out of the question: imperial planners of the eighteenth-century economy were motivated by the need to eliminate colonial competition to Spanish industry.

If Bourbon Spain now saw itself at the epicenter of its empire's economy, the designation of Buenos Aires as the viceregal capital, along with the wealth of its hinterland's soil and the access to goods from overseas, provided the city with the means to create a new center of economic and demographic power. By contrast, the cities of the interior reflected the stagnation of their own hinterlands' economies: their production and techniques, together with their greater dependence on silver production (whose profits were destined to decline), made for a very precarious economic future. Unfortunately, such differences would also assure Argentina of the antagonism among its peoples that would characterize the nation's history.

The animosity between Buenos Aires and the interior was also sustained by competing self-identities and perceptions of what comprised the *real* Argentina. Along with the increased volume of trade in goods that arrived at the port city came a flood of new political ideas and styles in the material culture. This intercourse remained concentrated in the viceregal capital; in the rest of the land, traditional habits of mind and value systems, along with time-honored techniques of production, remained in place. Thus, for example, in the region of Córdoba, located in the country's center, local merchants collected the cheap cloth woven on rustic looms by mestizas, or mixed-blooded women, in the humble shacks that dotted the hills. To the north, in regions such as Tucumán and Salta, which contained larger Indian populations, race and labor relations were intricately tied, serving as reminders of conditions in the sixteenth century, when Spanish conquerors replicated the hierarchical society of early modern Europe. Here the social hierarchy was significantly reinforced by medieval notions of privilege that accompanied the racial categorization.

Currents in Political Theory

Crucial turning points in Western political theory did not usually originate in Spanish America. Spain, too, was a marginal participant in the enthusiastic dialogue that took place among eighteenth-century political theoreticians in Europe.[13] This does not mean, however, that Spanish Americans failed to contribute their own dimensions to political theory, since the ingredient of the colonial experience surely provides a special quality not found among the great European political theoreticians. Moreover, the Spanish American elites were fully informed about the challenging new concepts of state power and citizens' rights emanating from France and England during the transitional era of the eighteenth and early nineteenth centuries. Indeed, one of the fundamental features of this age of independence was the competition for the hearts and minds of people caught between traditional and innovative views. Argentine historiography has long held that the line dividing traditionalism from progressivism was reflected in the differences between the urban centers of the interior and those of the littoral. The intellectual and legal historian José Mariluz Urquijo has pointed out that the interior's administrative districts had limited access to ideas and books authored by modern European intellectuals.[14] Perhaps what accounted for the differences in attitudes among these environments, however, had less to do with access to information than with a diminished number of interested and active supporters of modern political ideas.

The distinctions found among adherents of competing political theories were not really territorially determined; indeed, both conservatives and reformers could be found across different Argentine spaces. Some of the early revolutionary leaders, for example, had been trained by tradition-bound faculty in universities where the mode of learning and analysis was anti-Cartesian; that is, where the nature of inquiry was scholastic and prerational. Yet familiarity with enlightened European thinking and, for some, actual experiences in Europe undermined these habits of mind. Gregorio Funes, for example, a scholar from Córdoba who went on to contribute significantly to the cause of independence and the young nation, was an Argentine whose political concepts shifted as he became exposed to different intellectual currents. Having received a classical education at the prestigious University of Córdoba, a Jesuit enclave, Funes went on to study in Spain, where he expanded his awareness of European intellectuals. In contact with the literature of political innovators, such as Gaspar Melchor de Jovellanos, reformer of the Spanish legislative and judicial systems, he underwent a process of political reevaluation. Through a deeper reading of the seventeenth-century Protestant jurist Hugo Grotius, he came to understand and practice the art of balancing ideas in the face of changing conditions. Thus, he learned to set aside a propensity toward absolutist and dogmatic positions, inculcated throughout a lifetime of study in the Río de la Plata, coming to favor, instead, a pragmatism informed by pietistic sentiments.

The dramatic nature of this period caused a great deal of anxiety even among men who, like Funes, were committed to fundamental changes. Funes struggled with his own conflicts regarding the role of the state and the rights of individuals, a captive of the undercurrents of ambivalence in this era of change. His horror at what he considered to have been the political and military excesses of the revolutionaries in the early 1810s was accompanied by his unswerving commitment to independence from Spain. At the same time, his disdain for the antiquarian nature of Spanish government and social value systems—which he knew had become deeply rooted in the Argentine political terrain—was mixed with his concern over the damaging effects of the more liberal values of the English. Such values had inspired many of his revolutionary colleagues, who hoped to import English constitutional traditions to establish the basis for a liberal republic. This ambivalence is the subject of Tulio Halperín Donghi's essay on Gregorio Funes in this volume. He uses this quintessential actor in the independence movement to highlight the contradictory nature of the Enlightenment among the intellectuals of the turn of the century and to illuminate the shifting strategies the revolutionaries used to impose their vision of the new order.

But we are getting ahead of the sequence of events. By 1804, Spain had become a client state of Napoleonic France in the latter's diplomatic and military battle with Great Britain for European supremacy. Thus Spanish possessions in the Western Hemisphere were included in British strategic calculations. At the same time, Spanish American markets provided British industrialists and merchants with commercial opportunities.[15] In June 1806, a British fleet commanded by General William Beresford anchored off the coast and landed marines a short distance from the city of Buenos Aires. Viceroy Rafael de Sobremonte, after a weak attempt at resistance, fled with his retinue to the interior city of Córdoba, leaving the viceregal capital in the hands of the invaders and thus assuring his political doom as a traitor and incompetent administrator. To those who dreamed of political independence, this was a golden opportunity for a clean and bloodless secession from Spain. Protected by British military supremacy, they figured their chances for freedom were assured. Men like Juan José Castelli and Juan Martín de Pueyrredón, however, were soon disappointed by British attitudes, which were more consistent with those of an occupying army than with liberators. Within a few weeks, local resistance was organized under the leadership of Santiago de Liniers, a navy captain of French origin who served as the military coordinator of the militia forces. After heated skirmishes in the streets of the capital, the British forces surrendered on August 12. If the reconquest of the city did not lead immediately to a government independent from Spanish rule, it signaled the end of the political status quo. The military and political forces of the city now sensed the headiness that accompanied the defeat of the most powerful nation without the aid of Spain. They succeeded in transferring executive authority from Sobremonte to Liniers. The conventional date marking the start of the Argentine independence movement is 1810, but, in fact, popular will had made itself felt four years earlier.

The defeat of the British also signaled the start of a process that affected the militia in significant ways. The militia was not a novel institution in Spanish America. As Lyman Johnson's contribution to this collection demonstrates, the Bourbons had developed it into a considerable source of both revenue and expenditure, capable of affecting income level as its comprehensive needs drove up wages, especially those of skilled artisans. Yet the significant development lay in the process of increased militarization, a novelty in a region where the presence of a regular army was virtually unknown and where membership in the citizens' militia was more social than political. New militia companies were formed, each with its own uniforms and officers. Some were organized on the basis of the members' birthplace, giving a hint of the battles that ultimately would take place between armies defending their regional interests.[16]

A second British invasion of Buenos Aires, launched in June 1807, suffered the same fate as the first. This time, the invaders were defeated by the local militia with the aid of the citizenry. *Porteños* fought house to house, employing all weapons at their disposal, while *porteñas* poured boiling water and oil on English marines unaccustomed to urban guerrilla tactics. Once again, Liniers was the man of the hour. His military fortune, however, did not translate into political acumen, and he soon became a pawn of the many newly formed political circles. These groups were differentiated by their leaders' views regarding political action now that the region was, effectively, autonomous. Thus, the public environment of Buenos Aires consisted of opposites sharing the political spectrum: at one end, everyone felt the enthusiasm and confidence that accompanied two military victories over the British; at the other, the cabals' intrigues added to the considerable political tension.

This volume focuses on the erosion and subsequent restoration of order in Argentina. This is one of the most important historical problematics in the region, if not in virtually all of Spanish America. The historical tendency for the problem of political disorder to appear and reappear under a variety of political leaders, in diverse areas, and under different economic circumstances has long been problematic for historians, who are still searching for adequate ways to explain this complex social and political phenomenon. We know that divisionism plagued the nation throughout much of the nineteenth century, following independence. Yet dissension was already apparent prior to the revolution, when atomistic tendencies made consensus among political figures difficult to achieve. We can see the development of political rifts during the prerevolutionary era, between the first British invasion in 1806 and the town meeting, the *cabildo abierto*, on May 25, 1810, at which a revolutionary junta formally declared its intention to act as the governing body during the political vacuum left by the French invasion of Spain. The political "parties," as these pressure groups were called, represented very different views regarding the forms that the new government should take: some were looking for the opportunities to make a clean break with Spain; others hoped that, after an interregnum, the Spanish Crown, once restored to the power it lost to the Napoleonic invaders, would be thoroughly reformed into a liberal and constitutional monarchy; still others pursued a course of action designed to retain the status quo at all costs.[17] Each of these pressure groups had its own vision of what was needed, both in the long-term context of what shape to give the new nation and in the immediate sense of outmaneuvering the opposition.

Among the political figures who worked to achieve independence, men such as Manuel Belgrano and Domingo French had hoped for help from an external power, perhaps England. Eventually, however, they came to the realization that independence would be achieved exclusively by their own efforts. This group tended to avoid doctrinaire views; they were pragmatists who showed flexibility in strategies and recruitment to their cause. They hoped to achieve their goals without igniting a radical revolution. The members of this group, which Argentine historiography has labeled the Pro-Independence Party, shared a conservative view of political leadership. Fearing that their countrymen were not yet ready to embark upon the course of a liberal republic, they had originally preferred the safer political structure of a constitutional monarchy. Over time, some of them moved reluctantly in the direction of a republic. At first glance, their principal objective might be seen as being relatively narrow and nationalistic, yet they signaled a significant social change: the end of the Spaniards' hegemony in public office, and their replacement by Creoles.

In opposition to the pro-independence sector of political society were the men who formed the so-called Republican Party. Composed mostly of Spaniards, but with some notable exceptions, including Mariano Moreno, they came to dominate the *cabildo* of Buenos Aires following the victories over the English invaders. These men espoused a socially conservative view of public office (the continued domination of Spaniards in such posts) and a plan of leadership that would exclude Creoles from the highest positions in finance, commerce, and society. At the same time, they felt that Spanish authorities in the region had failed to understand local conditions and could not be counted on to defend their legitimate interests. They proposed a republican system of government that would begin with the formation of juntas through which they would channel their plans: only a total break from Spain would enable them to reconstitute the socially conservative regime that they felt had been lost in the wake of the reforms that accompanied the Enlightenment.

Neither of these two political pressure groups, however, held the needed instruments of force to make their views prevail. Such tools of persuasion were in the hands of the militia commanders, who now served as political brokers and enforcers. But enforcers of which ideological plan? These men were pragmatists who had little in common with the theoreticians of the center, the left, or the right; they shared a personal rather than a systemic vision of power. Thus, they tended to cohere around little else than their military offices and attendant privileges, but always within a nationalistic, antiroyalist context. In sum, they signified the beginnings of a framework of authority that rested fundamentally on militaristic traditions and a vision of power determined by personal considerations. By the time of the *cabildo abierto* of May 25, 1810, the pro-independence and republican groups had joined in a common front, which, while postponing the ideological rifts that would separate some of these men, would win the day with the support of the militia commanders.

Finally, Spanish bureaucrats in the viceroyalty formed their own pressure group. Transparently self-serving and holding the most limited political vision, they sought their preservation through the status quo, even if it meant serving a Spain under Napoleonic domination. Because of their rigidity and their limited ability to forge allegiances beyond their group and their families, they were the first to be swept away by the initial winds of revolution. Among the Spaniards who viewed the political debates as leading to the endangerment of their privileges were the many merchants who had been attracted to the Río de la Plata at the start of the free trade practices. Their fortunes were at risk: if the financial ties on which commerce with Spain depended were to be severed, so would the local bonds of clientelism that had maintained their hegemony.

In the end, the voices of change, however much they differed from each other in theoretical perspectives and operational plans, outnumbered and outmaneuvered the established authorities. The sum of the groups opposed to the continuation of the existing system was overwhelming: the traditional structure came tumbling down during the *cabildo abierto* of May 25, 1810, when viceregal authority was halted and power in Buenos Aires was transferred to a junta composed of Creoles. These men based their action not on a modern political concept but on a medieval tradition that, instead of being displaced, became invigorated by the progressive theories of the late eighteenth century: in the absence of effective and just rule by the king, power must be returned to the people.

Insofar as the change in the governing structure represented a step unilaterally taken by locally prominent men, the actions of the *cabildo abierto* signified the start of a political revolution. To the extent that the members of the revolutionary junta and many of its future appointees were Argentines, the changes were also social, but only in the restricted context of ethnicity, having virtually no implications for a distribution of wealth. This was, in sum, the initial stage in the forging of a new order, conceived as the Argentine state. Yet agreement over the meaning of this new order eluded both the revolutionary leaders and the generation that followed. Their subsequent struggles would continue to echo the sounds of discord, making the molding of the Argentine nation an elusive goal until the second half of the nineteenth century. Only then did elites begin to form a cohesive group with common goals and a national program of development.

For the first fifty years, however, the proposed versions of legitimacy were subjected to heated debate. Soon after 1810, the political discourse—which earlier had taken the form of treatises, parlor discussions, and arguments among individuals huddled closely, fearful of being suspected of plotting against the Crown—gave way to the terrible physicality of violence. Ultimately, in the absence of consensus over the nature and extent of the state's power, over whether or not to retain some or all of the traditional lines and sources of authority, over the extent of individual freedom, and over the right of provincial self-determination, the old Viceroyalty of the Río de la Plata underwent a schismatic process that severed the ties of important territories, including today's republics of Paraguay, Uruguay, and Bolivia. The search for a postindependence formula of governance turned a revolutionary spirit of independence, rooted in the liberal ideals of the French Revolution, into a protracted civil war. In the process, the basis for authority shifted dramatically from the figure groomed in civics and politics to the man strong in military assets. Thus, the ideals of political legitimacy held by the precursors of the revolution—who, depending on their ideological preferences, saw the possibilities of establishing either a conservative constitutional monarchy or a liberal democratic republic—were transformed into a more practical-minded authoritarianism based on personal rule, aimed at reestablishing a sense of order lost after 1810.

The Reverberations of Independence

The legitimacy claimed by the men of Buenos Aires to establish their leadership over the rest of the land was tested soon after the junta was formed on May 25, 1810. For the next decade, Buenos Aires tried, first by diplomacy and then by military means, to convince the rest of Argentina to join under its leadership. Much was at stake, including the notion of how to create a balance of power between the central authorities and the provinces, the location of the capital city, the taxation privileges of the provincial and local authorities, the geographic distribution of revenues collected at the ports, the safeguarding of the regional elites' privileges, the functions of the Catholic Church, and much more. These problems were not exclusively Argentine: many new nations, including the United States, underwent periods of experimentation with the nature and extent of central authority.

It soon became clear that the majority of provinces would not submit to any centralized authority emanating from Buenos Aires. For the next ten years, war was waged between unitarians and federalists; alliances were held together by evanescent personal agreements among regional caudillos, or military strongmen. It was a decade in which the vital human and productive forces were sapped of their strength; men and even young boys, especially the poor and the defenseless, came under the dreaded *leva*, or forced military conscription. Cattle and horses, which had been plentiful in the prerevolutionary age, were depleted to the point that they formed the basis of reparation payments.

The military campaigns between the unitarians and the federalists did not establish a clear winner until February 1820, when the apparent might of Buenos Aires came to an end. Allied forces from the littoral provinces of Santa Fe, Corrientes, and Entre Ríos defeated the last of the armies sent out by a city whose plans for centralist rule—with itself at the head—lay in ruins. The victorious forces did not capitalize on their success, however. Once the most important terms had been met—the payment of reparations in the form of 25,000 head of cattle, the abrogation of a constitution that had been drafted in 1819 with virtually no support from the other provinces, and the nominal renunciation of unitarianism by the leaders of Buenos Aires—the federalist caudillos simply went home.

But a tremendous amount of damage had been left in the wake of the wars. Just as important, the traditional lines of rights and obligations, which had governed social and political relations, had been radically changed. This was especially true of the countryside, where gauchos were recruited for the military troops and where estancieros had significant property investments. Ricardo Salvatore, an economist whose work focuses on the history of labor relations on the landed estates of the Uruguayan region of the Río de la Plata, here identifies the consequences of militarization in the rural areas, including the breakdown of social discipline. The effects of uprooting laborers, the arming of large segments of the population, and the social banditry that emanated from the erosion of traditional authority contributed to an increased sense of autonomy in the littoral. This process had long-term effects as the traditions of paternalism broke down, giving way to increasing tensions between the authorities, who supported the estancieros, and rural laborers, who were no longer as easily controlled.

In the deeper recesses of the northeast, by contrast, merchants and estancieros in the province of Corrientes managed to retain authority in the wake of the disorder that plagued other provinces.

In his essay, Thomas Whigham describes the consequences of the transition from colonialism to independence for the Correntino economy and society. The Argentine northeast depended on the flow of goods traded along a complex river system controlled by Buenos Aires. The political relations of the two areas were determined in great part by the regional considerations of commerce and freedom of trade. In provinces such as Corrientes and Misiones, therefore, merchants and producers formed a common front of interests. While areas such as Buenos Aires, Santa Fe, and Uruguay experienced a significant loss of social control, Whigham observes that anarchy was avoided in the rustic regions of the northeast; the northeastern economy maintained itself along lines of production and commerce that readjusted to the new conditions, even if the volume of trade remained modest.

For its part, the city of Buenos Aires accepted defeat and made the best of the imposed peace by turning its attention to what it had done best in the viceregal days: tend to its own lands, where cattle and their by-products permitted a dramatic economic growth. Peace, in effect, had liberated Buenos Aires to conduct its productive capabilities while exploiting its coastal advantages, thereby enabling it to become the dominant importer and exporter in what was now nothing more than an aggregation of provinces without any central guidance. Most of the provinces, in fact, continued to undergo slow economic decline and cultural isolation.

By contrast, Buenos Aires enjoyed an unprecedented growth in its material well-being during most of the 1820s. Moreover, it extended its territorial domain. Freed from waging war on its neighbors, the military forces of Buenos Aires turned their attention to battling the Indians on the southern frontiers of the province, extending its effective possession of the land. This expansion added significantly to the productive capabilities of the estancia, or cattle ranch. This unit of production became larger, as new lands were given to men who were already among the most prominent estancieros; therefore, the addition of available land was not successfully converted into an opportunity to expand the number of landowners. The campaign against Indians on the southern frontier provided opportunities for whites and Indians to interact; here they found a fluid region where law and lawlessness melded into a rapacious existence. The essay by Kristine Jones in this volume traces the historical and social dynamics of an Argentine region that generally has not attracted the attention of historians. Her study of the government's strategies of conquest coupled with containment and the Indians' reactions to such strategies depicts both the precariousness of life on the frontier and the limited options available to its residents.

Limits and Dynamics of the New Order

Nearly every figure of authority in postrevolutionary Argentina found it difficult to reestablish order, especially in the countryside. By the 1820s, Argentina had become a divided nation: suspicion underlay political relations among regional leaders, and the lines of authority that had been established during the colonial era disappeared forever without providing an alternative code of hierarchical relationships. New norms would not be established until after 1860, when a much stronger state became capable of dominating regional caudillos by combining greater military resources with techniques of political cooptation. Until then, however, rebellions were reported with regularity in the city's newspapers; so, too, were notices of marauders, bandits, and renegades prowling the hinterlands, sometimes being chased by posses.

One man opened his letter to a Buenos Aires newspaper in 1821 by calling for "Order! order!" His words typified the sentiments of a people bemoaning the sense of constant insecurity. He went on to complain about a regimen of regulatory and policy discontinuities, about the seemingly constant violation of the laws, and about the vanished sense of deference to established authority. Most upsetting was the sense that the government had failed to establish respect for its own policies.[18] These pleas characterized part of Argentina's collective conscience in the first half of the nineteenth century. The public's desire for order can be gleaned from a variety of sources, including personal memoirs, police reports, school authorities' notes on related issues of compliance and discipline, and the Buenos Aires popular press.[19]

Order and disorder served political purposes, of course, but by the 1820s we note a considerable overlap between liberals and conservatives concerning the need to deal heavily with disturbances lest they explode into rebellions. Consensus was building about the need for aggressive enforcement of the law; indeed, new laws and ordinances used the language of repression while the authorities' enforcement of those laws became more aggressive. Political and military turmoil had circumscribed more narrowly what was considered legal and orderly demeanor. Order stood for political stability; for efficient policing of the city's streets; for administrative processes based on consistent criteria; for equitable implementation of regulations; for a public morality that reflected the period's prevailing values, including those of the lower classes and the bourgeoisie; for an educational regimen that would produce men and women able to create a stable community; for a criminal justice system that mitigated the unstable political conditions. These expectations, among others, were shared by friends and foes of government alike, by people frustrated by the continued burdens of past practices, and by those who feared the forces of change. Juan Manuel de Rosas, Argentina's most notable caudillo, draped himself with the mantle of order by assuming the honorific responsibility of "restoring the laws"—of reestablishing order out of the chaos that had resulted (according to his supporters) from mismanagement at the hands of the generation of liberals, centralists, and the Europeanized gentry. Equally meaningful was the term "Party of Order," under whose banner gathered the same group of political figures that Rosas had accused of mismanagement. Among them were Manuel J. García, the liberal minister of finance, and Bernardino Rivadavia, provincial minister of government and ideological guide of the liberals during the 1820s.[20]

Two chapters of this volume are dedicated to the historical problematic of establishing social control in an age of military mobilization. Pilar González Bernaldo's contribution provides a description of the Buenos Aires countryside at the time that gaucho forces rose in support of Juan Manuel de Rosas at the end of 1828. Her analysis concentrates on the modes of information exchange in the pampas, where isolation, horsemanship, and loyalties to individual leaders helped to determine the motivations and directions of collective action. She points to the existence of different "spaces" of production and attendant social relations spread throughout the pampas. She discusses how political solidarities, the conditions that motivated allegiances, were shaped by factors such as the nature of the settlement (of long vintage and relatively close to the city of Buenos Aires, or more recent and closer to the Indian frontier); the nature of production (whether based on agriculture or ranching); the dimensions of the productive unit and the attendant labor relations (large estancias or family-sized units); and the territory of indigenous communities. Her conclusions deal with the complexity of rural sedition, which she sees as a consequence of the heterogeneous matrix of pampas society and the evolving nature of rural production.

Kevin Kelly's chapter deals with Juan Manuel de Rosas, the preeminent caudillo who dominated all aspects of life in Argentina from the 1820s until 1852. With Rosas's ascension to power in Buenos Aires, the old liberal order was forever changed. The immediate consequence of the *rosista* victory over the *porteño* liberals was, of course, the elimination of the latter from power, and, consequently, the beginning of a slow process of weaving together the informal ties among the provinces. In the longer term, however, liberalism itself would also become subject to sharp criticism from members of the younger generation of liberals who had grown up under the new authoritarianism. They observed that Rosas's power rested on the rabble that brought him to victory in the first place. In the new liberals' estimation, the popular classes were a fundamental source of the disorder that had plagued the country since its separation from Spain. Yet, as Kelly's contribution on *rosista* populism demonstrates, Rosas appealed to a wide cross section of Argentine society. He notes that the key to Rosas's stability was his success in keeping gauchos, estancieros, Indians, rural and urban dwellers, and Catholic conservatives in a balanced array of widespread internal support. In the end, only external forces could be gathered in sufficient strength to drive him from power in 1852. Only then did the new liberal order, wiser but much less democratic than its predecessor of 1810, begin the slow process of legal codification and state building that would culminate in a fully formed oligarchy by the 1870s. By then, Argentina had embarked on a process of legal codification and political institutionalization based on a complex matrix of political patronage inside the country and an intimate linkage with England in matters of trade and credit.

The chapter by Jonathan Brown, which deals with the rural economy and society of Buenos Aires, charts the changing political calculations and strategies of the elites and authorities from the late colonial era through the tumult of the postindependence age, past the authoritarian interregnum of Juan Manuel de Rosas, and into the age of greater estancia efficiency during the second half of the nineteenth century. Brown analyzes the changing nature of labor relations and forms of production, concentrating on the Buenos Aires rural area. In the process, he draws comparisons with a stagnating interior, whose forms of production and social exchange remained relatively unchanged by the dynamic market forces that would increasingly link Buenos Aires to the export sector.

As Argentine authorities of the second half of the nineteenth century succeeded in restoring a sense of political order and territorial coherence, they were still left with the problems occasioned by the divisions between one region of dynamic growth and another that increasingly lagged behind. The relative differences between the two were most visible at the level of economic performance. Yet behind the arithmetic of growth and stagnation runs an underlying current of disharmony that is not easily measurable. The restoration of the social order took place on the terms of the modernizing elites. Their interests were not motivated by, nor did they coincide with, the needs of the diverse peoples who inhabited the still-disparate regions that comprised Argentina. As the elites restored order, some of the conditions that had been problematic a century earlier were merely aggravated.

Notes

1. George Reid Andrews, "Spanish American Independence: A Structural Analysis," *Latin American Perspectives* 12 (Winter 1985): 105–32; Tulio Halperín Donghi, "Revolutionary Militarization in Buenos Aires, 1806–1815," *Past and Present* 40 (July 1968): 84–107; Mark D. Szuchman, "Disorder and Social Control in Buenos Aires, 1810–1860," *Journal of Interdisciplinary History* 15 (Summer 1984): 83–110; David Bushnell, "The Independence of Spanish South America," in *The Independence of Latin America*, ed. Leslie Bethell (Cambridge, 1987), 93–154.

2. Ronald C. Newton, "On 'Functional Groups,' 'Fragmentation,' and 'Pluralism' in Spanish American Political Society," *Hispanic American Historical Review* 50 (February 1970): 1–29; John L. Phelan, "Authority and Flexibility in the Spanish Imperial Bureaucracy," *Administrative Science Quarterly* 5 (June 1960): 47–65; John Lynch, *The Spanish American Revolutions, 1808–1826* (New York, 1973); Claudio Véliz, *The Centralist Tradition of Latin America* (Princeton, N.J., 1980).

3. José Luis Romero, "La ciudad latinoamericana y los movimientos políticos," in *La urbanización en América Latina*, ed. Jorge Hardoy and Carlos Tobar (Buenos Aires, 1969), 297–310; Romero, *Latinoamérica: Las ciudades y las ideas* (Buenos Aires, 1976).

4. The historical literature dealing with the struggles that took place over the course of the nineteenth century in Argentina is too extensive to mention here, but some of the more important treatments include Jonathan C.

Brown, *A Socioeconomic History of Argentina, 1776–1860* (Cambridge, 1979); Bushnell, *Reform and Reaction in the Platine Provinces, 1810–1852* (Gainesville, Fla., 1983); Andrés Carretero, *Los Anchorena: Política y negocios en el siglo XIX* (Buenos Aires, 1970); H. S. Ferns, *Britain and Argentina in the Nineteenth Century* (London: 1960); Halperín Donghi, *Revolución y guerra. Formación de una élite dirigente en la Argentina criolla* (Buenos Aires, 1972); Lynch, *Argentine Dictator: Juan Manuel de Rosas, 1829–1852* (New York, 1981); Thomas F. McGann, *Argentina, the Divided Land* (New York, 1966); David Rock, *Argentina, 1516–1982: From Spanish Colonization to the Falklands War* (Berkeley, Calif., 1985); Romero, *A History of Argentine Political Thought* (Stanford, Calif., 1963); James R. Scobie, *Argentina: A City and a Nation* (New York, 1971); Nicolas Shumway, *The Invention of Argentina* (Berkeley and Los Angeles, 1991); Richard W. Slatta, *Gauchos and the Vanishing Frontier* (Lincoln, Nebr., 1983); and Szuchman, *Order, Family, and Community in Buenos Aires, 1810–1860* (Stanford, Calif., 1988).

5. One of the earliest, and still valuable, treatments of the Bourbons' intendancy system is Lynch, *Spanish Colonial Administration, 1782–1810: The Intendant System in the Viceroyalty of the Río de la Plata* (London, 1958).

6. Recent studies of the local effects of the Potosí silver traffic on the local economy of Buenos Aires and the viceroyalty in general can be found in Herbert S. Klein, "Structure and Profitability of Royal Finance in the Viceroyalty of the Río de la Plata in 1790," *Hispanic American Historical Review* 53 (August 1973): 440–69; and Samuel Amaral, "Public Expenditure Financing in the Colonial Treasury: An Analysis of the Real Caja de Buenos Aires Accounts, 1789–1791," *Hispanic American Historical Review* 64 (May 1984): 287–95.

7. Jorge Gelman, "New Perspectives on an Old Problem and the Same Source: The Gaucho and the Rural History of the Colonial Río de la Plata," *Hispanic American Historical Review* 69 (November 1989): 715–31; Slatta, *Gauchos and the Vanishing Frontier*; Ricardo Rodríguez Molas, *Historia social del gaucho* (Buenos Aires, 1968).

8. For a case of Bourbon shortsightedness about regional administration, but with an emphasis on the newly created Viceroyalty of New Granada, see Anthony McFarlane, "The 'Rebellion of the Barrios': Urban Insurrection in Bourbon Quito," *Hispanic American Historical Review* 69, no. 2 (May 1989): 283–330.

9. For an overview of the premises and difficulties of the Spanish Enlightenment, see Luis Sánchez Agesta, *El pensamiento político del despotismo ilustrado* (Madrid, 1953).

10. Massimo Livi-Bacci, "Fertility and Population Growth in Spain in the Eighteenth and Nineteenth Centuries," *Daedalus* 97 (Spring 1968): 533.

11. Several demographic sources are available to account for the population shifts in the preindependence era, including Ernesto J. A. Maeder, *Evolución demográfica argentina de 1810 a 1869* (Buenos Aires, 1969), and Facultad de Filosofía y Letras, *Documentos para la historia argentina. Padrones de la ciudad y campaña de Buenos Aires* (Buenos Aires, 1919).

12. Susan M. Socolow, "Marriage, Birth, and Inheritance: The Merchants of Eighteenth-Century Buenos Aires," *Hispanic American Historical Review* 60, no. 3 (August 1980): 387–406; and Socolow, "Acceptable Partners: Marriage Choice in Colonial Argentina, 1778–1810," in *Sexuality and Marriage in Colonial Latin America*, ed. Asunción Lavrin (Lincoln, Nebr., 1989), 209–51.

13. For a general overview of the political currents that played into the movement for independence in Buenos Aires, see Halperín Donghi, *Tradición política española e ideología revolucionaria de Mayo* (Buenos Aires, 1985).

14. José M. Mariluz Urquijo, "Perfil del Virreinato entre dos siglos," *Boletín de la Academia Nacional de Historia* 32 (1961): 89.

15. For the best treatment of British interests in the Río de la Plata during the Napoleonic period, see Ferns, *Britain and Argentina in the Nineteenth Century*, esp. 17–51.

16. Halperín Donghi, "Revolutionary Militarization in Buenos Aires."

17. Carlos Alberto Floria and César A. García Belsunce, *Historia de los argentinos*, 2 vols. (Buenos Aires, 1971), 1:222–27.

18. *El Argos de Buenos Ayres*, 11 August 1821.

19. The historical literature on the problems of disorder and social control has proliferated in recent years. See Brown, "The Bondage of Old Habits in Nineteenth-Century Argentina," *Latin American Research Review* 21, no. 2 (1986): 3–32; Silvio Duncan Baretta and John Markoff, "Civilization and Barbarism: Cattle Frontiers in Latin America," *Comparative Studies in Society and History* 20 (October 1978): 587–620; Natalio R. Botana, *La tradición republicana. Alberdi, Sarmiento y las ideas políticas de su tiempo* (Buenos Aires, 1984); Slatta and Karla Robinson, "Continuities in Crime and Punishment: Buenos Aires, 1820–50," in *The Problem of Order in Changing Societies: Essays on Crime and Policing in Argentina and Uruguay, 1750–1940*, ed. Lyman L. Johnson (Albuquerque, 1990), 19–46; Manuel Augusto Montes de Oca, *Represión* (Buenos Aires, 1888); John Charles Chasteen, "Trouble between Men and Women: Machismo on Nineteenth-Century Estancias," in *The Middle Period in Latin America: Values and Attitudes in the 17th–19th Centuries*, ed. Szuchman (Boulder, Colo., 1989), 123–40; and Szuchman, *Order, Family, and Community*. On education and social control, see Szuchman, "Childhood Education and Politics in Nineteenth-Century Argentina: The Case of Buenos Aires," *Hispanic American Histor-*

ical Review 70 (February 1990): 109–38, and Juan P. Ramos in Consejo Nacional de Educación, *Historia de la instrucción primaria en la República Argentina, 1810–1910* (Buenos Aires, 1910).

20. Luis Alberto Romero, *La feliz experiencia, 1820–1824* (Buenos Aires, 1976), 194–95.

Lyman L. Johnson

The Military as Catalyst of Change in Late Colonial Buenos Aires

Among students of Argentine history, the military events of 1806–7 and 1809–10 are well known. During the first of these two periods, a small force of less than two thousand British troops took Buenos Aires, a city of more than forty thousand inhabitants, at the cost of one dead and twelve wounded. When news of the approaching British force was brought to Viceroy Marqués Rafael de Sobremonte, he fled, taking the treasury with him. After his flight only a perfunctory resistance was offered by the local military establishment. Although the victorious British general, William Carr Beresford, held the city for only six weeks before surrendering to a mixed force of local militiamen and Spanish regulars, his initial success mortally wounded the political and military structures of the colonial order.[1]

The defeat and surrender of Beresford and his entire force, together with the successful defense of Buenos Aires against a second attack in 1807 by a much larger military and naval force commanded by Major General George Whitelock, would produce a new regional political leadership recruited from the Creole officer corps of a profoundly transformed military establishment. This new military elite, in turn, would push aside the last vestiges of the colonial political order in two nearly bloodless military confrontations.[2] The first was the failed *golpe* of Spanish loyalists led by the Basque merchant Martín de Alzaga in 1809. The second was the successful *golpe* of May 22–25, 1810, which removed the Spanish viceroy, Baltasar Hidalgo de Cisneros, and established the first revolutionary junta headed by the Creole militia colonel Cornelio Saavedra.[3]

Colonial Military Reforms

The humiliating defeat of local regular army and militia forces by General Beresford in 1806 was particularly surprising given the Spanish colonial government's efforts after 1776 to strengthen the city's fortifications and modernize its garrison. Efforts in the eighteenth century by the Spanish government to improve imperial defense were provoked by substantial British and French challenges to both the political and commerical integrity of the empire. Imperial military planners viewed the Río de la Plata region as particularly vulnerable to attack. A Portuguese colony, Colônia, was already established on the eastern shore of the estuary and served as focal point for contraband trade. Here British manufactured goods were profitably exchanged for the silver of Potosí. Even Buenos Aires, the largest and most important Spanish city on the Atlantic coast, was a notorious center for contraband trade with Spain's European rivals.[4]

In order to end both the hemorrhage of silver through contraband trade and the territorial threat posed by Portugal and Great Britain, Spain created the Viceroyalty of Río de la Plata and made Buenos Aires its capital in 1776.[5] This political act coincided with the sending of a large military expedition to expel the Portuguese from Colônia and to secure from Spain what eventually became Uruguay. Although most of this expeditionary force was sent home once its primary mission was accomplished, Buenos Aires was assigned a vastly expanded garrison. In addition, efforts were undertaken by Spanish military authorities to enlarge and improve the urban militia forces.[6] By contrast, expenditures to upgrade local fortifications remained minimal. The city itself was in effect unfortified, although there was an adobe and brick fortress located on the city's central plaza. Because of the shallowness of the Río de la Plata, there was no need to protect the city against naval bombardment. Therefore, the location of the fortress near the riverfront meant that nearly the whole city could be occupied before its batteries could play a role in defense. In fact, the only significant effort to defend the fort against a hostile force was by the British under Beresford, and they were quickly forced to surrender.

In many ways, this increased investment in the defense of Buenos Aires after 1776 was typical in scale and character to military reforms undertaken throughout the empire by Spain's Bourbon dynasty. Historians of the Spanish colonial military establishment during this period have attempted to discover a relationship between the expanded military establishment of the late colonial period and the dominant political role played by Spanish American military officers after independence.[7] The three most comprehensive studies of the late colonial military conclude, however, that there was no direct link between the militarism of the early national period and the military reforms of the Bourbon period. Christian I. Archer argues convincingly for the Mexican case that it was the fiscal and military pressures of the decade after 1810, not colonial military policies, that led to the Praetorian political culture so visible after 1821.[8] Although there are no studies of the Río de la Plata region that provide similar levels of comprehensiveness and reliability, it is generally asserted in the existing literature that the Bourbon military reforms had no direct effect on the later development of military politics in Argentina. For Buenos Aires in particular and Argentina in general, historians assume that it was the two British invasions and the forced development of a new native-born officer corps that set the stage for the Argentine military's political vocation after independence.[9] Does this mean that the military reforms and enormous military expenditures of the late colonial period in Argentina had no effect on the subsequent development of the independent nation?

In this essay, I will examine the effort to reorganize and improve the region's military establishment during the period 1776–1810. I am particularly interested in looking for cyclical and secular trends in military expenditures. Changes in the character of military expenditures will also be discussed. The political and social effects of the two British invasions will then be outlined. Finally, I will attempt to test for a relationship between military expenditures and the performance of the regional economy.

It was obvious to Spanish planners in 1776 that the Platine region's underdeveloped grazing and agricultural resources could not support the enormous costs of viceregal administration and defense. As a result, Alto Perú (modern Bolivia) with its important mining sector was detached from the Viceroyalty of Perú and included in the new Viceroyalty of Río de la Plata. The fundamental fiscal dependence of the new viceregal government on the mining region of Alto Perú is clearly demonstrated by the importance of transfers from these treasuries to Buenos Aires relative to other sources of government revenue. Recent publications on colonial fiscal admin-

Table 2.1

Estimated Transfers from Subordinate Treasuries to the Treasury at Buenos Aires, 1781–1810

Years	Transferred from Other Treasuries (pesos)	Total Income Buenos Aires Treasury (pesos)	Transfer as % of Total Income
1781–85	5,534,642	8,073,014	68.6
1786–90	7,414,596	11,122,446	66.7
1791–95	8,149,169	11,113,906	73.3
1796–1800	7,452,644	10,231,514	72.8
1801–5	4,475,874	12,442,654	36.0
1806–10	4,880,104	12,268,635	39.8

Sources: John J. TePaske and Herbert S. Klein, *The Royal Treasuries of the Spanish Empire in America*, vol. 3, *Chile and the Río de la Plata* (Durham, N.C., 1982); and Tulio Halperín Donghi, *Guerra y finanzas en los orígenes del estado argentino, 1791–1850* (Buenos Aires, 1982).

Note: Because neither TePaske and Klein nor Halperín present data for the entire viceregal period, both sources were used to create the longest possible series for this table. Halperín Donghi presents his data in five-year aggregates beginning in 1791. TePaske and Klein begin their series for transfers from other treasuries to the Buenos Aires Treasury in 1781. Their series for transfers is broken by missing data for 1804–6. They also present no data for intertreasury transfers in 1810. This table, therefore, was constructed using Halperín Donghi's five-year aggregates for 1791–1810 and five-year aggregates based on the TePaske and Klein data for 1781–90. When I compared these two sets of figures for the overlapping period 1791–1810, I discovered that the total treasury income provided by TePaske and Klein was approximately 45 percent greater than that provided by Halperín Donghi. Both sources, however, were in near agreement on the total amount transferred to Buenos Aires by subordinate treasuries. In an effort to provide a more consistent estimate of the proportional significance of these transfers, therefore, I deflated the TePaske and Klein figures for total treasury revenue by 40 percent. This procedure appears warranted because of the discovery by Samuel Amaral that substantial amounts were moved from one treasury line to another, thereby tending to inflate the gross totals.

istration suggest that an average of approximately 60 percent of the income of the Buenos Aires Treasury came from this source alone.[10] Table 2.1 summarizes the available evidence for these annual transfers. Although the percentage of total government income derived from this source fluctuated, the clear connection between the loss of these funds after 1810 and the fiscal emergency that faced the first governments of the independence period should be clear.[11]

Any analysis of governmental expenditures during the late colonial period, then, must begin with the recognition of the fundamental structural weakness of the economy of Buenos Aires and its hinterland. Although the grazing industry provided most of the region's exports, most livestock and, therefore, most of the production of hides, tallow, and other items were located on the eastern shore of the river (modern Uruguay), not in the pampean region south of Buenos Aires. Agriculture was little developed in the province of Buenos Aires, and at the end of the colonial period the region was not dependably self-sufficient in the production of staples. After 1809, when the port was opened to neutral ships, the city became partially dependent on wheat imports from the United States. The city's artisan manufacturers were extremely limited in number and in scale of production. Contemporary census records indicate that only in the baking industry and in a small number of foundries were average work forces of ten employees found. There was an extremely low level of investment in machinery and plant, and very few of the city's artisans owned productive assets other than hand tools.[12] As a result, silver produced in Alto Perú, rather than local rural production or manufactures, remained the city's most valuable export throughout the colonial period.

Because the elaborate administrative and military apparatus of the new viceregal government was imposed on this narrowly developed and fragile regional economy, long-term and cyclical changes in the size and character of governmental expenditure tended to play a central role in determining local economic performance.[13] Table 2.2 provides a summary of annual expenditures by the viceregal government. The percentage of total expenditures devoted to military ends is displayed in column three. Expenditures for nonmilitary purposes rose dramatically with the creation of the Viceroyalty of Río de la Plata in 1776, then trended downward to 1786. The next decade was characterized by high levels of expenditures for civilian purposes, with expenditures in 1790 and 1797 nearly reach-

Table 2.2
Total Governmental Expenditure and Total Military Expenditure,
1773–1809

Year	Total Military Expenditures (in pesos of 8 reales)	All Other Expenditures (in pesos of 8 reales)	Percent Military
1773	4,323	847,699	0.5
1774	58,134	925,241	5.9
1775	12,950	1,169,645	1.1
1776	55,053	n.a.	3.0
1777	83,683	2,178,400	3.7
1778	61,535	3,763,156	1.6
1779	223,337	1,905,647	10.5
1780	78,640	1,820,777	4.1
1781	189,795	2,510,529	7.0
1782	108,030	1,242,523	8.0
1783	323,707	1,975,203	14.0
1784	462,862	2,100,156	18.1
1785	814,493	1,341,624	37.8
1786	751,204	1,002,956	42.8
1787	977,709	1,557,112	38.6
1788	794,510	1,712,381	31.7
1789	1,015,190	2,099,390	32.6
1790	1,249,286	3,059,898	29.0
1791	672,571	2,777,292	19.5
1792	868,163	1,993,187	30.3
1793	237,663	2,924,006	7.5
1794	706,965	2,448,747	22.4
1795	988,335	2,516,027	30.0
1796	895,323	1,544,022	36.7
1797	1,623,691	3,565,815	31.3
1798	1,290,398	1,137,163	53.2
1799	883,127	1,019,557	46.4
1800	1,020,524	1,614,945	38.7
1801	1,645,856	965,921	63.0
1802	1,079,857	3,303,317	24.6
1803	994,171	873,572	53.2
1804	1,569,749	2,296,623	40.6
1805	2,011,085	1,737,808	53.6
1806	n.a.	n.a.	n.a.
1807	1,042,354	1,324,924	44.0
1808	710,203	1,333,640	34.7
1809	842,001	2,477,887	25.4

Source: John J. TePaske and Herbert S. Klein, *The Royal Treasuries of the Spanish Empire in America*, vol. 3, *Chile and the Río de la Plata* (Durham, N.C., 1982). Reprinted courtesy of Duke University Press.

ing the level established in the peak year of 1778. During the final twelve years of the colonial period, however, civilian spending accounted for 60 percent of total expenditures in only four instances.

The military expenditure column found in Table 2.2 is an aggregate measure created from a diverse mix of defense-related budget lines. Included in this category are military salaries, payments to retired and disabled personnel, rations, uniforms and other supplies, construction and improvement of fortifications, frontier defense, local expenses for the Spanish fleet, and the supply and maintenance of coastal patrol vessels. Throughout this period, salaries claimed the largest share of the military budget. Total military expenditures averaged less than 10 percent of all government spending through 1782. This pattern was then altered, and total military spending moved steadily upwards to 1790. After a brief decline in the mid-1790s, the high levels of 1789 and 1790 were reestablished and maintained until the end of the colonial era. As of 1798, civilian spending tended to decline as a percentage of total expenditures, although 1802 and 1809 provide significant exceptions.

Spain's participation in the European wars of the late eighteenth and early nineteenth centuries clearly determined the cyclical character of military expenditures in this South Atlantic colony. Until 1806, military spending fluctuated cyclically in absolute terms and as a percentage of total expenditures in response to war or the threat of war. Disbursements among the various categories of military expenditure, however, remained unchanged. After the two British invasions, the essential character of military spending was altered. Between 1776 and 1805, most of the variation in the percentage of total governmental expenditure for the military was caused by changes in the level of capital expenditures for fortifications and naval infrastructure.[14] Expenditures for food, clothing, blankets, and other supplies also had a cyclical character, although the annual variation was much less important. Throughout the empire, the effort to improve fortifications proved to be an enormous drain on fiscal resources. In Cartagena, San Juan, and Havana, for example, major efforts to construct fortifications were constantly over budget and behind schedule.[15] For the Viceroyalty of Río de la Plata, improvements in fortifications in Montevideo and the construction of small frontier forts in the Banda Oriental and southern pampas had a similar fiscal impact, although at lower levels of actual expenditures. Wages, too, posed a major challenge (see Table 2.3).

Table 2.3
Percentage of Colonial Budget for Military and Civilian Salaries

	1791–95	1796–1800	1801–5	1806–10
Military Salaries	23.9	25.7	24.1	50.4
Civilian Salaries	7.9	8.4	6.8	8.3

Source: Tulio Halperín Donghi, *Guerra y finanzas en los orígenes del estado argentino, 1791–1850* (Buenos Aires, 1982).

The Military as a Social Institution

After 1805, the military threat posed by Great Britain to Buenos Aires and the other estuary ports transformed this pattern of expenditure. The military salary bill quickly grew to an insupportable level as resources were drained away from traditional commitments. During the final five years of the colonial era, salaries paid to military personnel reached an annual average of 35 percent of total government expenditures.[16] Expenditures for public administration, on the other hand, remained nearly unchanged throughout the viceregal period. The fiscal and judicial bureaucracies absorbed the lion's share of these administrative expenditures. Although there was some increase in absolute terms, civilian salaries never accounted for more than 10 percent of total government spending. The Spanish colonial administration successfully controlled the bureaucratic salary bill by using unpaid supernumeraries who served in the hope that they would be placed in future vacancies by a grateful Crown. Although salaries for colonial officials did increase during the late eighteenth century, the rate of increase appears to have been considerably less than that experienced in the private sector.

However, these aggregate figures for public sector salaries tend to disguise important differences in the levels of compensation received by civilian and military personnel in late colonial Buenos Aires. Both officer and enlisted ranks of the Spanish Army were underpaid relative to comparable sectors on the civilian side of the government. Lieutenants and captains received salaries similar to those paid to master artisans hired by the colonial authorities to supervise public works projects rather than to those paid middle-level bureaucrats.[17] Even the upper levels of the regular officer corps were paid significantly less than civilian employees with similar backgrounds and responsibilities. The colonel in command of the city's main infantry regiment, El Fijo, received an annual salary of 2,400 pesos and the commander of the region's most important mounted unit, the Dragons, received 2,880 pesos per year.[18] These salaries were generous indeed if compared with the annual wages of unskilled workers or journeymen and master artisans in the private sector. However, when compared with the salaries received at comparable levels in the administrative and judicial bureaucracy, the level of remuneration received by military officers was comprehensively inferior. The *contador mayor* of the Real Hacienda, for example, was paid an annual salary of 4,134 pesos. The four *ministros* of the Real Hacienda each earned 8,042 pesos per year. In the judicial bureaucracy, the *regente* of the Real Audiencia, had an annual salary of 6,000 pesos while the four senior *oidores* each received 4,920 pesos.[19]

In addition to low salary levels, officers in the Spanish military experienced fewer opportunities for promotion. Relative to the fairly limited number of individuals competing for promotions in the civilian bureaucracy, the comparatively large number of junior officers in the city's regular army units had few real prospects for advancement. As a result, very few sons of the urban elite—export/import merchants or career bureaucrats—entered the professional military. Even among the families of the less-well-off urban professional class, few sons were encouraged to seek careers in the military. Indeed, it is worth noting that marriages between professional army officers, even those of the highest rank, and the daughters of these wealthy and powerful groups were also extremely rare. Merchants were slightly more likely than other elite groups to arrange marriages between their daughters and military officers, since this type of alliance could produce enhanced access to procurement contracts or a means to pursue contraband trade. Yet, despite these potential advantages, few examples can be found of marriages between officers and the daughters of merchants.[20] Elite groups generally directed their sons toward more lucrative careers in the administrative and judicial bureaucracies or in commerce. This pattern was somewhat altered in rural areas. Before independence, the ranchers and farmers of the region, even those who controlled vast expanses of land, were generally poorer and politically less influential than the urban commercial and bureaucratic classes. Faced by more limited prospects, a larger proportion of the sons of this class entered the professional military. Members of the rural landowning class were also more enthusiastic in pursuing leadership positions in the reorganized and expanded militia, particularly in cavalry units. Nevertheless, only an extremely small percentage of all military officers in Buenos Aires were connected through family or marriage with the local elite.

Where, then, were local recruits for the officer corps of the regular army found? Generally, regular army officers entered the military as unpaid cadets—military apprentices in effect. Throughout Spain's American empire, these young men were overwhelmingly the sons, grandsons, and nephews of active-duty officers in line units. As a result, the upper levels of the officer corps were staffed by Spaniards who had entered the military in the metropolis while the most junior ranks were filled with their Creole sons, grandsons, and nephews. With the passage of time, this recruitment mechanism tended to create a closed, castelike, command structure. General José de San Martín, the hero of the independence struggle, is perhaps the best-known example of this career pattern.[21]

Throughout the viceregal period, severe recruitment problems depleted the enlisted ranks of the Spanish garrison. Salaries for enlisted men were low, approximately 75 percent of the average wage paid to unskilled workers in Buenos Aires, and were seldom paid on time.[22] As early in the history of the viceroyalty as 1776, the colonial government fell behind in paying the wages of enlisted men in the local garrison. Evidence suggests that at no time during the colonial period were full wages ever paid to enlisted men in Buenos Aires. For most of the late colonial period, enlisted men received only 50 percent of their statutory wages. Uniforms were irregularly provided in a three- or four-year cycle and, as a result, enlisted men were forced to choose between buying most of their clothing or appearing in rags. In Buenos Aires, even boots, blankets, and food rations were commonly provided by the soldiers themselves.[23]

The unpredictable character of military wage payments and the imposed cost of supplementing their inadequate provisions forced most enlisted men to seek part-time employment in the local economy. Many off-duty soldiers served as laborers in public works projects such as street paving and the building of a new seawall. Others were able to use skills learned earlier in civilian life to find part-time employment in the artisan shops of sawmills and brickyards. Particularly during the 1770s and early 1780s, the competition of enlisted men helped to depress wages in a broad range of lesser-skilled occupations in the private sector. It was only the significant expansion of Atlantic trade and a local building boom after 1786 that pushed up civilian wages to the levels found before the creation of a large military presence in 1776.[24]

Most enlisted men in the Buenos Aires garrison married local women. Many married soldiers lived away from the barracks and were able to escape close supervision and regular discipline. Desertion and absenteeism were chronic problems, and all the local line units were severely undermanned. Losses from desertion, death, and incapacitating illnesses were a continuing problem for the Spanish Army in America. The regular army infantry unit garrisoned in Buenos Aires maintained an expensive and largely ineffective recruiting station in La Coruña, Spain.[25] However, at no time did new recruits from Spain meet local manpower needs. Local recruitment seldom made up for this shortfall, and, as a result, the judicial system was regularly used to compel vagrants and criminals to join the army.[26] In some cases, convicted criminals petitioned the courts for the opportunity to gain an early release from prison by volunteering for military service.[27]

All of these recruitment vehicles worked overtime to reduce the percentage of European Spaniards in the regular army garrison of the city. By 1790, the regular army infantry and cavalry regiments of Buenos Aires both had Creole majorities. This problem was not unique to the city of Buenos Aires or to the Viceroyalty of Río de la Plata. A recent analysis of Spanish military records found that more than 80 percent of Spain's colonial garrison force was American-born.[28]

In 1802, the local commander reported that the regular infantry regiment of Buenos Aires was at 40 percent of full strength. Still the hemorrhage continued. Four years later, the *cabildo* announced that this same regiment had been reduced even further—from two thousand to fewer than two hundred active soldiers.[29] Although royal officials attempted to explain this deteriorating military situation to Spanish authorities by alleging that the cultural and racial inferiority of the local population promoted desertion, it is clear that the problem was structural in origin.[30] The irregular pay and low salaries received by the enlisted ranks could not effectively compete with the high wages and excellent employment prospects found in the expanding private sector of Buenos Aires.[31]

From Defense to *Golpe*

Most historians who have written about the two British invasions have concentrated their attention on Viceroy Sobremonte's inadequacy as a political and military leader. It is clear, however, that despite Sobremonte's failure as a political leader and military commander, little could have been done to defend Buenos Aires given the limited military assets on hand in 1806. One example can demonstrate the general lack of military preparedness. When the alarm was sounded following the British landing on June 25, only 129 of the 724 officers and men of the militia unit, the Voluntarios de Caballería, turned out to confront the invaders. There were only fourteen operative carbines to hand out to this small group. When the remaining men were issued pistols, it was soon discovered that most of the pistols lacked flints and that only four rounds per man of the correct ammunition was on hand.[32] After a perfunctory exchange of fire with Beresford's small invasion force, the Voluntarios de Caballería and other quickly mustered regular and militia units retired from the battlefield, leaving Buenos Aires undefended.

In the wake of this military disaster, both Creole and peninsular members of the local elite quickly moved to create a new, larger, better-trained, more disciplined military establishment. The immediate objective was to retake the city from the British. Once this task was accomplished, recruitment, reorganization, and rearming continued uninterrupted to the end of the colonial period. The second British invasion gave added urgency to these efforts. The relative cost of this expanded and reorganized military force is indicated in Table 2.2. Regular units, the El Fijo infantry regiment for example, were brought to full strength by raising enlisted salaries to statutory level and paying them on time, and by successfully manipulating the patriotic enthusiasms occasioned by the British occupation. While enlistments had remained at low levels and desertion rates had trended upward until 1806, the British invasions produced a dramatic alteration in local attitudes toward the military. Across the city's social landscape, military vocations were discovered by the thousands.

The militia establishment was completely reorganized by the city government and royal authorities, and a large number of new units were created. These new units were funded either directly by elite patrons—the Húsares de Pueyrredón, for example, were sponsored by a wealthy merchant—or by the municipal government, which created both new artillery and cavalry units. Ironically, both these private patrons of the military and the membership of the *cabildo* itself were overwhelmingly drawn from the city's merchant elite, a class that had always kept the military at arm's length. The individual most active in the period between the first British invasion and the failed *golpe* of 1809 was Martín de Alzaga, an important member of the *cabildo* and a wealthy Basque merchant.[33]

The enormous expenses associated with these new military commitments severely distorted both municipal and viceregal finances. Traditional obligations were ignored or dramatically reduced by both layers of government, and new taxes were imposed. Many of these new taxes were extremely unpopular consumption taxes, despite warnings from local exporters that the local economy would suffer.[34] Neither the anger of the urban pleb nor the protests of more privileged classes slowed this process. Voluntary contributions were also an important source of funds for meeting these extraordinary expenses, but after the defeat of the second invasion each new appeal to the elite for funds met greater resistance and produced less revenue.[35] As a result, "voluntary" contributions were more overtly coerced.

Prior to the second invasion, more than eight hundred Creole militiamen were activated and put on full salary, bringing the city's number of paid military to nearly four thousand. As Halperín Donghi points out, full-time employment in the militia or regular army proved particularly attractive to the native-born working class. Spanish immigrants of the popular class, whether artisans or clerks, tended to earn higher wages and had better prospects for advancement than did native-born workers with like skills. A similar pattern was present among merchants and professionals as well. Generally speaking, then, Spanish immigrants attempted to escape full-time military service while the native-born sought it. By 1810, nearly 30 percent of the city's adult male population was mobilized.[36] Once this military employment bubble was created by the special circumstances of the British threat of 1806–7, both the *cabildo* and the viceregal administration found it difficult to puncture without provoking dangerous social unrest. The fear of promoting political action by demobilized militia units, therefore, worked to slow efforts to reduce the cost of defending the city once the British threat dissipated.

These changes in military organization and recruitment had important political and social consequences for the city and the region. For the first time in the city's history, members of elite groups, both peninsular Spaniards and Creoles, actively sought leadership positions in the military—marking the end of the traditional social isolation of the military caste. Older members of the largely Spanish-born export/import merchant class provided funds for the recruitment, provisioning, and training of new militia units, but they attempted to avoid direct participation in the military.[37] Some of their sons and many Creole merchants, on the other hand, became officers, often prominent officers, in the city's expanded militia. Cornelio Saavedra, a merchant, and Juan Martín de Pueyrredón, the son of a merchant, would play important roles in the military events that marked the end of Spanish rule and the beginnings of independent government. Both men became prominent "military" leaders only in the aftermath of the British invasions. Martín de Alzaga held no military position but had been one of the heroes of the city during the second British invasion and used his influence with Spanish-born militia leaders to lead a military *golpe* in 1809.

Despite these important cases where members of the merchant elite moved into leadership positions in the military, however, the primary role played by this class during the emergency was financial. They organized and heavily supported a succession of patriotic subscriptions to help pay for new military expenses. They also accepted the imposition of new taxes on imports and exports and in some cases provided loans. Their enthusiasm diminished perceptibly, however, when it became obvious that these monetary demands would continue, despite the fact that Britain had become Spain's ally following Napoleon's invasion of the peninsula.

Not only was this new military establishment much more expensive than the traditional garrison it replaced, but it was also organizationally distinct. Many of the new militia units created after 1806 permitted some direct participation by enlisted men in the selection of officers. This type of popular participation was virtually unknown in colonial society. Even working-class organizations, like guilds and lay brotherhoods, excluded most of their members from direct participation in elections. Once this form of popular involvement in military government produced its first controversial results, the representatives of the elite moved quickly to guide the process toward the selection of officers drawn from or acceptable to the elite.[38] After the threat of invasion passed, the procedure was simply dropped in favor of direct appointment by responsible representatives of the political establishment. Some militia units, on the other hand, were completely the creatures of wealthy patrons. In these units, enlisted men were directly dependent on their commanding officers in ways that tended to subvert their loyalty to the state, or even to the military command structure.

Both popular participation and patronage promoted clientage and a personalist style of military leadership in the militia. Once planted, these seeds would quickly produce their first fruit on January 1, 1809, when the alcalde Martín de Alzaga led two militia units in an unsuccessful attempt to force Viceroy Santiago de Liniers from power. The viceroy survived because he was supported by a larger military force commanded by the Creole merchant Colonel Cornelio Saavedra. One and a half years later, Saavedra used these same forces to overthrow Liniers's successor, Baltasar Cisneros. In effect, these two events were military plebiscites that demonstrated the precocious political development of the new military leadership called into being by the two British invasions.

The political consequences of the two invasions and the creation of a new military establishment, then, are fairly clear: the development of a politically confident and militarily experienced Creole officer corps with close ties to the regional elite; the creation of a militarized Creole proletariat that was increasingly dependent on military salaries and tied to the new officer corps as clients; and, finally, the demoralization and marginalization of the region's professional officer corps and civilian bureaucracy. Here it is worth noting that the professional officer corps and the troops of the Spanish garrison played almost no role in the watershed events of 1809 and 1810. The increasing ascendancy of the military after 1806 did not develop directly out of the military reorganization undertaken by imperial reformers after 1776.

Military Expenditures and the Economy

The traditional social basis for the recruitment of both officers and enlisted men, the political and social isolation of officers from the elite groups, and the chronic structural problems of undermanning and poor discipline kept the old military order on the margin of political events throughout the era of Bourbon military reforms

(1713–95). In Buenos Aires, the dramatic increases in military expenditures that occurred during the Bourbon reforms did not serve as midwife for the later development of caudillismo and military interventionism during the independence and early national periods. Increased levels of military spending, efforts to reorganize and expand the local militia before 1806, and the presence of substantial regular army and naval garrisons all failed to alter significantly either the constellation of political forces in colonial Buenos Aires or the character of urban class relations. It was the special circumstances caused by the two British invasions that undermined the prestige and authority of the Bourbon military establishment and created, in turn, a new self-conscious Creole military leadership that essentially operated as the nation's first political party.

Although the city had grown rapidly after 1776, the urban economy continued to rely on transfers from Alto Perú and on its protected position as regional entrepôt. Even before the first British invasion, that silver-mining economy had been weakened in the wake of the disruptive Túpac Amaru Rebellion and the interruptions in Atlantic trade occasioned by the European wars. Under such circumstances, efforts to adequately fund the bloated payrolls associated with the city's new form of politicized defense decisions led over time to an increasingly confiscatory fiscal policy. In the end, this would drive a wedge between the new cadre of politicians in uniform and the urban elite groups that had initially spawned them.[39]

As a result, it is not convincing to portray the nation's early military politicians as class representatives or as agents of an emerging Creole economic elite. They were corporate, not class, representatives. The military emergency of 1806–7 and its long ebb tide forced an increase in total military expenditures and, proportionally, an even larger expansion of the military wage bill. The expanded military budget was imposed as traditional revenues were declining. This fiscal extravagance negatively affected both urban and rural elites as new taxes and voluntary contributions were put in place and was only sustained after 1808 by the coercive muscle of a self-interested military establishment.

The economic consequences of Bourbon military policy before 1806 are more difficult to discover, but the evidence suggests that military expenditures played an important role in determining the future course of this region's history. The figures presented in Table 2.2 indicate that after 1785 total military expenditures by the viceregal government fluctuated cyclically in the 700,000 peso to 2,000,000 peso range with a generally higher level of spending in the period 1797–1807. The military crisis of 1806–7 did not structurally alter the levels of military spending by the viceregal government. In fact, there was a slight decline in total spending by the viceregal government after 1807. In terms of military expenditures by the local agents of the Spanish imperial government, then, the period 1806–10 retained the essential character and scale of the program of military modernization begun in the 1780s.

Actual military expenditures in Buenos Aires during these years, however, increased well beyond the levels indicated in the aggregate data presented in Table 2.2. Nontraditional fiscal sources (private gifts, patriotic loans, disbursements from Crown monopolies, church funds, and, especially, municipal funds) were devoted in increasing amounts to military salaries and supplies after 1806. Although we cannot state precisely the total amount of money drawn from these sources, a rough estimate is possible. Between 1806 and 1810 more than 500,000 pesos in military expenditures were paid for by new taxes and patriotic contributions. From 1806 to 1810, the combined amounts drawn from these two sources were equal to 20 percent of average annual military spending by the colonial government.[40] Nearly half of the total 240,948 pesos donated for military purposes during this period was given in 1806. As time passed, the flagging enthusiasm of the citizenry can be measured by its diminished generosity. By 1809, only 6,450 pesos were donated to the military. This shortfall in voluntary support was made up by enhanced tax collection. New taxes and higher rates on existing taxes were imposed. By targeting economic sectors with significant Spanish participation or with large numbers of foreign nationals, the *cabildo* succeeded in limiting the political backlash generated by these new impositions. In the long run, however, the economic consequences of the fiscal policies of 1806–10 diminished savings and reduced levels of investment in both commerce and manufacturing production. The increased military wage bill, therefore, tended to promote consumption over production and punish the city relative to the countryside.

It appears indisputable that the period 1806–10 was a significant watershed in the political and economic development of both the city of Buenos Aires and of Argentina. At the center of the constellation of political and economic forces that eventually drove this region from Spain's colonial orbit was the creation of a large, politicized, and expensive military force led by Creole officers. The importance of this period and these men has been uniformly agreed upon since the nineteenth century, although debate still persists over the role ideology, class conflict, and changes in the international market played in these events. At the same time, relatively little effort has been devoted to exploring the connections between changes in the scale and character of public sector taxing and spending in the late colonial period and the form of export-led development that appeared after 1810 and persisted well into the twentieth century.

With the publication of Royal Treasury data for the Río de la Plata, we can begin to explore new areas of colonial history. Based on these records, Table 2.2 presents government spending for military and nonmilitary purposes. Unfortunately, students of colonial Argentina lack estimates for almost all other traditional measures of economic activity. There are no estimates for gross domestic product, for total wealth, or for the distribution of wealth. Given the nearly universal belief that the export sector played the leading role in directing economic growth in this region, it is perhaps more surprising that scholars have not yet published a reliable estimate of import and export volume for the period 1776–1810. The fragmentary data now available suggests that the total value of exports from Buenos Aires (primarily silver, hides, and other animal products) were uniformly lower than the local expenditures of the colonial government.[41] This has led some historians to suggest that these legal forms of commerce were only one part, albeit the biggest part, of the region's total import/export trade. Contraband trade, in fact, retained some importance in the regional economy after 1776, despite greatly expanded legal commerce and efforts by the colonial government to patrol the estuary. However, even if the average value of contraband exports reached 10 percent of legal exports, the total value of exports would not have exceeded average annual public sector spending during this period. It would appear, then, that alterations in government spending and tax policies must have played some role in determining the character and performance of the regional economy during the late colonial and early national periods.

In order to test this assumption, I created a number of time series variables for the period 1773–1810. These were used to supplement the two categories of governmental expenditure drawn from the Cartas Cuentas data published by John TePaske and Herbert Klein. Using contemporary account books from hospitals, monastic establishments, and governmental agencies, I developed three measures of broad economic performance: a consumer price index and two wage series. The price index is a weighted measure of articles of common consumption.[42] Included in this index are wheat, beans, sugar, chickpeas, salted beef, rice, yerba, wine, and average monthly rental costs for a one-room apartment.[43] Both imported (sugar, rice, yerba, and wine) and domestically produced goods are represented in this index. The commodities in this basket of common consumption goods were weighted to reflect actual consumption patterns of workers employed by ecclesiastical and governmental authorities.

The two wage series were prepared as part of a larger study of material conditions experienced by the colonial working class. The first is for unskilled wages. Unskilled workers, *peones*, constituted the largest sector of the urban working class of colonial Buenos Aires. Although the term *peón* was used contemporaneously to identify a diverse mix of skill and experience levels, there was actually an extremely narrow range of wages paid to these men. Skilled workers, artisans and trained mechanics generally received higher wages and enjoyed greater employment security. In order to create an index of skilled wages, I determined the occupational distribution of all skilled urban workers in colonial census records and then weighted the wage data accordingly. The occupations included are carpenters, bricklayers, iron workers, ship carpenters, caulkers, sail makers, arms makers and sailors.[44]

I then used stepwise multiple regression analysis to test the effect of consumer prices, military expenditures, and all other governmental expenditures on unskilled wages in Buenos Aires. The results indicate that changes in government expenditures for purposes other than defense had no measurable effect on the wages paid to unskilled workers. Both consumer prices and military expenditures, however, were strongly associated with changes in unskilled wages during the viceregal period.[45] Together these two variables explain 63 percent of the variation in unskilled wages. Although it appears that consumer prices were marginally more important in affecting changes in unskilled wages, changes in the level of military spending during the late colonial period also played a key role in determining this part of the local wage bill. The association found here between prices and wages was expected; the association between wages and military spending has not been suggested previously in the literature on colonial Argentina.

When the stepwise multiple regression was repeated with the index of skilled wages as the dependent variable, military expenditures proved to be more important than consumer prices in determining the variation in wage levels. The combined effect of all three independent variables—military spending, consumer prices, and other governmental expenditures—produced an R^2 of .50. Although this is substantially down from the .63 found for unskilled wages, it still indicates a strong association. This reduced effect should be expected given the more institutionalized, and hence less market-influenced, nature of skilled wages in preindustrial societies. The artisan trades of colonial Buenos Aires were never formally organized in guilds, but a well-established wage custom existed in the city for different trades and different skill levels in each trade. This custom informed and therefore tended to limit wage negotiations between individual workers and employers. As a result, changes in market conditions were always less immediately reflected in skilled than unskilled wages in colonial Buenos Aires.

It appears, then, that changes in the levels of military spending played a role in bidding up the cost of both skilled and unskilled labor in colonial Buenos Aires. Of these two categories, skilled wages were more powerfully affected by military spending. Although not observed or understood at the time, this process exacerbated already high local wage levels and worked to limit investment in labor-intensive sectors of both urban and rural economies.

Buenos Aires and its hinterland were particularly vulnerable to these pressures because the region suffered from a nearly permanent labor shortage. From the 1780s to the end of the colonial period, immigration and natural population increase failed to keep pace with a growing demand for labor. The creation of the viceroyalty in 1776 promoted a long-term building boom to house the greatly enlarged colonial bureaucracies and an expanding urban population. As a result, the construction trades experienced steady demand through the late colonial period. The expanded corps of officers and civilian bureaucrats, along with their households, added thousands of relatively affluent consumers to the city's growing number of well-off commercial and professional families. Demand for the goods and services of artisans and lesser-skilled workers remained high well into the national period, and the cost of labor consequently pushed steadily upward.

Throughout this period, wages were particularly high in both construction and port-related trades. Transportation trades experienced comparatively high wages as well. Even in the countryside, labor demands and therefore wages increased as ranchers and farmers moved to expand their output to meet greater urban demands for their products. These growing labor demands in the city and countryside could not be adequately met by the local population. Immigration from Europe and from Brazil was encouraged indirectly by colonial authorities, but remained at low levels. The African slave trade was freed from traditional legal constraints after 1790, and thousands of slaves entered the Buenos Aires labor market, providing some relief in manufacturing, service, and agriculture. Still, the government received complaints about labor shortages. Periodically, convicts, vagrants, and Indian laborers temporarily dispatched from Paraguay were all compelled by the *cabildo* to work during harvests. The benefits from these sources, however, were minimal. Although some amelioration was gained through population growth by 1800, the problem of limited labor supply remained well into the national period.

Contemporary commentators and some modern economic historians have noted the pattern of high wages in the region, especially in the countryside.[46] Since no consistent and reliable wage series was available before now, this argument was largely sustained by anecdote. The wage series used in this analysis not only confirms the existence of high wages in the countryside, but also demonstrates a pattern of relatively high wages across a broad range of skilled and lesser skilled occupations in the city itself. In Buenos Aires and its hinterland, the cost of labor inhibited both agricultural and manufacturing development. Given the cost of labor, the growth of the grazing sector, with its low inputs, is easily understood.

The findings presented here suggest that the Bourbon-era military reforms of the period before 1806 played an important role in determining the economic and political trajectory of independent Argentina. This connection has been masked by the unique character of the dramatic political events of 1806–10. Throughout the late colonial period there was a close association between the level of military expenditure and both urban and rural wages. This association began in the era characterized by capital expenditures for fortifications and naval infrastructure and remained constant after 1806 during the period of bloated military salary disbursements. Generally speaking, expenditures on behalf of the colonial military bid up the cost of skilled labor when artisans were attracted away from the private sector to work on large capital projects in the 1780s and 1790s. Then, after the British invasions, the creation of a large full-time military force bid up the cost of unskilled labor. As early as 1801, the military salary bill reached 70 percent of the value of all exports from the city. By 1807–9, these costs pushed beyond the value of all nonbullion exports from the region.[47]

The structural weakness present in the regional economy prior to 1776 persisted into the national period. Problems associated with low population density, inadequate infrastructure and high transportation costs, poor productivity and low levels of investment in producer goods, and scarcity of investment capital were ameliorated somewhat in the viceregal period, but continued to hold back the economy. These obstacles to development were disguised during much of the period after 1776 by the actions of the colonial state. Transfers from Potosí and other interior treasuries subsidized a dramatic expansion in public sector spending that promoted local consumption and generated significant new commercial activity. Direct and indirect demand by the public sector for goods and labor pushed wages and salaries upward. Yet the region's apparent prosperity was only tenuously connected to improved productivity.

Increased military expenditures contributed to the structural weakness of the economy by forcing up local labor costs and reducing the price competitiveness of the region's agriculture and manufacturing. With the collapse of the larger colonial economic and political systems after 1810, the state no longer had the resources to sustain its traditional redistributive role. In less than a decade this would lead to the economic and political ascendancy of the grazing sector.

Notes

1. An excellent firsthand account of the first invasion is found in the account of one of Beresford's officers, Alexander Gillespie, *Gleanings and Remarks collected during many months residence at Buenos Ayres and within the upper country* (Leeds, 1819).

2. The best short analysis of this important period is provided by Tulio Halperín Donghi in "Revolutionary Militarization in Buenos Aires, 1806–1815," *Past and Present* 40 (July 1968): 84–107. Halperín Donghi provides an expanded analysis in *Argentina. De la revolución de independencia a la confederación rosista* (Buenos Aires, 1972), 11–104. For a less traditional historical work that provides a feel for the city, see Alberto M. Salas, *Diario de Buenos Aires, 1806–07* (Buenos Aires, 1981).

3. See Halperín Donghi, "La Vida Política," in *Buenos Aires. Historia de cuatro siglos,* ed. José Luis Romero and Luis Alberto Romero, 2 vols. (Buenos Aires: Editorial Abril, 1983), 1:157–70.

4. The best history of this topic remains Sergio Villalobos R., *Comercio y contrabando en el Río de la Plata y Chile* (Buenos Aires, 1965). See also Jonathan C. Brown, *A Socioeconomic History of Argentina, 1776–1860* (Cambridge, 1979), esp. 23–27, and Zacarías Moutoukias, "Power, Corruption, and Commerce: The Making of the Local Administrative Structure in Seventeenth-Century Buenos Aires," *Hispanic American Historical Review* 68 (November 1988): 771–802.

5. Guillermo Céspedes del Castillo, "Lima y Buenos Aires: Repercusiones económicas y políticas de la creación del Virreinato del Plata," *Anuario de Estudios Americanos,* 3 (Seville, 1947), 669–874. See also Manfred Kossok, *El virreinato del Río de la Plata. Su estructura económica-social* (Buenos Aires, 1959), esp. 55–61.

6. Enrique M. Barba, *Don Pedro de Cevallos,* 2d ed. (Buenos Aires, 1978).

7. Lyle N. McAlister suggested this connection in his excellent book, *The "Fuero Militar" in New Spain, 1764–1800* (Gainesville, Fla., 1957).

8. Christon I. Archer, *The Army in Bourbon Mexico, 1760–1810* (Albuquerque, 1978), and "The Royalist Army of New Spain, 1810–1821," *Armed Forces and Society* 17 (Fall 1990): 99–113; Leon G. Campbell, *The Military and Society in Colonial Peru, 1750–1810* (Philadelphia, 1978); and Allan J. Kuethe, *Military Reform and Society in New Granada, 1773–1808* (Gainesville, Fla., 1978).

9. This argument is put forward in Halperín Donghi, "Revolutionary Militarization in Buenos Aires," 88–93.

10. See Halperín Donghi, *Guerra y finanzas en los orígenes del estado argentino, 1791–1850* (Buenos Aires, 1982), 26, and Herbert S. Klein, "Structure and Profitability of Royal Finance in the Viceroyalty of the Río de la Plata in 1790," *Hispanic American Historical Review* 53 (1973): 440–69. See also the important criticism of Klein's article by Samuel Amaral, "Public Expenditure Financing in the Colonial Treasury: An Analysis of the Real Caja de Buenos Aires Accounts, 1789–91," *Hispanic American Historical Review* 64, no. 2 (May 1984): 287–96. This article is followed by some commentary worthy of attention; see 297–322.

11. One effect of this loss of fiscal resources was the elaboration of a

shortsighted and destructive revenue policy by the first juntas. Taxes and forced loans (often on a confiscatory scale) were directed against the commercial and manufacturing sectors because these sectors had high levels of participation by Spaniards. As a result, scarce capital was invested in rural land or sent overseas to escape these taxes. One example of how tax policy altered a local industry is provided by Lyman L. Johnson, "The Entrepreneurial Reorganization of an Artisan Trade: The Bakers of Buenos Aires, 1770–1820," *The Americas* 37, no. 2 (October 1980), esp. 154–60.

12. As part of a larger study of the colonial economy, all surviving probate records for artisans and small manufacturers were analyzed. Among the members of this group, an average of less than 500 pesos was invested in tools, other equipment, and inventory. Five hundred pesos was the average annual wage of a master bricklayer.

13. Although the figures presented in Table 2.2 suggest that this point should be obvious, it is characteristic that the best recent discussion of the colonial economy does not even discuss the size and influence of public sector spending. See Brown, *A Socioeconomic History of Argentina*, esp. chap. 2.

14. There were only five fortified places in the viceroyalty: Buenos Aires, Montevideo, Colonia, Maldonado, and Ensenada. Major military construction projects were also undertaken in Patagonia and the Malvinas. For the purpose of this study, these expenditures have been included in the data for urban Buenos Aires, since artisan wages, tools, and other supplies were largely disbursed in the city's economy.

15. Juan Marchena Fernández has provided an excellent study of the military establishment of Cartagena in *La institución militar en Cartagena de Indios en el siglo xviii* (Sevilla, 1982); see esp. chap. 6, 275–322. Allan J. Kuethe pointed this out for Havana in a letter to the author. For an excellent discussion of the politics of military reform during this period, see Kuethe's "Los Llorones Cubanos: The Socio-military Basis of Commercial Privilege in the American Trade under Charles IV," in *The North American Role in the Spanish Imperial Economy, 1760–1819*, ed. Jacques A. Barbier and Kuethe (Manchester, 1984), 142–57.

16. Halperín Donghi, *Guerra y finanzas*, 30.

17. See Johnson, "The Entrepreneurial Reorganization of an Artisan Trade," 151, for a contemporary complaint about artisans earning more than officers.

18. Halperín Donghi, *Guerra y finanzas*, 3.

19. Archivo General de la Nación (hereafter AGN), División Colonia, Sección Contaduría, Caja de Buenos Aires, Real Hacienda, Sueldos de empleados de Real Hacienda.

20. This argument draws heavily from the published analysis of Halperín Donghi, *Guerra y finanzas*, 34–39. Susan Migden Socolow found that only 18 percent of merchant marriages were contracted with the daughters of

high-ranking military men. More telling, however, is the fact that among the ninety-seven export merchants for whom the occupation of the father was known, twenty-six were the sons of bureaucrats and only 6 were the sons of military officers (Socolow, *The Merchants of Buenos Aires, 1778–1810* [Cambridge, 1978], 37, 186).

21. The best one-volume biography of José de San Martín is by Ricardo Piccirilli, *San Martín y la política de los pueblos* (Buenos Aires, 1957). For an English biography, see J. C. J. Metford, *San Martín the Liberator* (London, 1950). A good biography of Cornelio Saavedra is Enrique Ruiz Guiñazú, *El presidente Saavedra y el pueblo soberano de 1810* (Buenos Aires, 1960).

22. Although statutory compensation for soldiers was 5 pesos per month, these wages were commonly in arrears or paid at a lower rate, often 3 to 3.5 pesos per month. In comparison, unskilled laborers, *peones*, regularly earned 6 pesos per month before 1790. After this date, unskilled wages rose steadily, reaching 8 pesos in 1808.

23. Carlos Roberts, *Las invasiones inglesas del Río de la Plata, 1806–07* (Buenos Aires, 1938), 87.

24. This discussion of wage levels is based on a comprehensive study of wages by the author. Wage series were created for eight skilled and unskilled occupations over the period 1770–1815. The data for these series were taken from contemporary governmental, monastic, and notarial records.

25. Demetrio Ramos Pérez, "La Ganadería de recluta de Galicia para los regimientos del Plata (1784–1800)," in Academia Nacional de la Historia, *Bicentenario del Virreinato del Río de la Plata*, 2 vols. (Buenos Aires, 1977), 2:7–57.

26. AGN, Criminales, Legajo 36, Expediente 15.

27. AGN, Criminales, Legajo 13, Expediente 20.

28. Marchena Fernández, *Oficiales y soldados en el ejército de América* (Sevilla, 1983), 300.

29. For the *cabildo* side, see Roberts, *Las invasiones inglesas*, 87.

30. Halperín Donghi, *Guerra y finanzas*, 40.

31. Johnson, "Salarios, precios, y costo de vida en el Buenos Aires colonial tardío," *Boletín de Historia Argentina y Americana Dr. Emilio Ravignani* no. 2, 3d ser. (1990): 133–58.

32. Roberts, *Las invasiones inglesas*, 88.

33. Ricardo Levene, *La Revolución de Mayo y Mariano Moreno*, 3 vols. (Buenos Aires, 1960), 1:234–50; and Halperín Donghi, *Guerra y finanzas*, 81–84.

34. Levene, *La Revolución de Mayo y Mariano Moreno*, 1:241–46.

35. Johnson, "The Entrepreneurial Reorganization of an Artisan Trade," 154–60; and AGN, División Colonia, Sección Gobierno, Archivo del Cabildo, Año 1810.

36. Halperín Donghi, *Guerra y finanzas*, 84.

37. Socolow, *The Merchants of Buenos Aires*, 143.

38. Manuel Belgrano, *Autobiografía*, in *Escritos Económicos*, ed. Gregorio Weinberg (Buenos Aires, 1954).

39. The military wage bill for 1807 was 1,862,996 pesos. In 1800 it had been 408,728 pesos. For the 1807 data see AGN, Gobierno de Buenos Aires, vol. 15, chap. 81. The 1800 data are from AGN, Caja de Buenos Aires, Carta Cuenta de 1800.

40. The John Carter Brown Library, Brown University, Providence, R.I., uncatalogued document, "Estado General que dé Orden del Excmo. Cabildo de esta Capital Forma su Contaduría para demostrar los Caudales" (published in Buenos Aires on February 10, 1810).

41. By region I mean the ports of Montevideo, Ensenada de Barragán, and Riachuelo as well as Buenos Aires. Since Buenos Aires presented costly obstacles to loading and unloading, other ports in the region were often preferred. A helpful five-year average of imports and exports for the period 1792–96 is found in Félix de Azara, *Viajes por la América Meridional*, 2 vols. (Buenos Aires, 1923), 2:185. Other bits and pieces can be gleaned from John Lynch, *Spanish Colonial Administration, 1782–1810: The Intendant System in the Viceroyalty of the Río de la Plata* (New York, 1969), 42–45; and Levene, *Investigaciones acerca de la historia económica del virreinato del Plata*, in *Obras de Ricardo Levene*, 3 vols. (Buenos Aires, 1962), 2:303–25.

42. AGN, División Colonia, Sección Gobierno, Archivo del Cabildo, 1770–1815; Obras Públicas, Canal de San Fernando, 1770–1808; Cabildo de Buenos Aires, Obras, 1805–6. AGN, División Colonia, Sección Contaduría, Culto de Buenos Aires, Mercedarios, Hospicio de San Ramón de las Conchas, Libros I, III, and V; Culto de Buenos Aires, Mercedarios-convento, gastos, Libros I, II, and III; Culto de Buenos Aires, Mercedarios, Convento Grade de San Ramón, Libro de Gastos, 1775–1815.

43. The weights for commodities are as follows: wheat (40), rice (10), chickpeas (2.5), yerba (7.5), sugar (5), French beans (2.5), salted meat (5), wine (7.5), and rent (20).

44. AGN, División Colonia, Sección Contaduría, Caja de Buenos Aires, 1770–1815. The accounts for each year were searched and each record of a wage payment was recorded. Medians were then calculated for each artisanal occupation. Finally, the eight occupations were assigned weights using the city census of 1778. The eight occupations and their weights are carpenters (20), bricklayers (15), iron workers (10), caulkers (10), ship carpenters (10), sail makers (5), arms makers (10), sailors (20).

45. The multiple regression analysis of variables affecting unskilled wages is $W = 30.092 + .4862P + .0196M - .0322o (+ = 4.37)^*(t = 4.11)^*(t = .10)$ where W = unskilled wages, P = consumer price index, M = military spending, and o = other government expenditures. $R^2 = .6346$, F-value = .15.63*, Std. Error = 22.56. *significant at the .05 level.

46. Luis Alberto Romero, *Buenos Aires: La sociedad criolla, 1810–1850* (Buenos Aires, 1980), 13; and Miron Burgin, *The Economic Aspects of Argentine Federalism, 1820–1852* (New York, 1971), 28.

47. Halperín Donghi, *Guerra y finanzas*, 30, 85. This pattern persisted in Buenos Aires after independence and then spread into the interior provinces as well. See Halperín Donghi, "Incidencia de los gastos militares en Córdoba, y Santa Fé (1820–1852)," in Universidad Nacional de Córdoba, Facultad de Filosofía y Humanidades, *Homenaje al Dr. Ceferino Garzón Maceda* (Córdoba, 1973), 253–65.

Tulio Halperín Donghi
Translated and Edited by Mark D. Szuchman

The Colonial *Letrado* as a Revolutionary Intellectual: Deán Funes as Seen through His *Apuntamientos para una Biografía*

Editor's Introduction

One of the exponents of revolution in the Río de la Plata, Gregorio Funes served as a rare intellectual bridge, crisscrossing the ideals of liberty with the notions of careful republicanism. Conscious of the need for peoples to find their leaders among the "thinking classes" endowed with enlightened ideas, he also witnessed and lamented the excesses of mass participation in political change.

Gregorio Funes was born in 1749 into a family from the city of Córdoba. Both of his parents could claim direct descendancy from the area's sixteenth-century conquerors. In a region where status and lineage fused into political prosperity, the eldest son of the Funes clan fulfilled the rites of passage required of all who followed the notables' path: he entered the secondary school of the Jesuits' principal house of learning, the Colegio de Monserrat, at the age of fifteen; he then continued his studies at the University of Córdoba, from which he received his doctorate in theology in 1774. After studying law in Spain, he returned to Córdoba in 1780 with a royal appointment as a canon in the ecclesiastical *cabildo*. Funes was well known and well connected; he rose along Córdoba's ladder of political ascent, fusing the two political art forms—the ecclesiastical and secular.

When news arrived of the events of the May 1810 revolution, Funes had been appointed *deán*, or dean, of Córdoba's cathedral. He also served as rector of the University of Córdoba, a formidably respectable and influential position. The members of Córdoba's *cabildo* appointed him as their emissary to the revolutionary junta's government in Buenos Aires. The authorities of Buenos Aires placed him in charge of the *Gaceta Mercantil*, effectively giving him control of the flow of official information and propaganda, as the governing body tried to find its way to independence and regional hegemony while minimizing estrangements. In many ways, Funes's own political life can be seen as exemplifying this difficult task of political survival and intellectual success. After alternating careers in public service and private life, Gregorio Funes died in Buenos Aires at the age of seventy-nine on January 10, 1829.[1] He died while strolling in a public garden, perhaps reflecting on the political reversal his countrymen were starting to experience: Juan Manuel de Rosas had been in power barely two weeks.

Reason as Political Mechanism

In the mid-1820s, having passed the age of seventy, Gregorio Funes, dean of the cathedral in Córdoba and prebendary of the archdiocese of La Paz, Bolivia, began to write his *Apuntamientos* (Notes), which he continued until his death in 1829. They were published after the fall of Juan Manuel de Rosas in 1852 by an anonymous "friend of the nation's servants," albeit without mentioning the autobiographical nature of the text.[2] The addition of an epilogue not written in Funes's hand (a fact left unmentioned in the publication) was remarkably inconspicuous, less because of the editor's skills than because of the nature of the dean's own text. Written in the third person and focused on his public life, the text was probably either the draft of an entry for a biographical dictionary or, just as likely, the draft of a prologue for Funes's collected works. Indeed, there is much in the text itself to suggest that it was the latter that figured in the author's mind.

The autobiography weaves the dean's career into the context of the old regime and the revolution, thereby offering a particularly valuable document for understanding the ways in which that historical transition affected one of the most representative members of an intellectual group characteristic of a mature colonial society. Funes's contemporaries were well aware that the intensity of the colonial experience continued to shape Funes's public image as a revolutionary figure, an image by which he hoped to be remembered. Domingo Sarmiento, elaborating on testimonies doubtless attributable to Funes's contemporaries, portrayed him as the archetype of "all the notable men of that era . . . like the ancient god

Terminus, with two faces, one oriented toward the future and the other toward the past."[3]

Funes, however, would not have recognized himself in that portrait; the picture he draws for us in his *Apuntamientos* shows his eyes to be fixed firmly on the future. This is in part, I am afraid, the result of a not-wholly-unconscious self-stylization. Thus, he presents his *Oración Fúnebre* (Funeral oration), given in memory of Charles III in the Cathedral of Córdoba, as "the first stone of the revolution" in a clearly tendentious manner.[4] However, beyond his understandable preoccupation with safeguarding his title as the precursor of the movement for independence, there is no doubt that, for Funes, his work as a writer gains meaning only in the context of an intellectual revolution that contained political corollaries, and of which he was keenly aware—even if he did not rush to write about them. Rather, he came to his analyses over time. This transformation began with a sudden and calculatingly quiet conversion that reflected both his reasoning and emotive abilities:

> Señor Funes was still a student when, as a result of the conviction of a soul naturally inclined toward all that is sound and true, he began to understand just how much he would have to step back from the path he had chosen and take a new route toward a literary education of his own making.[5]

This "new route," of course, was that of the Enlightenment, which converted knowledge based upon reason and experience into an engine capable of transforming the world. The dean was not ignorant of the presence of this new force, which provided continually changing contexts for his actions, beginning with his formative years during which "the darkness of Aristotelianism had started to dissipate from the curriculum" and extending to the revolutionary times when it reached beyond debates over ideas (*AB*, 1525). This transition had been so forceful that the monastic orders came close to spontaneous extinction for lack of callings, the novices having been scared off by the advances of the "spirit of the century" (*AB*, 1547–48). The revolution uncovered the political potential that hid within the movement for renewal. Knowing beforehand that this was to be its historical function, the dean awaited it fervently and, at the right moment, became an instrument of its birth. He had prepared carefully for this endeavor. For several years, he had dedicated himself to "reading those materials that corresponded more closely with the beginning new order" and had nour-

ished "his spirit with the works of Plato, Aristotle, Pufendorff, Con-
dillac, Mably, Rousseau, Raynal and others." He was not among the
many who spoke of the imminent revolutionary change "in a vague
and confused manner," but rather figured among the chosen few
who, "out of long and reflexive studies, were prepared to act" (*AB*,
1532).

It was thus that Funes prepared himself to experience a revolution
that he knew ahead of time would be necessary, but also to take his
place as one of its protagonists. His depiction of his own course of
action is essentially accurate: despite being over seventy years of
age, he was to surprise everyone—perhaps even himself—by the en-
ergy with which he (almost alone among Córdoba's elite) turned in
favor of a rupture with the old order in which, as he must have
known, he was risking his life.

In spite of all this, Sarmiento's impression of Funes's character
was not altogether unfounded. It is not a question of whether or not
Funes was a totally committed revolutionary: he could not be otherwise, as the revolution for him was the historical embodiment of all
those truths whose validity had so persuasively gripped his soul that
he had stripped himself of all that he had learned from his environment and teachers "in order to follow a new course and become a
self-taught man of letters." If this revelation drove him to undertake
a solitary and secretive exploration into this new world of ideas,
however, it did not dissuade him from advancing during four decades along a *cursus honorum* adjusted to guidelines elaborated under the sign of those older ideas whose shallowness had been so
clearly revealed to him at the start of his career. Once the revolution
broke out, transforming what had been an individual effort for internal renewal into a collective movement in search of a radical new
beginning, he immediately knew that it could not end until the
social order underwent an equally radical transformation. At the
same time, he seemed confident that the revolution would maintain his position—and indeed would consolidate it on the basis of
revolutionary principles founded on reason—within his own group
of *letrados*, even if that group had been fashioned by an ancien régime which he had long sought to eliminate.

Funes had reasons to be confident: he saw the revolution as the
political consummation of an intellectual regeneration represented
by the *letrados*. It was not too much for him to imagine that the
letrados would play an important role in the movement they had

inspired. The problem, however, was that Funes did not seem to notice that, within the framework of the mature colonial system, a *letrado* was both more and less than an intrepid seeker of truth, or a herald expecting to become a protagonist in the revolution that he naively thought had been announced merely by his presence. While a latter-day observer can understand immediately why the revolution would make it impossible for Funes to continue the contradictory ambiguity of the dual career he tried to carry on for four decades, thereby forcing him to choose between the risks and glories of a revolutionary and the less exalting destiny of a man of letters, it seems that Funes hoped that the revolution would eliminate the ambiguity altogether, not by forcing him to choose between contradictory positions but rather by forging them into compatibility.

Funes's hope was to be cruelly dashed for reasons that, although obvious today, remained a mystery to him. Identification with the ideological bases of the old order, which had defined the role of *letrados* in public life, was not the primary basis of the solidarities that bound men of letters to the ancien régime (indeed, Funes was far from being the only one who had repudiated such ideological identification in its essential aspects). Even when alienated, those *letrados* still formed a subsector of the colonial elite; they sought to expand the complex patrimony of their families by becoming part of the imperial bureaucratic apparatus, thus creating opportunities to influence decisions in favor of their families and network of friends and clients. At the same time, they expected that their literary production would enhance their reputations, adding weight to their opinions within the bureaucratic sphere and also allowing their families to bask in the reflected glow of their fame.

Dean Funes is very close to arriving at this ideal type, which reached maturity during the latter stages of the colonial period. What gives his *Apuntamientos* their peculiar tone is that he dedicates equal attention to his progress on the revolutionary path and to his growing literary reputation, following a particular image of the writer and his integration into society.

The Functions of Prestige

Because Funes's autobiography attempts to depict the life of a man of letters more than that of a public functionary or a politician, it is organized around the idea of acquiring prestige. This appears as the dominant theme of the work from its very first lines. His already notable family will have its reputation increased further by his literary fame. On both sides, Funes was descended from "patricians and founding fathers" who "were rewarded with the Republic's most honorable titles." Funes even records something as private as his mother's virtue from the vantage point of reputation and prestige: so eminent was that virtue that her "funeral eulogy, written by her confessor, was published" (*AB,* 1525).

From the very start of his autobiography, Funes rigorously separated the idea of prestige as a form of societal recognition based on the value given to an individual or a corporation, in instances in which it is obtained through intellectual activity, from the intrinsic validity of the activity itself. Thus, when speaking of his years of learning at the Colegio de Monserrat and at the university, both administered by the Jesuits at the time, he presents the most talented of his professors, Father Rospigliosi, as a "genius of the first order, doubtlessly capable of great progress in the sciences if only he had been lucky enough to have been born in a less unfortunate era" (*AB,* 1526). However, when rendering a general evaluation of the "Jesuit corps," under whose aegis he was first formed, he remembers it as

the most famous group in South America: famous for their riches, the austerity of their lives, their growing numbers—the majority having come from Europe—and for the vast reach of their control over the famous missions of Mojos, Chuiquitos, Paraguay and the other religious houses in adjoining provinces. It has been necessary to present this idea in order to appreciate the context in which the young Funes developed one of his literary careers. [*AB,* 1525].

Without even pretending to be impartial or critical, this passage articulates an ideal of Christian life that was particularly vulnerable to criticism after the Enlightenment (Funes is capable, for example, of admiring both the opulence and the austerity of the order in the same sentence). The passage also reflects, implicitly but unequivocally, a concept of intellectual prestige as one more element in a complex patrimony that also included wealth and power; each one of these elements strengthened the others. If at school and at the university Funes received from the Jesuits an education already considered questionable and antiquated, merely the fact of receiving it conferred a vicarious splendor on the first stage of his literary career—a consequence of the Jesuits' opulent churches, their vast influence, and the immense territory covered by their missionary work.

Funes's concern with standing was always influenced by the social dimension of intellectual recognition and reflected the prestige that was afforded him by the world in which he must prove his own worth. After the Jesuits' expulsion, Funes, who had been one of their favored disciples, immediately gained the favor of the Franciscans who replaced them at the University of Córdoba. Funes had something to offer: when the Franciscans entrusted him with a public presentation that covered "the whole of philosophy and another [presentation] on theology" they, too, hoped to surround themselves with the vicarious brilliance of the exceptionally talented student they had inherited along with the rest of the Jesuits' patrimony transferred by the Crown. In effect, the Franciscans proposed "to exhibit the progress made at the University under their own leadership" (AB, 1526).

Funes remained faithful to the collective values he understood so well when he finished with his first "literary career" and undertook his next one in Spain. These values continued to hold him in their sway when he contemplated them retrospectively as a veteran of the revolution that would provide him with so many surprises. While practicing as a lawyer in Madrid after completing his study of civil and canon law at the University of Alcalá, King Charles III bestowed upon him the charge of canon of the Cathedral of Córdoba. Thus he returned to his native city, favored by his sovereign early in his career, as part of the retinue of Friar José Antonio de San Alberto, bishop-designate for the diocese.

The relationship between Funes and San Alberto did not seem to have been particularly close, although we are assured in the *Apuntamientos* that the bishop used Funes's "talents in all the important diocesan matters" (AB, 1527). The reticence with which this doubtlessly unsatisfactory relationship was evoked reflected Funes's general attitude toward his colonial career: its discontinuities and setbacks would always appear in muted fashion. For example, it is difficult to guess from a reading of the text just what the expulsion of the Jesuits meant for Funes. His family retained a lingering nostalgic feeling for the expelled priests, but this had political implications that would likewise remain unexplored. Thus, the eulogy for Funes's mother, published by her Jesuit confessor, Father Gaspar

Juárez, during his Roman exile, bore a title that proudly displays the American birthplaces of both the eulogized woman and her eulogizer. Yet Funes alludes neither to the title nor to its implications.[6] His career is presented as a steady advance toward ever greater triumphs. While this image is not entirely false, it is also true that his advance had been irrecoverably blocked since 1804. In fact, Funes's possibilities of becoming a bishop became increasingly remote.

Funes's collaboration with Bishop Moscoso undoubtedly marked the happiest stage of his career, which advanced significantly during the bishop's tenure in Córdoba. Funes writes in detail how Moscoso recognized, used, and rewarded his talents. Funes casts himself first as an irreplaceable administrative assistant; next as an admirably efficient legal advisor (he was instrumental in the bishop's triumphs in jurisdictional disputes with Córdoba's Governor Rafael de Sobremonte); and finally, he was found to have equally useful talents as a man of letters. Thus, his collaboration was instrumental in the writing of a report "on the material and formal aspects of the Bishopric of Tucumán, which at that time also included that of Salta." When Moscoso became the target of an attack in the *Telégrafo Mercantil*, the first newspaper published in Buenos Aires, Funes "leapt to his defense in a tract published under the name of Patricio Saliano." When Moscoso, his friend and patron, died, Funes delivered the funeral oration, "both to immortalize the memory of this bishop and to give proof of his own gratitude" (*AB*, 1528).

Throughout his rise along the imperial bureaucratic hierarchy, Funes's capacity as a man of letters was always evident. His literary work had a clearly utilitarian orientation, not in the lofty sense with which the Enlightenment stamped its cultural creations, but in a more mundane sense, insofar as his literary productions were intended to achieve some immediate, practical effects in decisive moments of his career. Funes's utilitarian orientation derived from the events of his career, the framework of which permitted him to discharge specific functions. Because of his utilitarian bent, these efforts must inevitably be adjusted to the principles deemed acceptable in the latter stages of the colonial era. But it does not necessarily follow that, in rendering homage to those principles, Funes was simply sacrificing his convictions for the sake of career advancement.

Along with those convictions, which his works could not reveal at the time, Funes retained a greater affinity than he realized for the social and moral values that legitimated the position of the literary elites, even when his loyalty to them actually endangered his plans for advancement. For example, Funes includes in his writings the oration he prepared in memory of Bishop Moscoso. Acknowledging his patron seemed to him to be among the highest moral duties, and he is pleased to have done so even though he could no longer hope for further favors; however, publishing his oration threatened to attract the attention of the deceased bishop's adversaries, eager to punish Funes's overly zealous posthumous loyalty.

Ecclesiastical Solidarity

Funes felt a particularly intense obligation to remain loyal to the ecclesiastical estate to which he belonged. In Funes's judgment, the most important battle of his colonial career consisted of ensuring that the Jesuits were replaced in the institutions of learning by secular clergy, in keeping with the king's orders at the time of the Jesuits' expulsion.

Despite the definitive nature of the order, it had been conveniently ignored either because of intrigue or because of the favoritism enjoyed by the Franciscans in the eyes of Bishop San Alberto and the governor of Córdoba, the Marquis of Sobremonte. The [secular] clergy complained bitterly about the delay in implementation, but lacking the courage to demand their rights, they suffered patiently. . . . Unintimidated by power and prestige, Fr. Funes, after his return from Spain, energetically promoted the clergy's cause.

Finally, Funes achieved a greater triumph than he had anticipated when the king raised the status of the university in Córdoba to that of *Universidad Mayor* and immediately placed it in the care of the secular clergy. This was a costly victory for Funes, however, as he "had to suffer all the affronts of the subordinate despots charged with handling the Court's dispositions." These affronts were not just limited to the "insulting silence" that met his inquiries into the execution of the royal will. It was only in 1807, when Viceroy Santiago de Liniers took "command of these provinces," that the king's order was finally implemented (*AB*, 1529–30).

Not surprisingly, Funes preferred not to examine one aspect of this campaign, which was that its outcome would affect not only the corporate interests of his ecclesiastical estate but also his personal future. He was fully aware that, as the towering intellectual personality among the secular clergy, he would expect to acquire a dominant position within the University of Córdoba. This was indeed what occurred, as Funes writes:

> By virtue of the previous Royal Commands and new dispositions, the Rector of the University must be elected by the entirety of the faculty presided by the governor of the province. Juan Gutiérrez de la Concha, who occupied that position, convoked this body, and Señor Funes was unanimously elected on January 11, 1808. [*AB*, 1530]

Another aspect of this situation, however, was left unexamined by Funes for less obvious reasons. Funes's presentation of himself as a solitary fighter in defense of the rights of his threatened ecclesiastical estate reflects only one among several components of a complicated web of conflicts left in the wake of the Jesuit expulsions: the secular clergy's cause was especially important to anyone who remembered the exiles affectionately, and who thus faced the opposition of governors and viceroys. Yet Funes mentions none of these political passions and schisms; likewise, he makes it impossible for his readers to surmise that the dispute surrounding the governance of the university was tied to other disputes in which Funes and his friends were at odds with a group that had formed around the Marquis of Sobremonte. Funes's efforts and achievements in the viceregal court bore fruit in Córdoba only when Sobremonte, after he had been promoted to the office of viceroy following a brilliant performance as intendant of Córdoba, saw his career ended by his catastrophic failure in dealing with the English invasions of 1806 and 1807.

What Funes says is just as important as what he leaves unmentioned when recalling this episode. His document presents us with a figure who, fifteen years after the start of the revolution, was examining his career in light of the collective values prevalent in the colonial era, the flaws of which, he assures us with unquestionable sincerity, had been revealed to him with absolute certainty at the very beginning of that career. His battle for control of the university was waged according to the social and moral imperatives recognized by the intellectual elite of the ancien régime. This becomes clearer still when the highly stylized account found in the *Apuntamientos* is contrasted with the accounts of others, which, although equally compatible with the facts, would not be in the least attractive to Funes. He does tell us that, thanks to a positive resolution on the issue of governance, he was charged with reforming the university's curriculum. In doing so he endeavored

> to banish the unpolished style of scholastic disputation and, above all, to provide the mind with a commendable direction by way of a new method that . . . lifted learning from the dark circles to which it had been reduced and placed it on an environment based on reason so that it might reach its objectives [*AB*, 1531]

Such had been the outcome, or rather the version of the outcome, that Funes tried to inculcate in his readers, even if it was only an approximation of reality. He serendipitously admitted that the plan was less redeeming than it might have been, insofar as the new method did not reach "the point in which every intellectual faculty could be profitably put to use." Even so, the battle that preceded the curricular changes might have been described as a fight for new ideas based on reason, a point of view Funes wished to apply to his whole public career. Thus, it is even more significant that the key for interpreting and legitimating his role in the conflict is an elite code of ethics, the product of a society based on estates and on a bureaucratic and courtly system, where the basic duties are loyalty to patron and benefactor and to the corporate interests of one's estate.

Funes's triumph in the university was not the only sign that, after a long period of stagnation, his career had resumed its upward trend. The solid base of his position was confirmed in 1809 when the dean had to travel to Buenos Aires "to defend himself against the intrigue prepared at court by a rival endowed with the most depraved mischievousness." This difficulty was immediately resolved:

> Señor Funes's reputation was, by this time, too well established for him to lose his good name and the respect that all felt for him. In effect, Viceroy Liniers, who wanted to show Funes his gratitude both for his congratulatory speech given in Córdoba on the occasion of the defeat of the English of which Liniers was the hero and for his important services on behalf of the public good, offered Funes his hospitality. In the same vein, the judges of the Royal Praetorian Tribunal also honored him and settled the conflict to the entire satisfaction of his credit and of Justice. [*AB*, 1531–32]

Revolutionary Commitment

While the highest dignitaries of the old order were paying homage to Funes, he unhesitatingly readied himself to embark on the revolutionary career for which he had been preparing through his carefully chosen readings. He also established his first contact with the revolutionary circles in the viceregal capital, where he had occasion to "become friendly with Manuel Belgrano and Señor Castelli. It was to them that he first revealed what was in his heart" (*AB*, 1532). He was to show a steadfast loyalty to this revolutionary commitment from the movement's earliest and most uncertain moments; but then he also began to be surprised by a revolution whose features he had not clearly anticipated and for which his texts had left him unprepared.

He was surprised initially by the determination with which the revolution began cutting through the web of personal, family, and estate loyalties that previously had anchored his world and that would continue to influence him—in ways that we have already seen—even in his old age as a veteran revolutionary. When Cañete, a fellow student from Asunción, Paraguay, who was linked to Funes by an old friendship and deep mutual respect, informed the dean that Baltasar de Cisneros, viceroy-designate (and destined to be the last Spanish viceroy in Buenos Aires) had offered him the office of advisor general, Funes tried to persuade him to decline. He was guided by his concern for his friend's future and wanted him to avoid making a commitment to a regime that would soon crumble. But then, "Señor Cañete," Funes adds with melancholy, "betrayed the duties of friendship" by forwarding the dean's letter to Córdoba's intendant; only the opportune arrival of the liberating revolutionary troops from Buenos Aires saved the dean's life. Nonetheless, the military detachment that saved his life came equipped with altogether different and less pleasing innovations. When the fugitive leaders of the failed counterrevolution were finally captured, the dean shared with the expeditionary leaders his fear of disturbances if the prisoners were taken to the city of Córdoba, where they enjoyed widespread popularity.

[Hipólito] Vieytes [the political commissioner sent to accompany the Buenos Aires junta's troops into the interior] . . . then told him to calm down, since he had orders, which had been repeatedly confirmed, to shoot every captured fugitive, including the bishop. Señor Funes couldn't but shudder on learning of a decision as cruel as it was impolitic. [*AB*, 1535–36]

Along with the inhumanity introduced into politics by the revolutionary conflict, Funes was shocked to discover that the revolution did not legitimize the ideals that had guided his journey; in fact, loyalty and service to the revolutionary cause appeared as the antinomian rivals of those ideals. He quickly discovered that the new reality was even more dismal than his initial pessimism had caused him to suspect. In effect, the revolution did not eliminate the elites' old game of alliances and rivalries, which had guided them and shaped their loyalties in the colonial past; the game was merely transformed into a deadly affair.

Because the decisions made in this game now affected much more than mere success in the bureaucratic hierarchy or the accumulation of favors and prestige, those who played had to be willing to shed all remaining scruples. Thus, the dean was thrown into prison, despite his innocence, by the forces of the very revolution he had promoted. He now stood accused of conspiring against the revolutionary leaders in office in the same setting where he had earlier experienced spectacular triumph over other schemers, a victory afforded him by the then-moribund old order. This new incident, which struck him as horrendous, was nonetheless totally understandable within the framework of the new order whose birth he had helped to bring about.

The defeated party called for a counterrevolution but only the most heedless among them promoted it. And it was they who landed in prison once their plot was discovered. The trial followed a somber ritual that presaged death sentences. The most guilty among the accused was related to one of the three men then in power. His family used this relationship to interest the strongman in the prisoner's fate. It was then that this leader, using all the treachery of his character, told the family members of the accused that the only means to freedom was by implicating respectable people, including Funes, and he advised them to have the prisoner proceed accordingly. How could he [the accused] help but take advantage of an intrigue that might save his life? [*AB*, 1540–41]

While this is not the first time that Funes had to confront his adversaries' duplicity, what is new here is increased danger and a widened network of complicities, consequences of the heightened savagery of political conflicts. While in relating this episode he does not forgive the man whose slander might have caused his death, he offers him his melancholy sensitivity, describing him as a person willing to embrace a despicable, desperate plan in order to save his own life.

It is easy to understand why Funes was no longer attracted to this new, specifically political sphere of action to which the revolution gave him privileged access. In the end, he was released from prison because of the sagacity and spirit of justice of Secretary Bernardino Rivadavia and, above all, because ultimately "the heat of his persecutors cooled down" (Rivadavia, correct in his belief that premature freedom would harm them both, kept Funes in prison for months, long after he became convinced of his innocence). Funes then decided to immerse himself in his *chères études*, gathering materials for his *Ensayo de la Historia Civil del Paraguay, Buenos Aires y Tucumán.* "This peaceful retrenchment from political activities served to mollify the hostility of rivals and rekindle an enduring respect by the people," he writes (*AB*, 1541).

Paradoxically, it was only when Funes decided to abandon politics that he seemed to perceive clearly that politics had become a special sphere of action, distinct from any that had previously been accessible to him as a man of letters, lawyer, administrator, and advisor to high officials. Before, he had considered his new activities extensions of those that had occupied him under the old regime. The activities changed in method because of the profoundly altered environment in which they were being discharged, not because of shifts in their fundamental nature.

Much as he did before the revolution, the dean focused his literary talent on occasional publications, although now the opportunities were quite different. He was no longer commemorating the deaths of the monarchs and prelates who had inspired his earlier memorable panegyrics. Thus, when the revolutionary patriots lost control of Alto Perú, the "setback did not discourage the Junta. They put Señor Funes to work on a proclamation which reminded the people that the Roman senate had thanked the Consul Varro for not having given up on the Republic after the defeat at Cannas, which served to regain generous support." On other occasions, he was to go even further in adapting his old skills to new uses, as when the Buenos Aires revolutionary junta used "Señor Funes's pen in a virulent proclamation against the Brazilian States" (*AB*, 1540).

Similarly, Funes placed his electoral victories in the revolutionary political arena within a context containing direct lines to his successes during the colonial era. More than any other specific form of political support, these victories represented an acknowledgment of Funes's virtues and prestige. If on August 17, 1810, he had been elected as the delegate for Córdoba to the First Revolutionary Junta by "a large popular assembly of citizens deemed knowledgeable in such important affairs," it was "because of Funes's reputation as a just man whom no one could remotely hope to contest in the election" (*AB*, 1536). In 1816, he was reelected, although without the unanimity shown on the previous occasion. In Funes's view, "Córdoba, unable to overlook the honor he had brought and the good this compatriot had done for the nation, in effect, reelected him" (*AB*, 1542).

If this representative of the people patterned his relationship with the masses along the same lines as those that had linked him to the elite, he also continued to view his ties to political power—in which, according to the institutional concepts of the moment, he was a participant—as he had before 1810, when he had managed to establish his political position through royal patronage. Thus, his arrival in Buenos Aires as the representative from Córdoba to the First Revolutionary Junta in 1810 appeared as a reenactment of his previous year's triumph but within a new political system. If before the display of esteem by the viceroy and the *audiencia* had reflected "his already renowned reputation," it was the same high standing that motivated the many courtesies shown him by the revolutionary junta, including the homage, the military bands, and "the cheers of the people thrilled to have a figure who had already demonstrated his knowledge and patriotism in a classic fashion" (*AB*, 1537–38).

Funes's accommodation of new realities to old patterns became clearer still as the weight of the years and the disillusionments sapped the dean's revolutionary fervor. Admittedly, his separation from positions of leadership in the new government continued to protect him from the worst consequences of the frequent changes typical of the agitation within revolutionary politics. However, such protection was far from being totally effective; when "the convulsive and prolonged course of the revolution submerged completely" both Funes's private estate and his ecclesiastical income, he was obliged to seek employment, forcing him to renounce his intent to stay aloof from any further dangerous entanglements with rival revolutionary factions. Moreover, whenever the political convulsions turned fierce, they affected those individuals who had taken refuge in the private sphere even more successfully than Funes.

However, after the terrifying year of 1820, which closed a decade of revolutionary war, Funes's life finally seemed to return to an earlier course. The "Republic of the Arts" was reborn in Buenos

Aires, and the dean became one of the editors of *La Abeja Argentina*, the publication of the literary society "established under the influence of the government" of the newly created province of Buenos Aires. In 1823, in order "both to offer this service to the country and to succour his own needs," he became the editor-in-chief of *El Argos*, a newspaper dedicated to general news and current debates published by the same association (*AB*, 1548).

A Literary Beacon to the New Order

An external observer might see in all this merely the metamorphosis of the old *letrado* (who had no expectation that he might live off his intellectual talent) into a professional journalist. The dean, although doubtlessly aware of the plausibility of such an interpretation, preferred not to see things in this light, not even when his collaboration extended beyond *El Argos*, a publication dedicated to nominally newsworthy and cultural affairs, to the overtly political *El Centinela*. He would immediately note that the scope of his activities remained limited to his role as an intellectual, and, in any event, those activities had been occasioned by the Buenos Aires provincial government's projected ecclesiastical reform. While admitting that he participated in the founding of the newspaper, he pointed out that he had been responsible only "for its scientific, serious aspects." He insisted on viewing his participation in the political and ideological debates surrounding the proposed reforms as merely a return, albeit in a new context, to the more innocent practice of literary debating, which had been cultivated zealously by colonial intellectuals. Thus, he could portray his journalistic and political endeavors within the pristine context of intellectual discourse: "Another newspaper, *El Oficial del Día*, was published in competition with *El Centinela* and a very interesting and satisfying literary dispute took place between the editors, giving them an opportunity to display their knowledge of history, antiquities, politics, and ecclesiastical and civil governments" (*AB*, 1547–48). Funes would prefer to believe that, as had been the case in the past, differences of opinion are only a convenient opportunity for the debaters to win public admiration by displaying their knowledge and talents to full advantage.

In one way, the new order promised to award Funes a more distinguished place than the one that the ancien régime had reserved for him: the dean of Córdoba became the first author from the Río de la Plata area to be incorporated into a constellation of intellectuals that reached beyond the confines of the Hispanic world. The incident that provided him with this exalted position seemed so significant to him that, in what was an otherwise concise autobiography, he included a long and detailed account of it. Bernardino Rivadavia, who at the time was an agent in Paris on behalf of the revolutionary government, took it upon himself to disseminate the first two volumes of Funes's *Ensayo de la Historia Civil*, sending them

to various *sabios* of that capital city. One of them, M. Grégoire, whose name is renowned for his generous and religious philanthropy, as well as for his courageous and steadfast morals, shared with me his painful impression upon discovering that in this work the immortal Bartolomé de Las Casas, the most famous defender of the Indians during the Spanish conquest, was still being accused of having been the one who . . . promoted the idea of introducing the black slave trade in America. . . . He assured me that he had purified Las Casas's reputation from such a blemish, as atrocious as it was unjustified. [*AB*, 1543–44][7]

This vindication of the apostle of the Indians had been the subject of a memoir Grégoire had presented to the Institute of France, a copy of which he sent to Funes "in a most well-mannered and flattering way." The dean replied with a "memoir that took the form of a letter in which his respect toward that *sabio* [Grégoire] vied with the strength of his own arguments." When Juan Antonio Llorente published the debate in Paris in 1822 as an appendix to his edition of Las Casas's works, and Funes's winning argumentation was revealed to the reading public, he won recognition in the Old World as the literary voice of the New World.[8]

While thus rebuilding his public reputation, now as a universally respected writer, Funes's private fortune also began to recover. The manner in which this occurred demonstrated the similarity to the patterns found in the old order. Already compelled to take care of his material needs by writing for newspapers, Funes reluctantly decided to accept a seat as a salaried representative of Córdoba in the new Constitutional Congress that was to meet in Buenos Aires in 1824, thus returning to a "scene that more than once had been unlucky for him and in which he foresaw a struggle of lively passions." After Tomás Cipriano de Mosquera, minister plenipotentiary of Colombia, arrived in Buenos Aires, Funes heard detailed descriptions of

General Simón Bolívar, already known as the warrior who held the fate of South America in his hands. "Señor Funes believed he had a sacred duty to write a tribute to Bolívar and did so, praising him in his newspaper, *El Argos"* (*AB*, 1549).

As a result of this action and of the friendship forged between that affluent Colombian patrician and his unprosperous peer from Córdoba, Funes was designated to be Colombia's minister in Buenos Aires, while

President Bolívar and the Grand Marshall of Ayacucho [Antonio José de Sucre] . . . , once they became informed of how Funes had fought uncompromisingly during the revolution, of the ingratitude shown to him when he lost all his worldly goods, and of how the small income he received from his benefice would not be enough to assure a decent life during his old age, generously awarded him the Deanery of the Cathedral in La Paz in the Republic of Bolivia. Señor Funes accepted it and took possession of it through his proxy. (*AB*, 1549–50]

The Refashioning of Experience

Once again, Funes presented an episode in terms fashioned by the old order: the dean hoped to escape poverty by becoming an absentee prebendary, a sinecure won on the basis of his professional and literary services, among which the most important seemed to be his talent for artful flattery. Notably, this presentation of the episode, which sheds an ambiguous light on the dean's motives, ignored (undoubtedly in deliberate fashion) some important aspects that do not readily fit that archaic model of patronage. Funes's appointment as minister of Colombia was, in effect, part of Bolívar's attempts to forge an alliance with the Argentine opposition to the dominant group of centralists in the Constitutional Congress, a faction joined by the governor of Córdoba, whose political interests Funes knew he would have to defend against the majority of the congressmen.

But if Funes insisted on structuring his personal life according to patterns whose essential features were not recognized as being affected by that immense fact called the revolution, and if he examined the marks it left on his life by bemoaning his personal calamities, he remained a fierce defender of that cause which had brought him so much misery. Thus, Funes assured his readers (after recalling, for their edification, the tributes written to him by many authors) that none of these tributes flattered him as much as the libel published against him by the royalist Marquis of Casares, who had taken refuge in Rio de Janeiro after fleeing from the liberated city of Lima. Reactionary insults formed the best badge for a militant; they provided irrefutable proof of the "constancy with which Señor Funes has defended the nation's cause" (*AB*, 1550). Even more significant was his pride in having been accepted as a peer by a community of men of letters that was larger than the community that existed under the old regime; this makes him a citizen of a "Republic of Letters" embracing both worlds. Although Funes again preferred not to mention it, this was actually a community of militant men of letters, united in as open an opposition to the old order as the climate of the Restoration (1815–30) allowed. To that group belonged Henri Grégoire, former constitutional bishop of Blois and former member of the French National Convention, who retained residual prestige as "Membre de l'Institut" in Paris; Juan Antonio Llorente, the ex-Inquisitor who chose freedom and used it to reveal secret information about the institution he had served;[9] and Fr. Servando Teresa de Mier, an iconoclastic Mexican priest and political maverick who had also participated in the debate on Las Casas, and who for twenty years suffered constant persecution on both sides of the Atlantic, including jailing by the Holy Office.

Funes proclaimed his affinity with all these men. Even if he ultimately joined Grégoire in distancing himself from Llorente, when the ex-Inquisitor openly proclaimed his renunciation of Catholicism, he nonetheless devoted his final efforts as a man of letters to defending freedom of religion and the abolition of monasteries. Thus, Funes maintained until the end of his career an unwavering attachment to the ideals to which he had become committed from the start, when he decided to achieve that notability so cherished by the men of letters in his world. Then, as a notable, he challenged the system in which he had achieved his own eminence, until the time came to begin the process of dismantling the order that had sustained such values.

Funes's review of his career is an attempt to persuade both us and himself that he was able to achieve two fundamental goals despite their internal contradictions: that a world whose foundations he had helped to change and from whose violent death a new one had arisen would continue to offer him the same homage, and that the old order's illustrious son had become the venerable forefather of the system that replaced it.

Notes

1. Rodolfo de Ferrari Rueda, *Córdoba histórica* (Córdoba, 1943), 64–66.

2. Included under the title *Biografía* in *Archivo del Deán Gregorio Funes* (Buenos Aires, 1944), vol. 1.

3. Domingo F. Sarmiento, *Recuerdos de Provincia* (Buenos Aires, 1950), 71.

4. Funes published the oration and made sure it was widely disseminated. The commentaries it received, collected in *Archivo del Deán Gregorio Funes*, not only fail to examine this aspect of his inspiration (in no way a surprising fact), but point out that it bespeaks a certain posthumous flattering of the monarch. Yet, on May 30, 1810, at the time that he was preaching before the members of the revolutionary government in the Cathedral of Buenos Aires, Dean Zavaleta reminded his listeners of the interpretive code Funes himself subsequently preferred. On this point, see Tulio Halperín Donghi, *Tradición política española e ideología revolucionaria de Mayo* (Buenos Aires, 1961), 125–26.

5. *Apuntamientos para una Biografía*, in Senado de la Nación, *Biblioteca de Mayo* (Buenos Aires, 1960), 1530; hereafter abbreviated *AB* and cited in the text.

6. "Elogio de la señora María Josefa Bustos, americana, por D. Gaspar Xuárez, americano," Rome, 1797.

7. Henri Grégoire (1750–1831) was a French revolutionary and constitutional bishop of Blois. Grégoire figured prominently in French politics throughout the French Revolution and past the Napoleonic era. His liberal stands made him obnoxious to the ecclesiastical hierarchy. After his forced retirement in 1814, he pursued a literary career.

8. Juan Antonio Llorente, *Œuvres de don Barthelemi de las Casas, eveque de Chiapa, defenseur de la liberte des naturels de l'Amerique.* . . . (Paris, 1822).

9. In 1823, Gabriel H. Lovett wrote the introduction to the English publication of the work of Juan Antonio Llorente (1756–1823) dealing with the Inquisition under the title *A Critical History of the Inquisition of Spain, from the Period of its Establishment by Ferdinand V to the Reign of Ferdinand VII, Composed from the Original Documents of the Archives of the Supreme Council of the Inquisition and from Those of Subordinate Tribunals of the Holy Office.* For a reprint of the 1826 edition, see Llorente, *The History of the Inquisition of Spain* (Williamstown, Mass., 1967).

Ricardo D. Salvatore

The Breakdown of Social
Discipline in the Banda Oriental
and the Littoral, 1790–1820

The wars of independence in the Banda Oriental and in the Argentine litoral disrupted not only the material basis for rural production but also the network of social relations on which production was based. From an economy based on the estancia system, the region slid into a society dominated by direct appropriation of goods and by an almost total erosion of authority and social hierarchy. This disruption served to widen the space of rural workers' autonomy and acted as a serious obstacle to the restructuring of social relations in the countryside when, after 1815, foreign trade began to demand increasing volume of livestock products.

Why was it so difficult for the rulers and capitalists who emerged after independence to enforce forms of authority and social discipline prevalent in the previous period? Traditionally, the breakdown of social discipline that accompanied the wars of independence has been viewed as a result of the decomposition of the colonial elites, as the work of rural caudillos against urban-based classes, or as a temporary and necessary phenomenon associated with military mobilization.[1] I suggest that in order to understand this change in power relations, we need to pay more attention to the habits and attitudes of rural inhabitants and to their activities to escape the imposition of wage labor and landowner authority. Rural workers' traditions of freedom and illegality, once set within a framework of direct appropriation and the disintegration of social hierarchies, proved an important force opposing the attempts of hacendados, merchants, and local caudillos to return to wage labor and private property.

This chapter will evaluate the degree of autonomy that rural workers of Banda Oriental and the littoral experienced in two crucial periods, 1780–1810 and 1810–30, and will examine the conditions under which this autonomy was attained and preserved. It will show how, at the end of the colonial period, rural workers enjoyed an important degree of autonomy, both in the sphere of production and in rural society as a whole, and how the wars of independence enlarged this autonomy to a point in which society was organized almost independently of wage labor and of the authority of landowners. Under these conditions, the return to the estancia system became very problematic. At the end of the revolutionary wars, neither the economic bonanza opened up by foreign trade nor the activities of isolated caudillos and merchants sufficed to redress the problem of social discipline.

In the first part, the situation of rural workers at the end of the colonial period is examined, evaluating both their relations with estancieros and their degree of subordination to the Spanish colonial administration. The second part focuses on Artigas's records to see how the rural insurrection and the exodus of the *pueblo oriental*, as the people of colonial Uruguay were known, changed the organization of social life in the countryside. Social relations based on direct appropriation became the predominant form for satisfying needs, and this form was consistent with gauchos' cultural traditions and habits. Next, by utilizing the memoirs of a British merchant in Corrientes, the analysis turns to the limitations of merchant capital to rebuild the social relations of the estancia system.

Rural Workers' Autonomy at the End of the Colonial Era

At the end of the colonial period, rural workers managed to preserve an ample degree of autonomy within and without the estancia. Despite an acceleration of proletarianization, peons kept some independence from estancieros: they retained power to decide when to work for wages and when to quit, appropriated ranch products for their own use, managed to resist the imposition of work rules, and, on occasion, were able to impose their demands on the landowners. Outside the estancia, the social and geographical space where rural workers moved was hardly colonized by the end of the eighteenth century. Due to imperfections in the policies of colonial administrators, to the lack of cooperation of estancieros, and to the insufficient development of institutions of social control, gauchos continued to move freely in and out of legality and to live without respect for authority and law.

The Estancia Economy

Findings from a previous study on the Estancia de las Vacas, a large cattle ranch located in the East Bank, today Uruguay, near Colonia, are used to evaluate the extent of rural workers' autonomy in the sphere of production.[2] In this estate's records we found that occasional employment, high rates of turnover, recurrent labor scarcity, lack of labor discipline, and widespread robbery characterized the relations between estancieros and peons during the period 1791–1805. Long-standing traditions of rural inhabitants—illegal appropriation, freedom, and avoidance of permanent work, combined with absentee landownership and a fluctuating labor demand—made for the preservation of an ample degree of workers' autonomy within the estancia. Temporary wage laborers, working from ninety-five to 110 days per year, constituted the largest part of the ranch work force—48 percent of all wage earners worked less than three months and another 29 percent worked between three and six months per year.[3] Because of such practices, the estate's labor force had to be replaced at least three times each year, creating constant problems of labor recruitment for the administrator. Most temporary workers quit after receiving their first pay and never returned to Las Vacas.[4] Those who returned often moved to other occupations or to other ranches.

High occupational and geographical mobility on the part of rural workers, together with an irregular market demand for livestock goods, created recurrent shortages of labor. With time, labor supply accommodated to the fluctuations in demand but, in the short run, the estancia administrator was forced to delay some productive activities until new laborers were recruited.[5] Workers' refusal to engage in long labor contracts and the difficulties of finding economical substitutes for occasional laborers often resulted in losses of assets and sales to the estancia.

Within the estancia, discipline was lax. The owner of Las Vacas unsuccessfully tried to impose work routines and productivity standards on their peons. The lack of direct contact between the estancia's absentee owners and the labor force, and the refusal by both peons and foremen to obey instructions, rendered the owners' rules inoperative. Peons did not make the required roundups, did not produce the expected number of hides or sacks of tallow, and did not cut enough firewood.[6] In addition to the problem of work discipline, the administrator had to deal with customary appropriation of cattle, horses, and hides. Hardly a year passed without a reported robbery. Ex-peons used to steal horses and hides on their way out of the estancia while *agregados* (squatters) made their living by stealing cattle from the estate.

Gauchos' cultural traditions were an important factor in shaping the relations between estancieros and peons within the estancia. Their preference for leisure, their traditional mobility, their contempt for authority, and their customary appropriation of subsistence goods served as strong barriers to the estancieros' attempt to impose work discipline and deference. As the evidence of employment indicates, rural workers were able to decide when to hire themselves for wages and when to quit. They were able to resist work rules that contradicted their work habits. The possibility of living by means of direct appropriation gave rural workers some leverage in their relations with the estate's administrators: peons could abandon the estancia whenever they felt mistreated or badly paid.

Peons at Las Vacas attained their relative autonomy by the daily exercise of small oppositional acts. While in the estancia, peons appropriated meat, hides, and firewood for their own use, interrupted work to play or rest, and did not comply with instructions. At times, they demanded payment in cash, threatening to abandon the estancia if their requirement was not met. Some workers quit their jobs owing the estate for some unpaid goods while others stole the estancia's horses and hides in retaliation for unpaid differences. Unable to modify the attitudes and habits of rural workers, estancieros had to produce commodities for a widening market within a context characterized by high labor turnover, low productivity, theft, and lack of discipline.

Social Conditions for Rural Workers' Autonomy

To a large degree, rural workers' autonomy in the sphere of production was made possible by particular conditions permeating social relations in the Banda Oriental countryside. The existence of an open frontier between Spanish haciendas and Indian territory, the undefined nature of property relations, the inexistence or malfunctioning of the criminal justice system, and the customary toleration of illicit appropriation and trade in cattle created "territorial" and "social" spaces where gauchos were able to exercise their traditions of mobility, direct appropriation, and refusal to work. The existence of such free spaces was related to the failure of colonial authorities to gain control over the most mobile portion of the rural population, Indians and gauchos. There is ample evidence that, in the last two decades of the eighteenth century, colonial authorities tried to colonize, settle, pacify, and "bring order" to the countryside. However, for various reasons—lack of fiscal resources, hacendados' resistance, complicity between cattle merchants and gauchos in illicit trade, and solidarity among different segments of the rural working class—colonial policies fell short of controlling rural workers.

The existence of a "free frontier" appeared as a major factor conditioning the preservation of gauchos' cultural traditions. In the frontier, gauchos were free from the dependence on wage labor, free from Spanish criminal law, and free from the racial and social hierarchies of Spanish society. Colonial administrators were well aware that, in order to check gauchos' mobility and illegal activities, it was imperative to control these open spaces. Consequently, they tried to incorporate the frontier into the territory of Spanish law and civilization. By the end of the colonial period, however, the control of frontiers was by no means settled. In the north, Charruas and Minuanos raided Spanish towns, and Guaraní and Tupi Indians still moved southward to join gangs of bandits and smugglers. In the east, Portuguese smugglers continued their incursions, providing ample work for Indians and gauchos escaping from Spanish law or from the drudgery of estancia labor.

To the north, in the territories of the former missions, colonial authorities faced problems of poor discipline and depopulation. After the expulsion of the Jesuits, the mission Indians were robbed of their cattle by non-Christian Indians and by Spanish and Portuguese rustlers; they were also exploited by Crown administrators. Impoverished, Indians left their towns and went to Brazil, Montevideo, Buenos Aires, and the littoral, where some joined bands of bandits and smugglers and traded with the Portuguese while others became peons of estancias or settled around Spanish cities.[7] To settle the Indians and turn them into productive laborers, colonial authorities devised different schemes, among them a system of government stores and the abolition of Indians' communal organization.[8] Contrary to what colonial reformers expected, these policies created additional problems of discipline and more southward migrations.[9] As Félix de Azara reported in 1806, Indians from the missions of Santa Fe and Corrientes came and went as they pleased and received orders from nobody. They "knew no government, no community, nor the least subjection to anything."[10]

To the east, colonial authorities faced the threat of Portuguese invasions and, hence, of increasing illicit associations between Portuguese smugglers and rural inhabitants of the Banda Oriental. In order to contain Portuguese incursions, in 1800 Viceroy Gabriel de Aviles ordered the construction of frontier villages where settlers would be given land in exchange for territorial defense. The actual foundation of these villages, entrusted to Azara, did not go very far. A Portuguese invasion in 1801, together with the lack of fiscal resources, put an abrupt end to the plan. In 1805, a similar plan was attempted—this time contemplating the distribution of land belonging to large haciendas among poor residents—but the fierce opposition of the Gremio de Hacendados (Landowners' Guild) prevented its enforcement.[11]

The complexity and undefined nature of property relations created another space for the autonomous activities of gauchos. Because cattle hunting coexisted with cattle raising, estancieros had little stimulus to set limits to their properties. Hence, property boundaries were fussy and fences unknown. To the extent that large landowners were unable to exercise effective control over their own lands, a numerous population of squatters (*agregados*) was able to survive alongside with (and at the expense of) large estancias. Squatting provided rural inhabitants with alternative means of subsistence and, therefore, constituted a check against landowners' control of rural workers. The concentration of land property presented yet another problem for colonial authorities. The fact that only a few rich merchants and hacendados had titles to the land was detrimental to the settlement of population and the defense of the frontiers.

To solve these problems, colonial administrators attempted various "plans of land reform." In 1782 Juan José Sagasti suggested to the intendant of Buenos Aires that land be taken from the powerful and be distributed among the poor in small estancias.[12] The commander of the Montevideo countryside also presented a plan to push back the Portuguese and populate the frontier that included a maximum limit to the size of individual properties. In 1795, an anonymous proposal urged the distribution of lands belonging to absentee owners as the remedy for depopulation and vagrancy. Azara developed the most comprehensive plan for agrarian reform of this period in 1802. He argued, among other things, for the need to distribute land among those who would really populate the area, even at the cost of taking land away from those who had failed to do so.[13] Few of these plans were carried into effect; when attempts were made in this direction, the opposition of landowners prevented their enforcement. In 1805 a royal edict ordered the distribution of lands, twelve leagues from the Portuguese frontier, among poor families, providing for the expropriation of large estates and offering amnesty to cattle thieves for their crimes.[14] Large landowners opposed the edict, submitted a protest to the Crown, and obstructed its implementation.

Inefficiency in the operation of the rural police and in the system of criminal justice was yet another factor working in favor of gauchos' autonomy. Vagrancy laws, although in existence since the seventeenth century, were not used to curtail rural workers' mobility until after independence.[15] During most of the colonial period, they served to displace urban workers to agriculture at harvest time or to expel vagrants from the city.[16] In fact, the period between 1780 and 1810 produced no new legislation against rural vagrants. Instead, colonial authorities tried to regulate gauchos' leisure-time activities— gambling and drinking—as a means to reduce the time the latter spent out of work. Prohibitions against gambling had existed since the mid-eighteenth century but became more stringent in 1791, when a decree imposed harsher penalties on gamblers and on those who incited gambling. If previous prohibitions had tried to impose respect for religious festivities, the 1791 decree was oriented toward the transformation of gauchos' free time into labor time and toward the control of crime.[17] The same regulations that restricted gambling in *pulperías, canchas de bochas* (game of bowls), and horse race tracks also extended to ranch peons. In 1799, the *cabildo* ordered local authorities to control the river edges of estancias and apprehend all peons who were found gambling.[18]

In order to improve its control over the countryside, the viceroyalty organized a regular rural police corps in 1797. The corps of Blandengues (lancers), created to guard the northeastern frontier of Banda Oriental from Portuguese incursions and to control the illegal activities of smugglers, improved the security of the countryside slightly, but since the new corps was composed of the same kind of people it was supposed to repress, its efficiency in controlling rural crime must have been quite limited.[19] Desertion and lack of discipline characterized the new rural police.[20]

The landowners' complicity in the theft of cattle and hides made rural crime more difficult to control. Landowners used to give refuge to delinquents because they needed a labor force to smuggle cattle across the Portuguese frontier.[21] Cattle smuggling was still a collective enterprise shared by gauchos, estancieros, and merchants. Colonial authorities tried to separate the legal from the illegal trade of cattle by doing away with trade in unbranded cattle. In 1791, Viceroy Nicolás de Arredondo made the branding of cattle compulsory, ordering that all cattle be branded within the year and declaring that, after that time, all unbranded cattle would become royal property.[22] Spanish authorities moved against the activities of *pulperías*, where stolen hides and other cattle by-products were bought and sold. In the 1790s, various decrees regulating the sale of hides made it illegal for rural storekeepers (*pulperos*) to deal in stolen hides.[23]

Between 1780 and 1810, colonial authorities made various attempts to incorporate the labor power of poor rural inhabitants into productive labor. They devised plans for agrarian reform and settlement of rural population, passed laws for the legalization of commerce in hides and cattle, established a rural police for controlling cattle rustling and smuggling, stimulated landowners to evict squatters, and criminalized various leisure-time activities of the wandering working class. Despite these attempts, very little was gained in terms of reducing the territorial and social space of gauchos. Most plans of land reform stopped short of implementation. The persecution of criminals with a militia composed of criminals was almost an impossibility. Vagrancy laws, applied mostly against urban laborers, as yet did not constitute a threat to the mobility of gauchos. Prohibitions on gambling, drinking, and other leisure activities of rural workers were probably very difficult to enforce given the lack of a well-organized rural police. And, as landowners and merchants participated in cattle rustling and contraband, the enforcement of legislation on branding and theft control remained problematic as well.

Breakdown of Social Discipline after Independence

The revolutionary wars in the Banda Oriental and the littoral caused major disruptions in the social relations of the countryside. Cattle-ranching estancias were plundered and their owners driven away. A majority of rural inhabitants were mobilized into the revolutionary army. And the provision for this army converted direct appropriation or pillaging, used previously only as a complement to wage labor and subsistence production, into the predominant form for satisfying needs. Under these conditions, the small degree of labor and social discipline that existed in the late colonial period almost disappeared, and rural inhabitants found themselves freed from the influence of estancieros and political authorities. The revolutionary wars transformed the nature of rural society—a society based on the estancia system evolved into one based on direct appropriation and cooperative labor. Rural inhabitants took advantage of this social arrangement to fully exercise their cultural traditions of freedom, illegality, and avoidance of work.

Rural Insurrection and Exodus

After 1810, a chain of social and political events caused the loss of the Banda Oriental as a center of production and exports of hides. The revolution led by José Gervasio Artigas began the process by destroying Spanish estancias and cattle. The exodus of population from the region added to the destruction of the estancia economy, as migrants took along large numbers of cattle and horses to provision the army. The Artiguista army, once settled in the littoral, continued plundering estates as a means of subsistence. Artigas's agrarian reform of 1815 completed this process, shaking the basis of estancieros' power over the rural population. All these events uprooted the social relations of the old estancia system.

In the East Bank, the revolution of independence assumed the form of a rural insurrection against the policies of the Spanish colonial administration. Since the middle of the eighteenth century, the extreme inequality in the distribution of land in the Banda Oriental had been the source of many conflicts between absentee landowners and the actual occupants of the land. The bureaucratic cost and complication of registering a parcel had excluded many people from the possibility of becoming landowners. A few big merchants and landowners living in Montevideo or Buenos Aires owned most of the land while the largest proportion of the rural population owned no land. As many of the landowners were Spaniards, the Creole rural population associated this unfair distribution of land with the ethnic inequalities of the Spanish system.[24] Resentment of Spaniards' privileges combined with the injustice of the latifundia to create a growing class tension. In the last two decades of the century, the situation became explosive when landowners stepped up the eviction of squatters.

But the event that triggered the rural insurrection was the viceregal decree of 1810, which tightened the rules of landownership throughout the Banda Oriental.[25] This decree ordered all landholders to submit proof of their property to the colonial authorities and established a tax for all occupants without title, spreading discontent among the rural population. Squatters in particular resisted the new tax. That is why, when Artigas, a young, native-born officer of the Blandengues, decided to offer his services to the Buenos Aires Junta, many squatters were ready to enlist in his army. The revolution was as much an issue of squatters' defense of their lands as one of independence from Spain.

A vast mobilization of rural inhabitants was key to the early success of the Artiguista revolution. In two months, from February to April of 1811, Artigas's forces defeated the Spaniards in several battles—including the major Battle of Las Piedras—and began the siege of Montevideo. But when the Portuguese intervened, the government of Buenos Aires turned its back on Artigas and signed an armistice with Viceroy Francisco Javier de Elío in October 1811. The rural insurrection then turned into an exodus. Artigas, in order to resist this armistice, called upon the rural population to abandon the Banda Oriental territory. About 80 percent of the rural population responded to this call and followed him into the province of Entre Ríos. They abandoned estancias, took cattle herds with them, and destroyed all property that could not be carried so it could not be used by their enemies.[26]

In the beginning, people from all social classes participated in the rural insurrection and in the exodus. Landowners, rural merchants, squatters, peons, wandering gauchos, Indians, and slaves enlisted in the Artiguista army to fight against the Spanish forces.[27] Nevertheless, as the exodus reached the littoral, poor Creoles and Indians came to dominate the army, and the initial cooperation between members of different classes turned to conflict. Creole estancieros and merchants began to press Artigas for a reconstruction of the estancia economy, but gauchos and Indians, having learned to use the militias for their own purposes, were not interested in submitting to the relations of dependence and wage labor.

The need to find means of subsistence in a devastated countryside, the resentment against Spaniards, and the egalitarian ideas of their leaders moved the lower strata of the rural population to join the Artiguista army.[28] They saw in Artigas a faithful interpreter of their needs. Artigas wanted to eliminate social hierarchies based on heritage, blood, and color, which had dominated society under Spanish rule, and to diminish existing inequalities in the distribution of land.[29] In his *Reglamento* of 1815, he promised to redistribute land among the "most unfortunate members of society"—"free Negros, the Zambos of that class, the Indians and the poor Creoles" as well as "poor widows."[30] Gauchos and Indians added another ideal not shared by Artigas to the abolition of social hierarchies— that of common appropriation. During the insurrection and exodus, private property of cattle and food almost disappeared. Except for personal effects, all other forms of wealth were commonly appropriated by the population of each encampment.[31]

The rural insurrection and the exodus disrupted private livestock production and commerce. The ranchers who joined the insurrection had to abandon their estancias and drag along their peons and slaves. Those who opposed the insurrection had to escape, leaving their estates in the hands of majordomos or foremen. As slaves escaped their masters to enlist in the revolutionary militias, estancias lost a major source of permanent labor power. With the prolonged siege to Montevideo, landowners also lost a major market for their cattle and had to redirect sales to Rio Grande, Brazil. The siege also brought about a business collapse among Montevideo *saladeristas* (owners of plants that processed salted meat and hides) and merchants.[32] As a result, for more than ten years, the Banda Oriental lost its primacy as a maritime emporium and as the preferred pasture land for *porteño* landowners. Its exports declined drastically after 1810, and as late as 1824 its economy was still so "depopulated and desolated," so immersed in "misery and discontent," that exports remained negligible.[33]

But the war did more than stop livestock production; it eroded the threads of the social fabric of the countryside. The siege of Montevideo and the exodus destroyed the economic basis for the hegemony of large landowners and merchants residing in the city.[34] Local landowners, with the loss of cattle and land, lost most of their power over rural inhabitants. Freed from landowners' control, the lower strata of the rural population began to look for their own leadership and to experience new forms of subsistence not based on wage labor. As an independent way of life based on cooperation and direct appropriation came to replace the wage-labor relationship, the old system based on patron-client relationships began to fade away. An organization of social life into militias and gangs substituted for the estancia as the locus of human activity.

A Society Based on Direct Appropriation

After leaving the Banda Oriental, Artigas's army moved to the Argentine littoral, passing through the province of Entre Ríos and finally establishing its headquarters in Corrientes. From 1812 until the second siege of Montevideo in 1815, much of the rural population was mobilized into this army. To sustain this population, Artigas gave ample freedom to army officers and militia leaders to demand contributions from estancieros. Widespread appropriation of private cattle and horses and the wholesale destruction of estates followed the marches of the Artiguista army. Encouraged by Artigas, but also the product of gauchos' autonomous activities, banditry came to dominate large areas of Banda Oriental and the littoral, establishing for a while a different form for organizing social life. Direct appropriation of food and other resources replaced the previous organization of production centered on the estancia.

In 1812, the countryside of Banda Oriental, particularly the regions where the Artiguista army had passed, looked desolate. From his encampment, Manuel de Sarratea wrote to the Buenos Aires government: "there has not been a town which has not been plundered in a more or less deafening way, a house which has not been invaded or a family which has not been condemned to misery. . . . It is inconceivable the number of cattle which has been destroyed, there are no horses to mount."[35] Later that year, after having received several complaints from hacendados, he reported that the countryside "was inundated with ferocious bandits."[36]

One landowner described how the Artigas militias occupied his estancia several times during 1812. Different militia groups resided in the estancia's territory for months and appropriated large numbers of cattle and horses. Militiamen showed no respect for private property. "Whenever they want," the hacendado complained, "they come and gather a troop of cattle and take it away, and the most peculiar [feature] is that they do not ask permission of anybody as if it were an abandoned hacienda, they ignore the presence of the foremen and the peons who live in it."[37] Even more appalling to the landowner was the fact that part of the soldiery had organized a parallel production process for its own benefit. In a nearby land, militiamen used his cattle to produce jerked beef, tallow, and soap and had the audacity of selling these products to him and to the army.

Corrientes, the province Artiguistas made their home after the exodus, showed the same degree of desolation by 1815. J. P. Robertson, a British merchant doing business in the littoral, found the province submerged in a state of "anarchy and confusion, of bloodshed, robbery and violence." Due to Artigas's militias, landlords lived in constant terror. With little power over their property and practically no control over the rural population, landowners were at the mercy of "fierce and lawless banditi" who continuously devastated their estates.[38]

What Robertson and the complaining landowners described was a society based on direct appropriation in which gauchos or Artiguista militias appropriated from ranches what they needed for their sustenance and enjoyment. Within this society, private property of land and cattle were mere formalities. "Banditi," mostly gauchos and Indians recruited into Artigas's militias, held the actual control over the hacendados' property. As these gangs took cattle, horses, and peons from estancias and scared away their owners, many estates stopped all production for sale. Their assets became socialized wealth, which were used or consumed as use values. For the hacendados, this was a world turned upside down—the whole matrix of social relations based on the estancia had disintegrated.

The same was true in the sphere of movement. With production stopped, wagons were no longer needed and were scattered around the countryside; they served instead as shelter for the militias. Only gangs of robbers or Artiguistas could move cattle and horses from one point to another with ease. Water transportation also became difficult as pirates sailed along the Paraná River, seizing merchants' ships and taking their crews as prisoners.[39] Merchants shared the fate of the hacendados: their shops and warehouses suffered from constant pillage. A French merchant in Goya, who had stockpiled large quantities of hides, was attacked by Artiguista militias on three different occasions and robbed of all his money, his food, and the manufactured goods from his warehouse.[40]

Who were these bandits who threw the estancia system into chaos? Were they soldiers obeying orders from Artigas? Were they criminals preying on the confusion created by the war? Or were they peasants and peons redressing the injustices of the estancia system and realizing their traditional way of life?

Some of the bandits were Artiguista militiamen. Artigas had gathered an army of gauchos and Indians (Charruas and Minuanos). Not having resources to provide for their food, he allowed them to extort their subsistence from neighboring ranches.[41] Militiamen had to provide for their own subsistence by appropriating alien wealth. Although at first the ransacking of estates affected only enemy property (estates belonging to *malos americanos* and Spaniards), soon this method of appropriation generalized to include all estancias within the reach of militia gangs. There is ample evidence that, as time went on, the militias began to act more and more independently of their leader, and plundering could no longer be controlled. When Artigas, pressed by estancieros, tried to restore some order to the countryside, he was unable to control the delinquent activities of his own militias.

Some of the bandits were gauchos who had never served in the militia. Rafael Sosa Paraguay was one of them. He was caught in 1813 after having participated in the gang that stole cattle from Pedro García's estancia near Mercedes.[42] Others passed for Artiguista militiamen in order to steal hacendados' wealth without interference. Felipe Rivarola reported in 1812 how he and other landowners from Gualeguay in good faith delivered their horses to a band of robbers who said they were under the orders of Artigas.[43] Some of these robbers were members of the *castas:* blacks, mulattoes and Indians.[44] Other gangs stole cattle and hides from the state estancias (those taken under Artigas's laws from "bad Americans" and Spaniards) and sold these products to foreigners.[45]

Some of the robbers were ex-peasants who came into contact with Artiguista militiamen and learned from them the art of pillage. Robertson's report of a peasant dragged by the Artiguistas into one of these gangs is illustrative of this learning process. The peasant, although involuntarily involved in the ransacking of Corrientes, came back satisfied with his share of the spoils.[46] Even for those peasants who did not join bandit gangs, direct appropriation became a way of subsistence. Artigas reported in 1815 that peasants, more preoccupied with their own subsistence than with the preservation of collective wealth, were destroying the cattle herds.[47] So widespread was this practice that military commanders had to authorize their periodical appropriation of alien cattle.[48] Some acts of pillage carried out by peasants, however, had a different motivation. Encarnación Benítez became a popular hero in 1815–16 when his band roamed the countryside near Soriano, confiscated large landowners' lands and cattle, and distributed them among poor peasants. His bands' attacks on hacendados' properties were a way of redressing the unequal distribution of wealth prevailing in the area.[49]

The distinction between militiamen, errant gauchos, and peasants is arbitrary. Because there was a constant circulation of people from one category to the other during this time, it is more accurate to regard militiamen, peasants, and bandits as steps in the life experience of the region's rural inhabitants. As we saw during the revolutionary war, some peasants turned into robbers. Militiamen, having learned the art of pillage during their stay in the army, continued with this activity when they left. Desertion was so frequent that it was almost impossible to distinguish a group of Artiguista militiamen from a gang of deserters-turned-robbers. Gauchos uninvolved with the war also took advantage of the situation and gathered into bands with the purpose of ransacking estancias.

The passage from deserter to bandit became almost natural during these years. In 1814, one of Artigas's military commanders reported that deserters had formed bands more powerful than the government's armies and their "spoilations and excesses" were threatening the security of lives and property in the Corrientes countryside.[50] Desertion was so common that a recruiting officer estimated that very few of the soldiers recruited in Corrientes would arrive at Santa Fe, their final destination, and even if they did, they would disband when entering the city.[51] Lack of food supplies was sufficient reason for soldiers to desert the army and to move to other lands where they continued to exercise "their right" to extort cattle from estates.[52]

The bands roaming the countryside of Banda Oriental and Corrientes also included Indians. Artigas had given arms to Indians and had put them into contact with the rest of his army, which was composed mainly of gauchos.[53] Later, when the war was in decline, Indians and gauchos became partners in crime, developing a high degree of cooperation. This cooperation had already existed in the estancias, but was greatly intensified by the war mobilization. In one of the many robberies committed in Entre Ríos, it was reported that eight Indians had joined gaucho robbers and escaped to the Banda Oriental.[54]

For the lower strata of the rural population—gauchos, Indians, peasants, militiamen—appropriation of cattle and horses constituted not robbery but a form of life, a way of obtaining subsistence from wealth that existed in abundance in the estancias.[55] Artigas contributed to the legitimacy of this form of life by encouraging his militia leaders to ransack the enemy's property and to collect supplies for the army from estates. His policies of "socializing" the distribution of food among the population residing in his encampments also served to legitimize direct appropriation (and hindered the development of its opposite, consumption mediated by wage labor). Since Artigas created a system for the free distribution of beef among the numerous civilians who followed the soldiery, these people grew accustomed to receiving their sustenance from the army—from what was actually stolen cattle.[56]

The social system that emerged in Banda Oriental and Corrientes in 1812–15 was consistent with old gaucho traditions of independence and illegality. The war situation had only created an environment in which rural inhabitants were able to return to the times when they roamed freely through the Banda Oriental prairies, hunting cattle and selling it to Portuguese smugglers—a time when they lived on beef appropriated, slaughtered, and cooked on the spot; a time when they did not have to work for wages to earn a living. During the three years that followed the exodus, the social relations that had tied rural workers to landowners and merchants were destroyed. Freed from these ties, gauchos appropriated the land, destroyed the remnants of the old estancia system, and consumed the recently socialized wealth, returning for a while to their traditional way of life. The type of rural society that resulted from the Artiguista revolution gave gauchos opportunities to live according to previous life-styles and culture, and hence to better resist the reimposition of authority, private property, and wage labor.

Commercial Capital and Social Control

Whereas war mobilization and the problems of army provisioning ended in the littoral and the Banda Oriental in the mid-1810s, the problems of rebuilding cattle ranches and of regaining social control lasted at least until the late 1820s. Political segmentation of the territory, conflicts between caudillos, and the lack of consensus among estancieros delayed the normalization and control of the countryside. Rural inhabitants grew so accustomed to the mode of direct appropriation that it became extremely difficult to reintroduce previous systems of labor recruitment and social control.

In a society characterized by plunder and pillage, merchant capital appeared as a possible way to rebuild the estancia economy. Providing an outlet for the spoils of plunder, merchant capital could valorize livestock products deprived of exchange value by the war. Reintroducing money in a devastated economy, merchants could lure peasants and gauchos to collect local produce for sale. But, would this suffice to put rural inhabitants to work under the social relations of the estancia? Here, we examine a case in which foreign merchants, through their commercial activities, tried to rebuild the ranches and the relations of subordination on which they were based. Their effect, as we shall see, was negligible. As long as widespread direct appropriation of cattle subsisted and gauchos found alternatives to ranch work, merchants were unable to rebuild the traditional relations between landowners and peons.

John Robertson and his brother William came to the Río de la Plata region in 1811 and 1814 to open a commercial operation for the collection of hides from centers in Corrientes and Goya. With youth, entrepreneurial drive, and the capital of their relative in Bath, England, they soon organized a successful business.[57] Four conditions proved essential for the success of their enterprise in Corrientes: the use of money and credit, the control of transportation, the payment of high wages, and the help of an authoritarian manager to discipline gauchos. The economy of Corrientes had been greatly demonetized by the time the Robertsons arrived in 1814. The revolutionary wars and the collapse of trade that it brought about had reduced the use of money to a minimum. Robertson found boys and girls peddling their wares door to door; some of them were offering their goods for money, but many were demanding other goods in exchange.[58] As the Robertsons began to import gold doubloons from Buenos Aires and to pay for local produce and labor with gold, however, money once again started to replace this primitive mode of exchange.[59] The Robertsons used money as credit, giving cash advances to collectors for future deliveries of local products. Although this way of doing business was very risky, it was the only accepted commercial practice in the interior.[60] Whereas local merchants traditionally had profited from large differences between buying and selling prices, the Robertsons offered high prices for the local produce and charged low prices for their wares. In a countryside devastated by war and banditry, this strategy allowed them to do away with competition from local merchants and to reconstitute the threads of commerce.

Transportation had constituted a bottleneck since the start. On one occasion, for example, the Robertsons' *capataz* (foreman) traveled as far as fifty or sixty leagues from Corrientes to find an estanciero who had stockpiled as many as ten thousand hides. The owner, due to the disarray in transportation and the labor scarcity created by the war, had been unable to send this production to Corrientes. As he had neither wagons nor bullocks nor peons, he was only too happy to sell the produce to whomever had the means of carrying it westward. As soon as the Robertsons realized that existing stocks of hides or cattle herds were scattered throughout the province, they saw the need to have their own transportation system. With the help of Pedro Campbell, the *capataz*, they organized three troops, each containing eighteen to twenty wagons, three hundred bullocks, and twenty to thirty saddle horses. The labor force was organized similarly to that of an estancia: for each troop there was one foreman, one or two assistants, five or six *bueyeros* (drivers of relay bullocks), and as many drivers as wagons (eighteen to twenty).[61] In total they employed between seventy-five and eighty-one people.

In order to mobilize these workers, they used the power of money, paying peons high wages in cash. As William Robertson recalls: "Our three capataces were, in their line, the finest fellows we could pick out in the province; and their having, on the other hand, our orders to pay the highest wages for the best men as their assistants and peons, our three troops of carts were like three crack regiments in the army of the nation."[62] But paying high wages made the operation extremely expensive. The Robertsons invested about five thousand pounds in the troops of wagons and had operating expenses amounting to five hundred pounds per month.

When the Robertsons arrived at Corrientes, a state of class fear prevailed among estancieros to the point that carrying out the normal operations of a cattle ranch seemed almost an impossibility. As Campbell put it: "There is not an estanciero that has the liver . . . to go to his own estate; peep out of his own window; slaughter one of his own animals; carry ten dollars in his pocket; take time to sip a mate; or venture to light a segar after dusk."[63] Under these conditions, finding a man who could provide the owner with protection against bandits and soldiers was essential for running a ranch. If the same person could command respect and admiration from gauchos, so as to be able to organize and discipline them for ranch work, the estanciero had very good chances of setting up a workable and stable ranch.

Pedro Campbell, the Robertsons' *capataz*, was such a person.[64] An Irishman in gaucho attire, Campbell had gained the admiration and fear of others. Being very close to Artigas, he had military authority over the militias while his bravery and ability with the knife gave him the respect of gauchos. He was, according to William Robertson, "the most feared and respected man in the province." The Robertsons hired Campbell at the outstanding wage of 1,200 pesos a year.[65] His services included the protection of the Robertsons' property and persons, the organization of the wagon business, the hiring and firing of peons, and the supervision of the collection and transportation of hides. Of these, the most important task consisted of disciplining the labor force, of turning gauchos into obedient peons. With the use of authoritarian methods—which included whipping and solving conflicts with a knife—Campbell was able to impose labor discipline among the unruly Creole peons.[66]

In order to collect as many local products as possible, Campbell was to induce estancieros "to return to their estates and collect hides, skins, horse-hair, and wool." But when estancieros found it difficult to hire peons and to make them work in the estancia, Campbell's activities as organizer extended toward his suppliers' estates. With his own peons, he helped ranchers repair their houses, improve their corrals, build wagons, and collect cattle and horses.[67]

This was a clear case in which a merchant's activities extended over to the social relations of production in order to have commodities for purchase.

How effective and widespread were the Robertsons and Campbell's restructuring of relations of production? According to William Robertson, his own purchases coupled with Campbell's work in disciplining the labor force and rebuilding estancias generated a rapid economic revival of the region.[68] However, it is likely that Robertson extrapolated the image of intense activity from his own business to the whole economy. In a short period of time his business grew to levels of activity previously unknown in the region. During the nine months he stayed in Goya, Robertson collected fifty thousand oxhides, one hundred thousand horsehides, and many bales of wool, mobilizing large numbers of workers and keeping high levels of work intensity. His "lieutenants, capataces, peons, carters, sailors, and others, were from sunrise to sunset in a constant, busy, and animated train of action."[69] But intense activity was probably restricted to his own business. After all, his troop of oxcarts was the only one in operation in the region, and the purchase of hides and wool by other merchants paled in comparison to his own.

Examining the nature of production a little closer, one finds reasons to doubt the ability of our enterprising British merchants and their disciplinarian *capataz* to reestablish relations of production throughout the region. Concerning trade, undoubtedly the Robertsons had the capacity to mobilize the work of many independent producers and sellers of hides, but this does not imply that they promoted actual production in estancias. At least three-fourths of the hides the Robertsons purchased during their stay in Corrientes came from wild cattle, gathered by parties of gauchos on the open prairies. Only one-fourth of their purchases came from domesticated cattle, that is, from production in settled estancias. This reveals the limited degree to which the Robertsons' purchases contributed to the rebuilding of ranches. Regarding labor discipline and the settlement of new ranches, Campbell was able to convince only a dozen landowners to take his services to organize production. The lion's part of his job, however, consisted in organizing gauchos for cattle-hunting expeditions.[70] Besides, as Campbell was happy to admit, he was the only one (probably one among few) who had enough power in the Artiguista army and enough respect among rural inhabitants to re-create the relations of discipline among the latter.

Estancieros who could not hire his services or those of other caudillos had little chance to gather enough peons, put them to work, and maintain some degree of authority over them.

Even if the Robertsons' and Campbell's activities had stimulated trade and created labor discipline beyond the limits of their own business, the effects of their actions were not long-lasting. After all, the Robertsons stayed in Corrientes province for only a little over a year. Having arrived late in 1814, they left for Buenos Aires in October of 1816, with no intention of returning. After they collected all their hides at Goya, loaded them on their own riverboat, received all the oxcarts from Campbell, and paid the last wages to their *capataces*, peons, and servants (it was like "the disbanding of a little army," William Robertson commented), rural workers went back into the countryside to go on with their wandering habits.[71] Campbell, the disciplinarian, returned to his military position in Artigas's army, later becoming commander of the navy. The reasons the Robertsons gave for their withdrawal from Corrientes help us to understand why this kind of activity could not last. First, there was a problem of personal security. Several times the Robertsons had been detained by different parties of the conflict and at least twice had been incarcerated.[72] Second, their commercial strategy was based on the shortrun; they had to collect enough hides to make a large shipment to England and then return.[73] As the hides available for purchase were the surplus product of a society based on plunder and direct appropriation, not the product of ranch production, their activity could only be short-lived.

When W. R. Robertson returned to Corrientes in 1817, he saw the region in a state of great commercial activity. Population was multiplying in Goya, and small dealers had taken the place the Robertsons had left in the hide business.[74] But this situation did not last long, nor did it change the nature of social relations. In 1819, Andresito, an Indian leader belonging to Artigas's army, occupied the city of Corrientes. With the province under Indian rule for almost a year, owners abandoned their estancias in fear, leaving them to the pillage of bandits and soldiers.[75] Once Artigas was defeated and his militias dispersed, the Indians concentrated on the western bank of the Uruguay River in Corrientes and made organized robbery their main business.[76] The situation of the military was no different in 1828 than in 1815; army officers could not control the pervasive cycle of soldiers turning into deserters, and deserters turning into robbers.[77] Widespread banditry and misery in the countryside continued well into the late 1820s, despite the efforts of Governor Pedro Ferré to curb rural crime and lawlessness.[78] As Indians, deserters, and bandits continued to appropriate the estancias' wealth long after Artigas's militias were disbanded, the Robertsons' dreams of transforming Corrientes into a secure place for estancieros remained elusive, at least until the next decade.

Conclusions

From 1790 to 1820, rural society in Banda Oriental and the Argentine littoral evolved from a situation where the estancia system was prevalent to one in which large segments of the population subsisted by means of direct appropriation. This change brought about a widening of the autonomy of rural workers vis-à-vis the government and the landowning class. Although at the end of the colonial period rural workers already enjoyed an ample degree of autonomy within and without the estancia, this autonomy expanded after independence with the breakdown of wage labor and the paternalistic relationships that characterized the estancia system. As rural inhabitants entered different social arrangements—joining army encampments, militia gangs, or groups of robbers—they were able to exercise more freely old traditions of freedom, refusal to work, and direct appropriation of subsistence. Society came to be organized around use value (direct appropriation to satisfy needs) and, consequently, achieving social control became even more difficult.

Whereas in the late colonial period, the relative autonomy of rural workers was related to the failure of colonial administrations to curtail the mobility and the alternative sources of subsistence of rural inhabitants, in the postrevolutionary period, it was the very destruction of the estancia system—brought about by war and pillage—that prevented the new rulers from enforcing some degree of social control over the rural population. The war created the need to change the mechanisms of appropriation and distribution of wealth, and this led to the gradual erosion of traditional hierarchies and to an undesired decentralization of authority. The space without law, once restricted to the areas close to Indian territory, now embraced most of the Banda Oriental and the Argentine littoral. Banditry by mounted groups also periodically ravaged rural populations of Córdoba and Santa Fe well into the 1820s. None of these incidences, however, ever reached the epic dimensions of the Artigas rebellion.

Under the new social milieu, the activities of isolated merchants and ranchers proved insufficient to rebuild the basis of the estancia system. Although the combination of authoritarian foremen and metallic money were able to mobilize some temporary labor power for the collection of hides, the strategy could not be extended to the entire rural population, particularly in the areas where bands of militiamen and robbers still reigned supreme. As colonial reformers knew well, the enforcement of property rights on cattle and land and the existence of wage-labor relations required the use of an effective public force—rural police and a system of criminal justice—that could criminalize rural inhabitants' alternative sources of subsistence and reduce the territorial and social space of wandering gauchos. Only after Artigas's fall, the new leaders of Banda Oriental and the littoral recognized this truth and tried "to bring order" to the countryside.

Notes

1. See, for example, Tulio Halperín Donghi, *Revolución y guerra* (Buenos Aires, 1972), 293.

2. Ricardo Salvatore and Jonathan Brown, "Trade and Proletarianization in Late Colonial Banda Oriental: Evidence from the Estancia de las Vacas, 1791–1805," *Hispanic American Historical Review* 67, no. 3 (August 1987): 431–59.

3. Ibid., Table IV, 442.

4. Out of a total of 1,252 recorded wage payments between 1791 and 1805, our records registered 903 different names.

5. In 1794, administrator Posadas blamed the lack of peons for the ongoing difficulties in collecting and processing grease and tallow. A report on the conditions of estates in 1795 stated that the lack of workers prevented the roundup and branding of cattle so that domesticated animals escaped to the wilds or to neighbors' herds. In 1799, as a result of labor shortages, the administrator was unable to fill existing contracts for tallow and grease due to lack of laborers.

6. Salvatore and Brown, "Trade and Proletarianization in Late Colonial Banda Oriental," 452–57.

7. Between 1768 and 1800, 53,000 Indians out of an original population of

96,000 had fled from their villages (John Lynch, *Spanish Colonial Administration, 1782–1810* [New York, 1969], 186–89).

8. In 1783 Viceroy Juan José de Vértiz implemented a system of government stores that sold goods on credit (*socorros*) to Indians in order to make them cultivate their own plots or sell their labor to the most prosperous in the community. The plan, first applied in Paraguay and Cochabamba, was not implemented elsewhere due to the opposition of the intendants. In 1803, a *Cédula Real* abolished the government in communities and gave freedom to all Guaraní and Tupi Indians, loosening even more the already lax discipline (ibid., 197–98).

9. To integrate the Indians completely, Indian communal property had to be abolished and Indians given full rights to trade and work with other races. A Plan of the Junta in 1806 recommended that land, cattle, and other possessions of the communities be distributed in private property to the Indians, and that all Indians be given the right to work, to buy, to sell, and to own property. All Indian tributes were to be abolished and Indians had to pay taxes every other Spaniard paid. The plan was never implemented.

10. Félix de Azara, "Informe sobre el govierno y libertad de los indios . . . ," in *Memoria sobre el estado rural del Río de la Plata y otros informes* (Buenos Aires, 1943), 246–51.

11. José P. Barrán and B. Nahum, *Bases económicas de la revolución Artiguista* (Montevideo, 1968), 95–96.

12. Ricardo Rodríguez Molas, *Historia social del gaucho* (Buenos Aires, 1968), 80–83.

13. These programs of agrarian reform and others are analyzed in Barrán and Nahum, *Bases económicas*, 96–104.

14. Ibid., 109–10.

15. Sending vagrants to the army or using them for public works was not an innovation of the late eighteenth century (Rodríguez Molas, *Historia social del gaucho*, 109).

16. Legislation prior to 1780 reveals that it was customary to expel city vagrants from Buenos Aires, sending them to the prison of Montevideo or to the Malvinas Islands. In 1774, Viceroy Vértiz issued a *bando* ordering all those "who did not live from their work nor have any occupation or master" to leave the city, or to be sentenced to four years of deportation in the Malvinas. Urban laborers, on the other hand, were subject to forced labor, an extreme expedient used to solve situations of shortage of hands during harvest time. Since the early eighteenth century, it had been common practice to force colored artisans to suspend their activities and hire themselves out during the wheat harvest. In 1753 and again in 1777, the colonial government closed all brick furnaces around the city of Buenos Aires to compel brickmakers to pick up the harvest.

17. In 1746, there was a prohibition against playing cards in *pulperías*. In 1756, a *bando* forbade horse races during work days. In 1776, the opening of *canchas de bochas* was forbidden during the time of *cuaresma*. In 1777, many games were banned together: cards, dice, *taba, pato,* and others. In 1791 a *bando* punished with prison the simple incitation to gambling (Rodríguez Molas, *Historia social del gaucho,* 89–91).

18. Ibid., 170.

19. In order to attract recruits, the colony offered soldiers salaries above those of *dragones* and extended an amnesty to all deserters, smugglers, and criminals who joined the Blandengues for two years (Washington Reyes Abadie et al., *La Banda Oriental: Praderas, fronteras, puerto* [Montevideo, 1965], 77, and Barrán and Nahum, *Bases económicas,* 108).

20. In 1798, for example, of the fifty-two Blandengues sent to pacify an Indian uprising, eleven deserted. In 1801, Azara complained that the defense of the northeastern frontier, a responsibility of the Blandengues, was ineffective to prevent Indian attacks (Barrán and Nahum, *Bases económicas,* 84, and Azara, "Informe sobre el govierno y libertad de los Indios," 171–72).

21. Luisa Sala de Touron et al., *Estructura económica-social de la colonia* (Montevideo, 1967), 152.

22. Barrán and Nahum, *Bases económicas,* 92–93.

23. Prudencio de la Cruz Mendoza, *Historia de la ganadería argentina* (Buenos Aires, 1928), 92–93.

24. See Juan Pivel Devoto, *Raíces coloniales de la revolución oriental,* 2d ed. (Montevideo, 1957).

25. Barrán and Nahum, *Bases económicas,* 88–89; Agustín Beraza, *La economía de la Banda Oriental, 1811–1820* (Montevideo, 1961), 14–15; Nelson de la Torre et al., *Artigas: Tierra y revolución* (Montevideo, 1967), 37–38.

26. Halperín Donghi, *Politics, Economy, and Society in Argentina in the Revolutionary Period* (Cambridge, 1975), 275. On the exodus, see Florencia Fajardo Terán, *Significación histórica del año once* (Buenos Aires, 1959).

27. De la Torre et al., *Artigas,* 33–36; and Beraza, *La revolución oriental, 1811* (Montevideo, 1961), 22–27.

28. Because the masses who made the revolution were illiterate, it is difficult to evaluate the ideals that moved them to fight. Artigas's system of ideas included federalism, social and economic equality, and an incipient form of nationalism, but it is likely that it was Artigas's egalitarianism that appealed to the lower strata of the rural population (De la Torre et al., *Artigas,* 24).

29. Artigas wanted to "wipe out the excesses of despotism" and "the accursed custom of a man's high social standing being decided on the cradle" (letter to J. Silva, April 1815, in Halperín Donghi, *Politics, Economy, and Society,* 297).

30. Barrán and Nahum, *Bases económicas*, 122.

31. Beraza, *La revolución oriental*, 68.

32. Beraza, *La economía de la Banda Oriental*, 16–22.

33. Robert A. Humphreys, *British Consular Reports on the Trade and Politics of Latin America 1824–1826* (London, 1940), 19, 40.

34. Halperín Donghi, *Politics, Economy, and Society*, 275.

35. Manuel de Sarratea to Gov. of Provincias Unidas, Salto Chico, 23 June 1812, in José Artigas, *Archivo Artigas*, 20 vols. (Montevideo, 1950–81), 9:6–7.

36. Sarratea to Gov. of Provincias Unidas, Santa Lucía, 29 December 1812, and Sarratea to Eusebio Valdenegro, Salto Chico, 16 August 1812, in ibid., 10:138, 313.

37. Eusebio M. Calcena y Echeverría to his father, Mandisoví, 13 August 1812, in ibid., 10:128–29.

38. "He [Artigas] robbed, pillaged, plundered, drove the owners of *estancias* from their homes, and the cattle to the eastern bank of the Uruguay. . . . The estancias became depopulated, the herdsmen were seized upon for soldiers, all the natural ties of society were broken or relaxed; the country was overspread with fierce and lawless banditi . . . and rare was the mounted (gaucho) to be met with, who was not a robber or assassin or both. . . . The huge wagons which were wont to convey the hides from estancia to estancia, and to the different ports of shipment, were dismantled and scattered over the country, to serve as tents or bivouacs for the erratic plunderers, who, half naked, wholly reckless, subsisted on the cattle they could take with their lassos, and enjoyed the luxury of spirits, gambling, and segars." J. P. Robertson and W. P. Robertson, *Letters from South America*, 3 vols. (1843; reprint New York, 1971), 1:22–25.

39. José Luis Domínguez to Director Supremo de las Provincias Unidas, Corrientes, 25 February 1814, in *Archivo Artigas*, 14:107.

40. Robertson and Robertson, *Letters from South America*, 1:143–45.

41. Francisco de Chagas Santos to Diego de Souza, San Borja, 30 March 1813, in Artigas, *Archivo Artigas*, 11:302.

42. Francisco Bustamante to Bruno Méndez, Mercedes, 5 August 1813, in ibid., 12:154–55.

43. Felipe Rivarola to Francisco Javier de Viana, Lucas, 26 September 1812, in ibid., 10:191–92.

44. De la Torre et al., *La revolución agraria artiguista 1815–1816* (Montevideo, 1969), 51.

45. Commander of Supplies, Maldonado, 10 July 1813, in Artigas, *Archivo Artigas*, 12:103.

46. "When he got there (Corrientes), he saw his friends begin to disperse about the town, to enter shops, houses and stores, and to help themselves to whatever they fancied, without any apparent displeasure, certainly without

any resistance on the part of the real owners of property. . . . The marauders once more formed into a body, and each carrying his own share of the spoil, they trotted leisurely out of the town, while the old Chacarero found himself on his way home, with a large cut of good lace cloth, a new hat, a couple of pieces of nice printed calico, and two or three dollars in money. . . . He exclaimed: Pillaging has been a good thing!" Robertson and Robertson, *Letters on South America*, 1:151–52.

47. J. Artigas to Cabildo de Montevideo, Cuartel General, 12 November 1815, in Archivo General de la Nación, *Correspondencia del General José Artigas al Cabildo de Montevideo, 1814–1816* (Montevideo, 1946), 48.

48. In 1815, Pablo Pérez, one of Artigas's officers, authorized several *vecinos* from Partido de la Cruz to enter alien property and slaughter alien cattle for their own subsistence. "It is not fair that they die of starvation," he said (De la Torre et al., *La Revolución agraria artiguista*, p. 54).

49. Ibid., 142–43.

50. José León Domínguez to José Artigas, Corrientes, 23 February 1814, in Artigas, *Archivo Artigas*, 14:98–99.

51. Ignacio Alvarez to Director Supremo de Santa Fé, 11 March 1814, in ibid., 14:146.

52. Cabildo de Santo Domingo Soriano to José Artigas, Santo Domingo, 16 July 1813, in ibid., 12:14–15.

53. Barrán and Nahum state that after the exodus most of Artigas's militias were made up of gauchos and Indians (Barrán and Nahum, *Bases económicas*, 115).

54. Pablo Areguati to General in Chief of the Army, Salto Chico, 9 December 1812, in Artigas, *Archivo Artigas*, 10:297.

55. Eusebio M. Calcena reported that soldiers' relatives were accustomed to entering the estancias in daylight; they appropriated eight to ten loads ("cargueros") of beef, and this was not considered robbery (Artigas, *Archivo Artigas*, 10:129).

56. Juan José Durán to Bruno Méndez, Migueletes, 14 May 1813, in Artigas, *Archivo Artigas*, 12:28–29.

57. See Vera Blinn Reber, *British Mercantile Houses in Buenos Aires 1810–1880* (Cambridge, Mass., 1979), 95, and H. S. Ferns, *Britain and Argentina in the Nineteenth Century* (Oxford, 1960), 81.

58. "Salt for candles," "tobacco for bread," "yerba for eggs," "tomato for sugar," they cried aloud in front of the houses. From this observation, Robertson inferred that Correntinos predominantly relied upon barter to satisfy their daily needs (*Letters on South America*, 1:52–53).

59. "We ourselves," claimed the Robertsons, "gradually introduced the use of money in our domestic economy." Readily available money constituted "the very soul" of the British merchants' business (ibid., 1:52–53, 283, 287).

60. "The universal system of doing business in the interior parts of South America, is giving what are called 'habilitaciones,'—that is, advancing to the grower or collector of produce a certain sum in money and goods, which he engages to repay in his produce within a given time, and at a stipulated price. If you want wheat, hides, mineral ores, wool, yerba, tobacco, or any other product of the country, in large quantities, you must advance the money in the first place, and then trust to the honesty of your debtor for fulfilling his part of the contract." Ibid., 1:174.

61. Ibid., 1:180–81.

62. Ibid., 1:183.

63. Ibid., 1:63.

64. Campbell was an intriguing and unique character. Born in Ireland, where he had worked as a tanner's apprentice during his youth, he joined the British army and came to Río de la Plata with the invading forces of 1807. After the defeat of his regiment, he remained in the region and went to Corrientes where he worked in a tannery for a while. Soon he adapted to the gauchos' ways of living and even surpassed their skills. When the insurrection in the Banda Oriental broke out, he joined the Artiguista forces and promptly became an assistant to Artigas.

65. Robertson and Robertson, *Letters on South America*, 1:28–39, 63–64.

66. "No small difficulty was experienced at first in bringing back all the peons or Gauchos to their old habits of labour and subordination as servants, so completely had they been demoralized by the lawless life which, as Artigueno soldiers, many of them had led. But high wages, regularly paid, worked wonders. In many parts, indeed, the bolder and more reckless of these men would now and then show an inclination to upset the good work which was going forward. But Campell's sway was omnipotent, and he reduced the worst of them to submission and obedience. His physical strength—his undaunted, if not ferocious, courage when roused—his dexterity with his knife, and his ready appeal to that, or to his gleaming sabre, sowed all spirits less daring than his own, and left him undisputed master of the field." Ferns, *Britain and Argentina in the Nineteenth Century*, 61.

67. "The higher class of estancieros, seeing the new order of things established, and knowing they had now a sure and profitable market for their hides, were gradually up and stirring, many availing themselves of Don Pedro's help to re-organize their estancias, and to collect again their herds of cattle" (Robertson and Robertson, *Letters on South America*, 1:176–78).

68. "In these various ways the country, as if by magic, started into industrious life and mercantile activity, in every section of its wide extent. Herds and flocks gathered together, thousands and tens of thousands of the wild cattle were slaughtered for their hides; and in all directions the creaking of the large wheels of huge and ponderous wagons, laden with the produce of estancias and villages, gave token of renewed prosperity and peace, where a

few months, nay a few weeks, before, all had been rapine, desolation, and decay." Ibid., 1:179.

69. Ibid., 1:251.

70. Ibid., 1:65–66.

71. Ibid., 2:35–37.

72. Their lives had been in danger even though they commanded a passport from Artigas. "We had suffered too much from irregular, unlawful, or violent aggression," the Robertsons commented to General Miller. So they sailed for Buenos Aires in the hope of finding a "more civilized policy" and the protection of both the British community in Buenos Aires and of the British navy in Rio (Ibid., 1:59, 2:40).

73. Ibid., 2:40.

74. Ibid., 2:58.

75. An account of Andresito's occupation is reported by Miss Postlethwaite in ibid., 2:161–78, and John Street, *Artigas and the Emancipation of Uruguay* (Cambridge, 1959), 315.

76. "Accustomed to pillage [they] constituted themselves into bandits and this was the bait which attracted outlaws and deserters from neighboring armies and towns." Their exclusive occupation was to rob cattle, from the *estancias* in Corrientes or from those of the Portuguese in Misiones, selling the stolen cattle to those from Entre Ríos who come to buy them in exchange for goods appropriate to the Indians's use, especially brandy." *Memoria del Brigadier General Pedro Ferré* (Buenos Aires, 1921), 27.

77. See letters quoted in Hernán Gómez, *Historia de la Provincia de Corrientes*, 3 vols. (Corrientes, 1929), 3:70–71, 126–27, 134–36.

78. Thomas Whigham reports that due to constant *levas* and pillage of tobacco plantations, subsistence agriculture prevailed in Corrientes until the late 1820s (Whigham, "Agriculture and the Upper Plata: The Tobacco Trade, 1780–1865," *Business History Review* 59, no. 4 [Winter 1985]: 563–96). Even at the end of the decade, when the powerful caudillo Pedro Ferré strengthened his control of the province, other Indian gangs occupied the town of Corrientes, once again bringing pillage and destruction.

Kristine L. Jones

Indian-Creole Negotiations
in the Southern Frontier

Civil wars and political disarticulation shook the Americas in the
first half of the nineteenth century as colonial societies struggled toward independence and national unity. Colonial boundaries
and intercultural frontiers between different native societies contracted, shifted, and reformed. Internal conflicts between centralists and federalists drew efforts away from boundary definition and
maintenance, allowing political movements, refortifications, and
confederations to flourish among autonomous Indian societies,
often incorporating Europeans escaping western society. In North
America, Mexico lost half of its territory in the Treaty of Guadalupe
Hidalgo to the United States, along with its responsibility for defense against Apache and Comanche raids. When the United States
turned its attentions east toward resolution of the Civil War, these
and other plains societies enjoyed a cultural and economic renais-
sance. In the Southern Cone, the Araucanians reclaimed territory in
the Chilean cordillera; they pushed into the pampas grasslands and
up to the margins of Argentine settlement. The temporary resurgence of political sovereignty and military power among "hunting
and gathering" societies in the North American plains, Chilean cordillera, and Argentine pampas at this time was clearly related to
uniquely American conflicts in state building.

Because of postindependence political disunity, responsibility for
resolution of Indian-white hostilities throughout the Americas re-
verted to frontier settlements. Locally raised militias (Indian as well
as European) organized for defense, and, even more commonly, locally negotiated treaties provided temporary and localized peace
through regular payments of goods to the Indians. When the resolu-

tion of internal civil wars and national political consolidation permitted unified national policies and centralized military policies toward the Indians in the 1870s and 1880s, the new American governments faced more formidable and better organized Indian forces. National—and nationalistic—histories of the subsequent conquest depict a militarily superior "white" society that subjugated hemispherically undifferentiated and (ergo) inferior "Indian" society. The costs of the resulting Indian wars of the 1870s and 1880s, throughout the hemisphere, are seemingly obvious by any perspective. The loss of lives, livestock, and control over frontier commerce provided a rationale for national policies of conquest. These very policies of dispossession, extermination, and genocide prompted equally fierce opposition from Indian societies.

The costs of earlier policies of "pacification" are much less understood. One such policy pursued by newly developing nations involved the payment of regular nations of annuities in exchange for negotiated peace. This approach to frontier conflict negotiation, long established in the western tradition, is often overlooked because the expenditure often appears to have been insignificant in the context of national budgets. In the broader context, though, the costs as well as the benefits had wide-reaching consequences.

This chapter will look more closely at the direct costs and benefits to both Indian and Creole society in the southern Argentine pampas that resulted from peace negotiations involving annuity payments in the mid-nineteenth century. That this "profligate bribery"[1] existed is well known; less understood are the intricacies at the local level, especially negotiations involving politically astute Indian caciques and the better-known Creole caudillos. Focus on these frontier dynamics leads to greater insight into the indirect costs and benefits of nation building in the uniquely American context. While the annuity payments and political alliances were in place, Creole society was able to recover from civil wars, expand livestock interests, and consolidate political systems. For part of the time, Indian societies were able to enjoy the same benefits (respite from intertribal hostilities, expansion of trade in livestock, and florescence of powerful tribal confederations) while maintaining political and cultural sovereignty. When the payments ended, however, the balance shifted, and the Argentine state faced a more formidable and understandably hostile force.

The Southern Frontier: The Colonial Background

In the late colonial era, to facilitate expeditions south to the Indian-controlled Salinas Grandes for salt (which could not be obtained through trade with Brazil or other European traders because of trade restrictions imposed by the Spanish) the *cabildo* (municipal government) of Buenos Aires authorized a series of agreements (usually including gifts "out of respect for them")[2] with Pampas, Tehuelche, and Araucanian leaders. Along the southern frontier of Creole settlement, conflicts over use rights to grazing and wild herds hunted for their hides sometimes resulted in locally negotiated treaty agreements specifying rights to trade and commerce, as well as gifts. Terms and conditions for trade often included exchange of goods for the redemption of Creole captives occasionally captured by the Indians.

By this time, Indian societies in the pampas had already been altered through indirect contact with European society. The incorporation of the horse, the spread of disease, and the shift to new technologies all led to modifications in indigenous social structure long before extensive direct contact with European society. A picture of indigenous societies emerges in reports and comments from military expeditions, missionaries, and other travelers of the mid-1700s. Especially important are the accounts of two Jesuit missionaries, Padre José Cardiel, who worked among the Pampas groups he called the Serranos, and Padre Thomas Falkner, who contacted both Pampas and Araucanian groups.[3] While their missionizing attempts failed to Christianize or to settle the natives of the grasslands onto small farms, the first sensitive depictions of these groups appear in their accounts.

The subsistence pattern of the Pampas Indians (those indigenous to the pampas) in the mid-1700s depended upon the herds of wild horses and, to a lesser degree, wild cattle. The territorial range of the various bands of Pampas Indians had increased with the acquisition of the horse from the precontact seasonal range involved in following the guanaco and avestruz. Horse meat now predominated in a diet that also included guanaco (a large, woolly animal related to the llama), avestruz (South American ostrich), and wild plants in season. Horsehide mobile *toldos* (tents) served as shelters, and clothing included decorated skin capes.

The Pampas groups moved seasonally over the grasslands in bands of ten to thirty people. Early observers compared their movements to those of "gypsies," but it is clear from early missionary accounts that movements coincided with the seasonal offerings of the land. Falkner noted, for instance, that the months of July, August, and September attracted hunting parties north into the grasslands utilized by Creole ranchers. The hunt organized their movements, and the formation of the hunting party seemed the only social form recognizable to Europeans, who likened them to military operations.

Although incorporated within native social categories, the ready availability of the horse freed the Pampas Indians from dependence on seasonal hunting and gathering. Now they could engage in intensified hunting and trading. Intertribal trade in textiles and slaves expanded to include cattle and horses. This had consequences for social organization. For instance, the gendered division of labor began to shift in favor of the mobility of men and to burden the load of women, who were charged with preparing the skins.[4]

Spanish accounts of the caciques (native spokesmen) and their *tolderías* (mobile tent encampments) often imposed Spanish ideas about political authority and leadership, ascribing perhaps more authority than a cacique actually held. Others, however, noted the limitations that caciques faced in keeping their followers in line: "They do not subordinate themselves to their caciques and they leave one to go to the other whenever they desire. And if the cacique decided to undertake a project, he had to tell the group, and each person gave his opinion."[5]

This loose social organization did extend beyond the family or band level. Not only did people "leave one [cacique] to live with another," but temporary and more formal alliances were effected as well. Two or more bands would often forge alliances to retaliate against liberties (spying, kidnapping) taken by another. In some cases, these band alliances were capable of raising war parties of forty men.[6]

Marriages provided formalized ties between bands. By the mid-1700s these kinds of relationships moved outside Pampas Indian networks to include the Tehuelche groups to the south in Patagonia and the Araucanian groups to the west in the cordillera.

There were many opportunities for intergroup trade, not only between different Indian groups, but also between the Indians and the

Spanish. At this time a clearly defined trading network, rooted in pre-Columbian systems, operated on the pampas. In exchange for horses and other leather goods, the Pampas Indians received ponchos and other textiles from Araucanian groups in the west. Occasionally, the Pampas groups would provide a slave (often a captured Creole woman) for the Araucanians, although they themselves did not practice slavery.

Araucanian hunting and trading parties, primarily from the Lake Nahuel Huapi region and the Pehuenche homeland in the foothills south of Mendoza province, became an increasingly notable force in the humid grasslands. Trade probably accounted for the Araucanian predominance in this intercultural sphere. Although Pampas and Tehuelche Indians traded as a means of supplementing their subsistence, the Araucanians were linked into trade with Chilean Creoles on the Pacific coast. Araucanian place names and other linguistic markers began to predominate in a kind of lingua franca that developed in this trade. Their language was reported to have been the most generally understood among the Indian populations in the pampas, and bilingual speakers were common.

It is sometimes generalized that Araucanians were established on the pampas by 1725. Archival documents, missionary accounts, and travelers' journals, however, do not indicate that the Araucanians were physically located in the pampas, only that they regularly sent hunting and raiding parties there. Intertribal contacts with the pampas groups intensified, and language and other cultural concepts were exchanged, but actual Araucanian settlement in the pampas was an early nineteenth-century development, when the push of colonization in Chile and the attraction of trade in the Argentine pampas encouraged the permanent establishment of groups, like the followers of the famous Araucanian cacique Calfucurá.

In the mid-eighteenth century, the trade route to the west was the most prominent, but another pre-Columbian trade route to the north still functioned. While the Charruan and Littoral Indians to the north had mostly disappeared by the eighteenth century (decimated by disease and incorporated into the Guaraní missions), Spanish traders had stepped into their place and continued to supply the preexisting demand for tobacco and yerba mate.

Following the establishment of the Viceroyalty of the Río de la Plata in 1776, the increased commercial activities in Buenos Aires linked into and attracted the exchange and flow of goods in the pampas. The Spanish now took the largest role in the trading net-work. Buenos Aires became the eastern focus and center of the flow of goods; estancias in Mendoza and Chile were the western foci. What had been a fluid, interband Indian system now had strong pull to the east and west coasts, linking into the Creole markets.

As Indian and Creole interactions increased, the Spanish felt constrained to better understand Indian societies. Explorers, military men and those interested in commercial endeavors like the expeditions to the salt mines began to recognize differences between the indigenous societies they contacted. They began to discern the contrasts between the Araucanians and the Pampas groups and noticed ethnic divisions. They reported on distinguishing characteristics in clothing, beliefs, and funeral practices. Creoles found it to their advantage to recognize divisions and intertribal enmities in order to trade with the various tribes (and often to exploit them). At times, Creoles also entered into these local-level conflicts.

The impact of the Bourbon reforms extended into the sovereign Indian societies. Because the reforms obtained throughout Spanish America, similar patterns of expanded presence on the part of Creoles were experienced in both Chile and Buenos Aires. On the one hand, access to the regions defined by new military boundaries was denied the Indians; on the other hand, increased demand for the resources of the unconquered grasslands resulted in increased trading relations. One of the first moves of the new viceregal order was to throw out a net of fortifications along the frontier of Creole settlement, more as an attempt to control the commercial activities already flourishing there than as a defensive measure against presumed foreign pretentions against Spanish territory. The Bourbon reforms also liberalized trade policies, officially opening the port of Buenos Aires to wider trade possibilities, which stimulated the expansion of Creole settlement and ranching into the pampas. This led to conflict with the Indians already living there over the same resources.

The Araucanians of the cordillera stepped up their hunting and trading excursions into the pampas, and began to appropriate control over the few remaining herds of wild cattle and horses. Increasingly displaced by expanding Creole society from the central-south valleys of Chile, Araucanian populations began to concentrate more and more on the eastern slopes of the cordillera. Some Araucanian groups began to shift to a more mobile life-style.

This dispersal of the Araucanians into the pampas increased the number of hunting parties and created strains among the indigenous Pampas Indians. Araucanian place names, language, and kinship systems came to predominate among non-Araucanian groups, mirroring Araucanian predominance in the trading networks. These shifts were more than simple accommodations; they had an impact on the social, political, and economic organization of the Pampas groups. Consensus leadership began to give way to more hierarchical systems of political authority. Social groups grew larger, with bands of forty to fifty more common than the smaller family groups seen in the mid to late eighteenth century.

Intercultural exchanges among the various Indian societies in the pampas included the exchange of women. By European standards, marriage among the Araucanians were "made by sale"; that is, they practiced wife exchange. The Pampas and Tehuelche groups placed less importance on this practice, though they did obtain captives for trade with the Araucanians. In some cases these captives included Creole women captured in raids against isolated ranches. The women were then incorporated within the Araucanian social structure.

The individual Araucanian's status in society was determined through patrilineal descent, with preference for cross-cousin matrilateral marriage. That is, eligibility (and the exchange of bride price) was unidirectional, through the "mother's brother." Marriage was sanctioned by compensation to the wife-giving family.[7] Under such a system, a young man's opportunity to obtain a wife or wives was limited. Of the many attractions of the pampas for Araucanian hunting parties, the opportunity to accumulate bride wealth and status ranked high for unmarried warriors. Trade, and eventually warfare, provided the means to obtain the livestock, captives, and glory with which to acquire wives.

When Creole settlement began to push farther south in response to the trade stimulus of the Bourbon reforms, the newly reauthorized Spanish militia moved to protect—that is, to control—this frontier, and a series of peace treaties with various caciques in the 1790s allowed conditions for Creole settlement of lands north of the Salado River.[8] The terms of these treaties, effected through the interpreting skills of León Rosas, father of Juan Manuel, provided not only the one-time presentation of "gifts" in exchange for peace, but also access to local trade, monitored by the colonial forts and conducted in the *pulperías* (trading posts). This institutionalization of trade in the frontier stimulated increased Indian participation in local commerce. Pampas and some Araucanians traded salt, hide, furs, weavings, feathers, and other products for spirits, mate, and tobacco, all supplied by *pulperías* that were often directly or indirectly controlled by local hacendados.[9]

Early Independence

After independence, increasing trade opportunities and the riches of the southern grasslands continued to draw an increasing number of Araucanian Indians out of the cordillera and into the pampas. But at the same time, Creole ranching and commercial activities pushed south of the Salado River.[10] Conflict was inevitable. Loosely organized bands of Pampas Indians turned over increasing political authority to those caciques skilled at negotiating with Creoles, and new political alignments and tactical intermarriages with intruding Araucanian encampments resulted in more hierarchical and military political formations in what is commonly called the "Araucanization of the desert."

The scattered and locally negotiated peace treaties of the 1790s broke down after 1812, especially when the Indian monopoly over salt sources in the Salinas Grandes collapsed with the legal import of salt and the appearance of commercial *saladeros* (meat-packing establishments). Hostilities increased, ushering in the first epoch of nineteenth-century raids called *malones*.

The atomization and militarization of Argentine society during early independence disrupted the few existing alliances and placed Pampas Indians along the frontier in an almost perpetual position of war.[11] Political forms began to change as "peace chiefs" assumed increasing political authority, transcending their traditional roles as lineage leaders. These leaders' influence extended beyond the band level to include authority over several bands. A hierarchy of leadership replicated the band-level lines of authority on a larger scale. Not yet organized tribally, different Pampas societies forged temporary alliances with Araucanian interlopers.[12]

Royalist forces took advantage of inherent conflicts; Chilean General José Miguel Carrera forged an alliance with the Araucanian Ranqueles, who had recently settled in present day La Pampa, in his actions against the insurgents. The cacique Llanquetruz and his

Araucanian followers moved to settle permanently in the pampas, and they maintained a royalist or autonomous stance. Araucanian raiding from the cordillera intensified, and the *malones* put pressure on frontier settlers to negotiate.

Ranchers in the southern districts of rural Buenos Aires organized to provide support for locally raised militia. These ragged troops, often rounded up under new measures against gauchos, vagabonds, and criminals, were outfitted with horses, colts, and a few pesos obtained through the donations of the landowners in the frontier *partidos*.[13]

By the 1820s, economic self-sufficiency was no longer possible for the local indigenous groups pulled into trade and commerce in the frontier. As subsistence shifted from a hunting economy to specialization in horse and cattle trading, dependency on Creole markets increased. Trading relationships became increasingly specialized. Trade no longer supplemented and filled temporary shortages; it had long since become a necessity for survival. As Creole and Indian competition intensified, Creole control of commerce effectively pushed the Indians (as well as the nonpropertied Creoles) out of the commercial networks. Creoles noted that treaty negotiations with cacique spokesmen, which provided specified annuity payments, worked quite well in controlling the unlicensed commerce. An incipient ranchers' organization, the Sociedad de Labradores y Hacendados,[14] after generating its own local *guardia* (frontier militia), now began to provide compensation in the form of annuities for the settlement and pacification of the "true owners of the land."[15] Following a military expedition led by Martín Rodríguez between 1825 and 1828—and encouraged by Colonel Juan Manuel de Rosas—a plan of "peaceful dealings with the Indians" established terms of coexistence in the grazing lands south of the pampas. The government guaranteed the purchase of Indian goods, specifically for skins of lion, fox, deer, skunk, and so on, "but this would be only in the case that they [the Indians] don't find someone who would pay more, because in this case the only interest of the government is the good of the Indians."[16] Government licenses formalized the terms of peace, named specific hacendados as protective patrons of the new allies, pledged support against enemy Indians, and specified the providers of the annuities through the Sociedad. As in the past, these agreements included exchange (redemption) of Creole captives and "gifts" marking the terms of agreement.

Inspection of the individual peace treaties reveals complex internal factionalism and diversity among "the Indians." In the treaty of 1825, for instance, thirty-nine caciques and fifty representatives of other mostly Araucanian groups south of Buenos Aires, Santa Fé, and Córdoba agreed to return Creole captives in exchange for the right to trade with Creole settlements (to be carried out under military escort). But they specifically retained sovereignty over that territory west from the Sierra del Vulcán, Tandil, and Curico.[17] More commonly, individual bands (numbering around forty people and scattered throughout the settled pampas) were approached by government emissaries who, following explicit instructions written by Colonel Rosas, established the terms of peace. In addition to gifts, compensation for land, compensation for redeemed captives, and guaranteed markets for "Indian products," each cacique received a printed form, a *"papeleta,"* guaranteeing safe passage within the Creole frontier established by treaty. This *papeleta*, not coincidentally, clearly identified Rosas as patron.[18]

Some caciques (mostly Pampas) opted (out of desperation) to remain within newly defined Argentine territory. They agreed to a system of patronage and licensing, and settled in camps near Tandil and Tapalquén.[19] In compensation for land lost to Creole ranchers, Rosas arranged for annuity payments to these Pampas groups, raised once again through the new cattlemen's association. These newly negotiated treaties permitted the Creole ranching frontier to move south of the Salado River in the 1820s. Seventeen new guard posts, also provisioned through regional "donations," threw a tighter net over commercial as well as military and political activities in the southern frontier.

Indian reliance on the trade from which they were now being excluded is hinted at in the volume of annuities they demanded to replace commerce. The total estimated value of commerce in the entire southern frontier in 1811 amounted to only 60,588 pesos (valued in pesos of eight reales).[20] Annuity payments at only one fort, called Independencia, amounted to 74,200 pesos in 1826. Authorities at Independencia reported that they gave the Indians a variety of goods in 1826 (see Table 5.1).

The extent of the payments to Indians in this one fort suggests why the explosion of commerce in the pampas now made it more profitable to the Creoles to fulfill Indian demands through direct annuity payments rather than through access to trade in the *pul-*

Table 5.1
Breakdown of Annuity Payments to Indians at Fort
Independencia, 1826

Goods	Value in Pesos
500 mares	12,500
100 *tercios* (8640 kg.) of Paraguayan mate	10,000
100 ropes of tobacco	6,000
Aguardiente, clothes, and stirrups	10,000
Compensation for returned captives	30,000
Purchase of captives' dependents	1,000
Purchase of captives' horses	1,500
Expenses and interpreter's fees	1,200
Total	74,200

perías. By removing the Indians from commercial networks with the annuity agreements, ranchers were able to protect, control, and take over the trade. While commerce in Buenos Aires province continued to expand, the Indians were now locked out of participating in it.

In 1828, having ensured and stabilized the security of this flourishing ranching and commercial arena, the government decided to extend its boundary south and east to Bahía Blanca, a new zone of production. Once again Creole settlement and activities had extended beyond the fortifications. Once again Rosas was enlisted to carry out the pacification arrangements following the military campaign of Colonel Frederick Rauch. Rosas built on his earlier negotiating success, according to one contemporary observer. The British observer Sir Woodbine Parish noted that "the influence of his name went far to induce the more peaceably disposed tribes to enter into treaties for their lands and to engage and cooperate in defending them against the hostile Ranqueles."[21]

Another traveler in the south, Narciso Parchappe, a French surveyor who in 1828 joined the expeditionary forces founding 25 de Mayo, a new fort in Cruz de Guerra, commented on the friendly terms of Indian-white relations at the time.

The Indians, who at this time lived in peace with the Christians, habitually frequented those places and there were villages along almost all the main lagoons. Some Christians, among whom was our guide, trafficked with the Indians and exchanged brandy, tobacco, yerba, and other trifles in exchange for skins, hides, ponchos, reins, etc. They were very well received by the savages, and the day of their arrival was an important event for the Indians, who communicated it from one village to the next by way of smoke signals, in accord with the customs of these clans. . . . Many Christians of both sexes are found among these Indians, having been made captives in previous wars. . . . A great many of these captives feel sincerely attached to their masters, who treat them kindly, and they refuse to take advantage of opportunities to escape.[22]

In Bahía Blanca, however, Rosas met the opposition of those Pampas led by the cacique Chocorí. Not coincidentally, in 1806 Chocorí had allied himself with royalist forces in the defense against the British invasion. He was then defending certain rights granted as a result of unsuccessful missionizing attempts in the late eighteenth century, and certainly supporting territory granted in the 1790 treaties.[23] Although these Pampas groups around Bahía Blanca came to a temporary agreement with Rosas in 1828, they soon began to "repeatedly terrorize the frontier settlements."[24]

After Rauch's campaign of 1828, interprovincial and interregional struggles distracted the subsequent maintenance of the "peaceful commerce with the Indians." At the same time, drought and epidemic disease battered away at weakened allied Indian bands between December 1828 and April 1832. The annuities, though now increasingly critical to life itself, disappeared. What had begun as freely chosen participation in a frontier economy now became coercive integration through the oppressive circumstance of starvation. Hostile tribes, discovering the frontier garrisons were significantly weakened, burst in upon Creole and allied Indian frontier settlements, raiding for livestock and captives. The interdependency of the frontier political and economic order was breaking down, and a new political order would eventually emerge, this time operating out of a national rather than regional arena.

The Campaign of the Desert of 1833

The pacification treaties and annuity payments worked out within locally organized and relatively autonomous frontier society during the provincial government between 1825 and 1828 had provided two things. First, by establishing an alliance structure, they laid the foundation for the subsequent success of Rosas's military campaign in 1833, which vaulted Rosas into national prominence. Second, they ensured not only the economic dependency of the Indians involved (while at the same time denying nonallied groups access to local commerce) but also ensured a political dependency that was to provide Rosas a political base upon which to build his rise to national power.

General Rosas's famed military campaign of 1833 split the Indians into cooperative and hostile groups. Reliance on the patronage systems created by the pacification treaties of the 1820s ensured the participation of allied Indian troops, who joined together to drive nonallied groups to the south. Contrary to what might be expected, these political allies did not coalesce along tribal or even ethnic lines. Instead, they reflected the settlements with individual Pampas and Tehuelche band chiefs and Araucanian leaders. Dependence on annuities, rather than ethnicity, tied the allied groups geographically to specific territories in local-level alliances with specific caudillos, most of whom were loyal to Rosas.[25] The military campaign of 1833 pitted band against band, family against family, as military actions forced "pacified" Indians against competing groups of Pampas, Tehuelche, and Araucanians.[26]

In a three-pronged military campaign operating out of Mendoza, Córdoba, and Buenos Aires, General Rosas built upon the alliance network so that his Division of the Left was able to push the military frontier south to the Río Negro, effectively freeing the humid grasslands (*pampas húmedas*) from hostile Indian raids most of the time. In the settlement with the defeated Indians, Rosas arranged for the redemption of 634 Creole captives, not all of whom wished to leave their Indian families. The care and training of most of these individuals was turned over to the Benevolent Society. The foundation charitably prepared them to serve as domestic help in the burgeoning port city of Buenos Aires.[27]

Rosas left his Indian allies to defend the new military boundary. When Charles Darwin stopped along the Patagonian coast at the mouth of the Río Negro in 1833, he commented on the military pressure to which the Indians were now subjected. Rosas prevented these allies from operating farther north at the same time that they had to confront Araucanian raiding parties still operating out of the cordillera. "The general," commented Darwin, "thinking that his friends may in a future day become his enemies, always places them in the front ranks, so that their numbers may be thinned." In this way, Darwin noted that the "escape of the Indians to the south of the Río Negro, where in such a vast unknown country they would be safe" may have tempted the allied Pampas Indians. However, escape to territory claimed by Tehuelche Indians was "prevented by a treaty with the Tehuelches to this effect; that Rosas pays them so much to slaughter every Indian who passes to the South of the river, but if they fail in doing this, they themselves shall be exterminated."[28]

Following independence, rapid growth of commerce depended on trade integrating widely varied Indian and Creole interests. Out of this trade, a distinct frontier society with its own set of social relations developed. Building on local-level successes, Indian and Creole leaders were able to consolidate political authority to their advantage in negotiations for access to territory in the treaty negotiations. The temporary advantages obtained by those Indians who opted for rations, however, removed them from access to opportunities for continued participation in the frontier markets. In contrast, the dynamism of the frontier allowed greater access to Creoles like Juan Manuel de Rosas.

Peaceful Commerce with the Indian, 1835–59

The new military hero, Rosas, took steps to consolidate his political power when he moved into national office. One of the early actions he took was to convert responsibility for the annuity payments from the frontier landowners' association to the rest of the nation. Beginning in 1835 and continuing until 1859 (annually only until 1851) the Argentine government authorized payments to allied Pampas and Araucanian tribes. The account books registered these annuities as "Peaceful Commerce with the Indians."[29] Beginning with an initial payment of 98,227 pesos for payments to the liberated captives, the value of rations distributed to dozens of specific caciques began at 41,041 pesos in 1837 and climbed to 202,981 in 1851. Additional bands over the years also opted for the annuity plan. Rosas granted lucrative government contracts to loyal supporters, further consolidating his political network to the disadvantage of often victimized and shortchanged Indian allies. The increasingly detailed records of the new state bureaucracy reveal the kind of important tactical information about Indian leadership and population that also worked to Indian disadvantage in the frontier wars that were to erupt later that century.

Although nonallied Araucanian war societies continued to plague the frontier south of Mendoza and Córdoba with *malones*, a frontier held primarily by unitarian supporters, Rosas's successful treaty negotiations of 1825–28 and his subsequent military campaign of 1833 allowed federalist ranching concerns in Buenos Aires province (north of the Río Negro and east of the Salinas Grandes) to take their expansionistic course in peace. In contrast, properties south of Córdoba and Mendoza suffered as a direct result of the alliance network Rosas had forged. Unitarian landowners in these interior provinces complained that certain raiding parties actually were carried out at Rosas's order. While Rosas and his supporters profited economically during the next two decades, his Creole political opponents suffered. The position of the allied Indians also grew more desperate because Buenos Aires officials violated the treaty, expropriated Indian lands, and reduced annuity payments. In contrast, nonallied Indians began to confederate under Araucanian leadership. They increasingly operated in concert to maintain political autonomy and sovereignty over their remaining territorial stronghold. Much as Juan Manuel de Rosas was able to translate his locally constituted power into the national arena as a result of cagey understanding of frontier relations, Indian leaders also moved to consolidate political power.

When the Araucanians moved permanently into the pampas, they brought with them their kinship system. They interacted with and also married into different Tehuelche and Pampas bands. Most often, non-Araucanian women were integrated into Araucanian groups, and this quite often resulted in political alliances between the Araucanians and non-Araucanian wife-giving groups.[30] One of the consequences of this intercultural exchange was an ever-widening circle of exchange between Indian groups with a definite tendency to favor the Araucanians. To illustrate, once an Araucanian bought a woman from a nonrelated pampas group, members of her lineage were then eligible to his relatives for marriage. Because of the Araucanian preference for patrilocality, meaning that wives would stay with the husband's family, Araucanian societies expanded.

The interrelations between different bands in the pampas linked them into complex exchange systems that depended upon the transfer of women from wife-giving groups in exchange for bride wealth. The spoils of *malones,* ever larger numbers of horses and captives, provided compensation to the wife's family. At the same time, the interconnectedness, abetted by increasing pressure and conflict with the Creoles, provided the structure for the amalgamation of several bands into tribal organizations.

Powerful personalities began to emerge as prominent political and military leaders when distinctive tribal unities coalesced. Llanquetruz gained fame as leader of the Ranqueles in the interior of present-day La Pampa. He attracted marginal Creole deserters escaping recruitment into the militia. Calfucurá, after assassinating the Indian leader Mariano Rondeau, who had been an ally of Rosas, headed the Voroganos, an Araucanian group that had permanently settled and controlled the area of Salinas Grandes. Sayhueque rallied support of the mostly neutral Araucanians settled south and west in the "País de las Manzanas" (in present-day Neuquén). All of these leaders attracted, through intermarriage and offers of protection, increasing bands of scattered Tehuelche and Pampas Indians. In contrast, those Pampas, Tehuelche, and Araucanian groups that had fallen dependent on the annuity payments began to look to the Pampas leader Juan Catriel and his two sons, Cipriano and Juan José Catriel. When the annuity payments ended in the late 1850s, coinciding with the fall of Rosas, they shifted their allegiance to the great military leader Namúncura, son of Calfucurá.

Because Argentine authorities provided annuities to maintain the peace in Buenos Aires province, livestock production there expanded more or less unimpeded. The nonallied Voroganos and Ranqueles, however, organized hunting parties to raid unprotected estancias for livestock and women. There is no question that such raids, though no doubt necessary to subsistence, were clearly perceived as acts of war by the Indians as well as the Argentines. The *malón* was no longer a simple raid for subsistence; it was now an ideological military crusade. Some groups, like the Manzaneros, chose not to join this crusade. According to a contemporary spokesman for Sayhueque, it was contrary to their interests.

Our contact with the Christians in the past few years has produced yerba, sugar, biscuit, flour, and other luxury articles that were unknown to us before, but which have now become necessary. If we make war on whites, we would not have a market for our ponchos, hides, feathers, etc., and, consequently, it is in our interest to remain on good terms with them.[31]

Even though the Manzaneros maintained their neutrality, they continued to control the mountain passes and to allow the passage of livestock that had been obtained in warfare by other Indians.

Livestock acquired in the *malones* carried out in territories not protected by annuity systems contributed to a large and important informal market. This was no longer simply a tactic of subsistence. Indians traded, husbanded, and herded cattle to market, especially in Mendoza and San Luis. In Chile, even more overt cattle markets existed to purchase these cattle, which had been herded in long drives along the course of the Río Negro and through the low passes in the cordillera controlled by the Manzaneros. Such transactions, though extralegal, characterized the mid-nineteenth century livestock markets.[32]

Once the Indians had been denied access to the commercial markets in Buenos Aires province, few alternatives remained. Those who chose the annuities and forfeited territorial rights found themselves unable to meet basic subsistence needs. Those who sought alternative markets and maintained territorial claims continued to flourish; they met their needs by demanding annuities from the provincial government or by organizing *malones* against undefended Creole interests.

Conclusion

When Juan Manuel de Rosas fell from power and opposition figures no longer deemed it necessary to continue what they considered the profligate bribery of the annuity payments—which, after all, protected only the southern ranching interests—the "peaceful commerce with the Indian" came to an end. There followed three more decades of military hostilities along the southern frontier, which reached unheard-of excesses in terms of economic and social costs. Great confederations forged from Vorogano, Ranquel, and Pampas forces sent war parties to raid the southern frontier. They captured hundreds of thousands of head of cattle and thousands of women and children in highly organized *malones*.

The Argentine national government finally turned its attention once again to the consolidation of its southern and western national boundary after the close of the Paraguayan War in 1871. But this time it discovered more formidable and better organized Indian forces, in sharp contrast to the politically and economically interdependent alliances between Creole and indigenous groups forged earlier in the century. The benefits of pacification, with its costs incurred in the payment of annuities for the short-term advantage of protecting and monopolizing frontier commerce, turned out to be a much greater loss to the nation. The policies of the Rosas provincial government ultimately forced the Indians to respond with better organized and more hostile military actions that threatened livestock interests, the basis of the Argentine economy. Policies of pacification, annuities, and rationing, cloaked in humanitarian ideologies of civilization, meant even greater losses for the Indians. They were left with no other choice but warfare in the face of these policies of exclusion and dispossession. In 1879, the federal government launched a force of soldiers, armed with modern repeating rifles, which finally defeated the Indians, freeing up the southern pampas and Patagonia for white settlement.

Notes

1. A popular expression used by opponents of the practice in the mid-nineteenth century.

2. Archivo General de la Nación, Buenos Aires (hereafter cited as AGN), Sala 9, 1-4-3, Comandancia de Fronteras.

3. José Cardiel, "Diario del padre José Cardiel en su viaje a Buenos Aires hasta el Vulcán y Arroyo de la Ascensión," in *Colección de obras y documentos* ed. Pedro de Angelis, 8 vols. (Buenos Aires, 1960), 4:59–66, and Thomas Falkner, S.J., *A Description of Patagonia and the Adjoining Parts of South America*, with introduction and notes by Arthur E. S. Neumann (Chicago, 1935).

4. The French ethnographer Alcides D'Orbigny first commented on these consequences in *El Hombre Americano* (Buenos Aires, 1944), 244.

5. "Observaciones extraídas de los viajes que al Estrecho de Magallanes han ejecutado en diferentes años los almirantes y capitanes Olivares de Noort, Juan Childey, Tomás Candish, Juan Narborough, y noticias adquiradas en las expediciones ejecutadas desde esta isla por las Franceses con la fragata 'Aguila,'" in *Colección de obras y documentos*, 4:144: "No tienen subordinación a sus caciques, pues cuando quieren, dejan a uno y van a vivir con otro; y si el cacique emprende tiene que hacer alguna empresa, a todos se lo comunica y cada uno da su parecer."

6. Falkner, *A Description of Patagonia*, 133.

7. Louis C. Faron, *Mapuche Social Structure: Institutional Reintegration in a Patrilineal Society of Central Chile*, Illinois Studies in Anthropology

No. 1 (Urbana, Ill., 1961). Archival documents and travelers' accounts corroborate Faron's contemporary ethnologic analysis.

8. AGN, Sala 9, 24-2-6, Legajo 14, Expediente 26, 1790.

9. Kristine L. Jones and Claudia Wentzel, "Frontier Commerce in 1811 Rural Buenos Aires," unpublished manuscript.

10. In his "Diario de un viaje a Salinas Grandes," in *Colección de obras y documentos,* 4:3–45, Coronel Pedro Andrés García commented on Creole settlement and trading deep in Indian territory. He remarked on itinerant *pulperos* who traveled directly to the *tolderías* to trade.

11. Tulio Halperín Donghi, *Politics, Economics, and Society in Argentina in the Revolutionary Period* (Cambridge, 1975), 380.

12. For an anecdotal account of such an alliance, see Maria Graham Calcott, *Journal of a Voyage to Brazil and Residence There during Part of the Years 1821, 1822, 1823.* (London, 1824).

13. La Plata, Archivo Histórico de la Provincia de Buenos Aires (hereafter cited as La Plata), "Negocio pacífico con el indio 1825–28."

14. Coronel Juan Antonio Garretón, *Partes detalladas de la expedición al desierto de Juan Manuel de Rosas en 1833* (Buenos Aires, 1975). The powerful Sociedad Rural Argentina that dominated late nineteenth- and early twentieth-century politics in Argentina grew directly out of the Sociedad de Labradores y Hacendados.

15. La Plata, "Negocio pacífico con el indio 1825–28."

16. "pero esto será en el caso que no encuentrasen quienes les pague más, pues en esto no lleva más interés el Gobierno que le bien de los Yndios" (ibid.).

17. Juan Carlos Walther, *La conquista del desierto* (Buenos Aires, 1970), 71.

18. La Plata, "Negocio pacífico con el índio 1825–28."

19. Rómulo Muniz, *Los Indios Pampas* (Buenos Aires, 1966), 131.

20. Jones and Wentzel, "Frontier Commerce in 1811 Rural Buenos Aires," from AGN, Sala 3, Entradas 20-7-7, 20-7-8, 20-7-9, and Salidas 20-7-10 and 20-8-1.

21. Sir Woodbine Parish, *Buenos Ayres and the Provinces of the Rio de la Plata* (London, 1852), 203.

22. Narciso Parchappe, *Expedición fundadora del Fuerte 25 de Mayo en Cruz de Guerra Año 1828* (Buenos Aires, 1977), 93.

23. *Acuerdos del extinguido cabildo,* Serie IV, Tomo II, Libres LIX, L, LXII 1805–7 (Buenos Aires, 1924).

24. Garretón, *Partes detallados de la expedición al desierto,* 18.

25. An interesting and important exception is the alliance between the Ranquel leader Cipriano Urquiza, whose name reveals the patronage of Rosas's nemesis, Justo José de Urquiza.

26. A discussion of ethnicity pertinent to this complex inter-Indian con-

text can be found in Marta Bechis Rosso, "Interethnic Relations during the Period of Nation-State Formation in Chile and Argentina: From Sovereignty to Ethnicity" (Ph.D. diss., New School for Social Research, 1983). When Bechis and I crossed paths in 1986, we discovered our mutual research interests and interpretations. At the same time, Leonardo León Solís was working on a Ph.D. dissertation at the Institute for Latin American Studies in England on Araucanian expansion from Chile in the late eighteenth century. Also working independently, José Bengoa at Sur Profesionales in Santiago, Chile was writing *Historia del Pueblo Mapuche: Siglo XIX y XX* (Santiago, 1985), and Raúl Mandrini was conducting research on the Araucanians in Buenos Aires province.

27. Academia Nacional de la Historia, *Juan Manuel de Rosas y la redención de cautivos en su campaña del desierto (1833–34)* (Buenos Aires, 1979).

28. Charles Darwin, *Charles Darwin's Diary of the HMS Beagle,* ed. Nora Barlow (London, 1933), 173.

29. "Negocio Pacífico con los indios, rendiciones de cuentas," AGN, Sala 3, 17-8-5, 17-8-6 (1835–39 and 1840–58).

30. This is the expected pattern in a patrilineal system with patrilocal rules.

31. Guillermo Alfred Terrero, *Caciques y capitanejos en la historia de Argentina* (Buenos Aires, 1974).

32. See Alberto Recart Novión, *El Laja: Un río creado* (Santiago de Chile, 1971), for discussion of cattle markets in Chile.

Appendix

Habiendo el Gobierno facultadome, como á comisionado en el negocio pacífico con los indios, para disponer lo conveniente en los que como rindieron servicios en las últimas expediciones á los infieles, y están mandados considerarse pertenecer á la Comisión que ejerzo á este respecto, he resuelto en su virtud, por haberlo hallado conveniente, que durante estubiere encargado de la Comision entre tanto el expresado   no fuese por mí llamado á servir cuando se formen las guardias, ó cuando la necesidad reclamare sus servicios, pueda retirarse á trabajar donde se le proporcione ocupación, sin que por nadie bajo de pretexto alguno se le incomode, ni moleste, no faltando al órden, ni al respeto á las autoridades, ni al que se debe á las personas. Para todo lo que respondo de la legitimidad del resguardo y de mi autorización, á fin de que las autoridades ordinarias, territoriales, y militares respeten esta papeleta.

Buenos Aires,   de 1827.

Juan Manuel de Rosas

Having been charged by the government as the agent responsible for establishing peaceful interactions with the Indians, and in order for me to do whatever is necessary regarding those who provided services in the last expeditions against the infidels and who are required to continue being part of the special military detachment under my leadership, I have resolved that as long as I am in charge and for as long as [*] is not called by me to serve when the units are formed, or when the need arises to draft him to service, he may retire to work wherever he is given a job, but that under no circumstances whatsoever is he allowed to cause discomfort or trouble for anyone, nor may he fail to conduct himself in an orderly fashion, nor may he fail to show respect to the authorities nor anyone else who deserves it. In order to carry out the legitimate basis of this preventive service and of my authority, I charge all local, regional, and military authorities with heeding the contents of this document.

Buenos Aires, [+] of 1827

Juan Manuel de Rosas

* = name of the individual would be filled in here

+ = date of the document would be filled in here

Samuel Amaral
Translated by Patricia Jepsen
Edited by Jonathan C. Brown

Free Trade and Regional Economies: San Juan and Mendoza, 1780–1820

Although its commercial monopoly in the Americas did not end until independence, Spain undertook some liberalization of trade in the last decades of the eighteenth century. These reforms had widespread implications for both Buenos Aires and the interior of the Viceroyalty of the Río de la Plata. As early as 1620, forty years after its founding, Buenos Aires had not been permitted to trade either with Spain or with other countries. Restrictions fostered contraband trade, especially after 1680, through the Portuguese settlement of Colônia do Sacramento across the river. Many goods produced in the interior enjoyed de facto protection, the natural consequence of the limited market presented to such goods over this contraband route. Later in the eighteenth century, this longstanding situation for the interior was altered with the establishment of the viceroyalty and its capital in Buenos Aires in 1776, and with the enactment, two years later, of the free trade ordinance that opened the port city to direct trade with Spain.[1] After the revolution of 1810, all restrictive regulations were eliminated, and ships of all nations, particularly Great Britain, began to trade at Buenos Aires.

For a long time, Argentine historians have believed that the modifications brought about by the creation of the viceroyalty and the establishment of free trade hurt the regional economies of the vast hinterland while Buenos Aires benefited. In their view, free trade stimulated the commercial growth of Buenos Aires but caused depression in the interior, where products would have been displaced by cheap European imports. More recently, it has been argued that not all regions in the interior suffered to the same extent. Those specializing in the production and export of one principal product,

such as Mendoza and San Juan, two provinces at the eastern foothills of the Andes known collectively (along with the province of
San Luis) as Cuyo, were the most severely affected by overseas competition.

"What has become, oh colonists, of the riches of your grandfa-
thers?" lamented Domingo Sarmiento in mid-nineteenth century
when he compared the alleged colonial prosperity with the gloomy
present. How did the colonial golden age come to an end? Was the
decline the bitter fruit of free trade? This chapter analyzes the consequences of the liberal trade policies of the late eighteenth and
early nineteenth centuries on the economies of San Juan and Mendoza, through the supply of trade, production, and marketing conditions related to their wine and *aguardiente* (brandy distilled from
wine). We shall see the nature and extent of crisis—whether as the
consequence of free trade or, as Sarmiento suggested, the result of
the civil wars—that affected the economy of Cuyo. The answers will
challenge those long-held views about free trade and the regional
economies in late colonial and early independent Argentina.

Free Trade

After the royal decree of October 16, 1765, a regime of gradual free
trade began to appear in Spanish America. This decree opened up
the sea routes between Cuba, Santo Domingo, Puerto Rico, Trin-
idad, and Margarita and suppressed various taxes. Another royal
decree in 1770 incorporated Yucatán and Campeche into the free
trade regime. The decree of January 17, 1774, removed the ban on
commerce between the Viceroyalties of New Spain, Perú, and New
Granada. On July 10, 1776, Buenos Aires was included in this inter-
American free trade regime. Finally, the free trade bylaw of October 12, 1778, decentralized the relations between Spain and America by allowing free trade and navigation among fourteen Spanish
and nineteen American ports including Buenos Aires. Only New
Spain (Mexico) was excluded from this arrangement and did not
receive these benefits until 1789.[2] In spite of the restrictions that
were still in force (non-Spaniards were banned from trading with
America, among others), these measures meant free trade and price
competition within the empire. The merchants had only to take
into consideration the product cost in port and the freight charges to

the point of destination. They also had to consider the transit taxes, which were not affected by the liberal measures. Trade between Spain and Spanish America grew appreciably. In the last quarter of the eighteenth century, Spanish exports (half of which came from Northern Europe) to the American colonies increased by 300 percent.[3]

Until recently it was supposed that the effects of the free trade laws had been catastrophic for local production in the interior of the Viceroyalty of the Río de la Plata.[4] This opinion began to change when Tulio Halperín Donghi pointed out that artisans' textiles proved resistant to competition from manufactured imports. This exception, he says, did not reach the zones wherein "the Spanish colonization had created small replicas of the Mediterranean agriculture." Spanish wines, oil, and nuts supposedly arrived in Buenos Aires at a cheaper price than similar products from Cuyo.[5] San Juan and Mendoza were said to have gone into depression.

To illustrate the consequences of free trade on San Juan's economy, two sources are generally used: a 1785 report by Marquis Rafael de Sobremonte, the governor intendant of Córdoba, and another report made in 1806 by José Godoy Oro, delegate from the Buenos Aires Consulado.[6] The marquis stated that the trade in wine and *aguardiente*, the foundations of San Juan's economy, had "fallen into decline motivated by the abundance of the Spanish products." According to Godoy Oro, Buenos Aires had been "the only market for the people of San Juan . . . until the European trade was cleared, and even worse with the introduction of brandy by the Portuguese." He was referring to the 1778 law, and to a 1795 decree, permitting trade in black slaves and colonial products between Buenos Aires and Brazil.[7] Both sources, however, are suspect. The first lacks credibility because it was based on information provided by the local businesses; the second, because its goal was to eliminate the taxes imposed on wine and brandy in Salta, Córdoba, and Buenos Aires.

These testimonies do not present an impartial view of the situation; rather, they were intended to solicit certain benefits. In an economy where market forces were limited by rigid institutional conditions, complaints were more effective than the reduction of production and marketing costs for obtaining a redistribution of income or larger market shares. The producers in Cuyo had had good luck with earlier complaints in the eighteenth century, when they successfully obtained royal decrees suppressing taxes on the wine and brandy trade in Córdoba and Buenos Aires.[8] The Consulado's delegate was arguing in favor of the suppression of taxes and, therefore, had to exaggerate the image of poverty.

Information about the export of wine and *aguardiente* from San Juan and Mendoza is scattered and sketchy. Eighteenth-century travelers do provide some help. At the beginning of the 1790s, Mendoza, according to Thaddaeus Pereginus Haenke, exported 32,000 arrobas of wine to Buenos Aires alone (each arroba equaled approximately thirty-five liters). Félix de Azara reports that the average quantities exported to Buenos Aires and Montevideo during the five years of peace (1792–96) was 6,166 arrobas of wine from Mendoza, and 15,884 arrobas of *aguardiente* from San Juan. Around 1820, the export of wine from Mendoza to Buenos Aires was 7,000 arrobas, and, seven years later, was 12,600 arrobas of *aguardiente* and 16,000 of wine.[9] The analysis of the impact of the liberal measures cannot be based on this scant information.

Our study will be based, therefore, on a homogeneous source that, although problematic, does not have the partiality of the official reports. Our source provides more consistent and systematic data than do the eighteenth-century reports and travelers' accounts. The data come from books in which officials registered the receipts of the *sisa*, an excise tax collected for the maintenance of a fort on the southern Indian frontier of Mendoza. The excise tax consisted of the payment of two reales per load of wine or brandy leaving San Juan and Mendoza, or, stated another way, one real per *botija* (a jug of wine, thus the tax was called the *real de botija*), as two *botijas* comprised one load that weighed four arrobas.[10] From this source, we have reconstructed the volume and regional distribution of the export of wine and *aguardiente* from San Juan between 1783 and 1817 and in 1824 and from Mendoza between 1780 and 1810.[11]

The Export of Wine and Brandy

The long-term trend in wine and *aguardiente* exports from San Juan does not support Godoy Oro's picture of depression. An annual average of 3,600 arrobas of wine and 10,900 arrobas of *aguardiente* in 1783–91 grew to 9,000 and 18,600 arrobas respectively in 1804–8. This implies annual growth rates of 4.9 percent for wine and 2.9

percent for *aguardiente*. Growth from 1752–54 and 1783–91 was 6.9 percent, which means an annual growth rate of approximately 0.2 percent.[12]

Although the few available figures from before 1783 do not distinguish between wine and *aguardiente*, this first attempt to quantify the levels of exports does not reveal a crisis attributable to the opening up of trade in 1778. It is even harder to accept the existence of that crisis if one keeps in mind that the sum of the annual average export of spirits from San Juan in 1804–8 (27,600 arrobas) shows a 90 percent growth over the annual average of wine and brandy exports in 1783–91 (14,500 arrobas).

The average volume of wine exported in each decade (not considering the years for which there is no information) was 3,388 arrobas in the 1780s; 3,115 in the 1790s; 7,190 in the 1800s; 9,243 in the 1810s; and 4,038 in 1824 (see Figure 6.1). The average volume of *aguardiente* exported was 10,756 arrobas in the 1780s; 13,623 in the 1790s; 19,901 in the 1800s; 19,905 in the 1810s; and 13,866 in 1824 (see Figure 6.2). Thus the average of wine exports registered in the 1810s is 173 percent greater than the average registered in the 1780s; and the average of *aguardiente* exports is 85 percent greater. These figures mean annual growth rates of 3.7 percent for wine and 2.3 percent for brandy. What is more, the 1824 exports, although less than those of the 1810s, were 19 percent higher than the average of the 1780s for wine and 28.9 percent higher for *aguardiente*.

In periods of peace, exports fluctuated, and there was a certain growth in the periods of war. But the high points do not coincide strictly with the beginning and ending dates of these conflicts. In fact, the average volume of *aguardiente* exports shows considerable stability as of 1799. Taking the average of the peacetime period of 1784–96 as base index of 100 (10,409 arrobas), we have 177 in 1797–1801 (war); 201 in 1802–4 (peace); 183 in 1805–8 (war); and 192 in 1810–17 (peace).[13] The ups and downs of the brandy exports, therefore, cannot be explained by the effect of the international conflicts.

Wine exports show slightly different results. Taking the average for the period of peace, 1784–96, as base index of 100 (3,287 arrobas), the index rose to 137 in 1798–1801 (war); 97 in 1802–4 (peace); 309 in 1805–8 (war); and 270 in 1810–17 (peace). Even though growth is seen in wartime (especially in the second wartime period), the average of the last period of peace is 170 percent above that of the first. The introduction of spirits was not completely closed off in war-

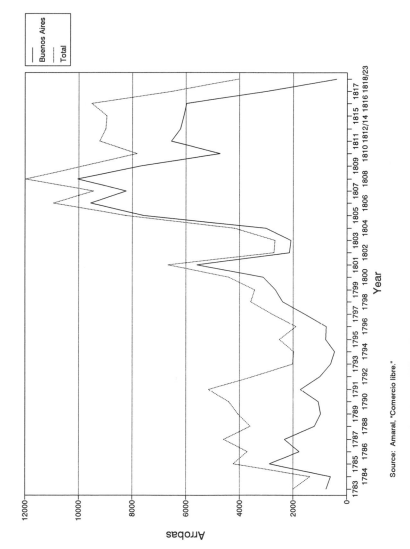

Source: Amaral, "Comercio libre."

Figure 6.1. San Juan: Wine Exports, 1783–1824.

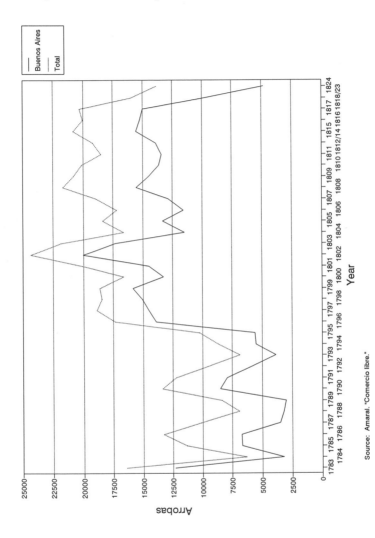

Source: Amaral. "Comercio libre."

Figure 6.2. San Juan: Brandy Exports, 1783–1824.

time. The measures taken to relieve the effects of the interruption of trade with Spain, such as permitting trade with neutral countries in 1797, allowed the import of sugarcane *aguardiente* from Brazil. The same thing happened in 1805–6 when the "Portugalization" of ships (changing the Spanish flag for that of Portugal) was allowed.[14] The variations in percentages of the Cuyo exports from one year to another show that instability is a central characteristic of the wine production, much more noticeable in wines than in *aguardiente*. In effect, the export of wine suffered extreme variations of 207 percent in 1785 and −59 percent in 1802; *aguardiente* exports, from 80 percent in 1785 to −62 in 1784. The explanation for the fluctuations in export volumes should be sought, as we shall see, more in supply than in demand at Buenos Aires.

As far as markets were concerned, Buenos Aires was always the largest consumer of Cuyo wine and brandy. Regional distribution of the exports in 1783–1824 shows that 68.9 percent of Cuyo's *aguardiente* was destined for Buenos Aires; 12.9 percent for the center of the country (Córdoba, San Luis, and Santa Fe); 13.5 percent for the north (La Rioja, Catamarca, Santiago del Estero, Tucumán, Salta, and Jujuy); 3.3 percent for Alto Perú; and 1.4 percent for other places. At the same time, 64.7 percent of the wine went to Buenos Aires; 20.8 to the center; 11.8 to the north; 0.7 to Alto Perú; and 2 percent to other destinations.

It has been claimed that because Buenos Aires imported wine and *aguardiente* from Spain after the free trade law was instituted, San Juan's trade consequently reoriented itself toward the north.[15] The importing of Spanish spirits was not, however, a novelty introduced in 1778; Spanish wine and *aguardiente* had always had an open door to Buenos Aires. Moreover, the Crown's policy had been contrary to the development of wine and grape production in America, but Spain only grudgingly tolerated the wine industry in Cuyo and Chile because it was impossible to supply certain colonies from Spain, and also because colonial wine produced revenue for the treasury.[16] If some market reorientation occurred after 1778, it was because Buenos Aires's share as a final destination for the exported spirits from San Juan actually grew. After independence in 1810, about 65 percent of the wine was exported to the ex-capital of the viceroyalty, even though all foreign wines could now freely enter the port. Another fact, even more revealing, is the regional distribution of brandy exports. Between 1796 and 1817, Buenos Aires purchased from 68 to 85 percent of the total brandy exported from San Juan. In the case of both wine and *aguardiente* markets, there was a fall in the northern share from the middle of the 1790s and later almost a total disappearance of other destinations. If there had truly been some reorientation because of the 1778 liberalization, it turned favorable for Buenos Aires. The Alto Perú markets were supplied by the *aguardiente* from the valleys of Arequipa, so the growth of San Juan exports can only have been due to a temporary fall in that area's production or circumstantial difficulties in its marketing.[17]

The average volume of wine exported per year in each decade was 13,183 arrobas in the 1780s; 20,724 in the 1790s; and 20,306 in the 1800s (see Figure 6.3). The average yearly volume of *aguardiente* exported was 1,129 arrobas in the 1780s; 2,074 in the 1790s; and 1,818 in the 1800s (see Figure 6.4). Thus exports of wine registered a 54 percent increase in the 1800s over the 1780s while *aguardiente* exports grew by 61 percent. These figures represent annual growth rates of 2.2 percent for wine and 2.4 percent for *aguardiente.*

The export figures available for wine and *aguardiente* from Mendoza do not differ much from those of San Juan. Using the average from the peacetime period of 1784–96 as a base index of 100 (13,735 arrobas), wine exports moved to 117 in 1780–83 (war); 220 in 1797–1800 (war); 109 in 1802 4 (peace); 187 in 1806–8 (war); and 127 in 1809–10 (peace). Despite the decreases suffered during periods of peace, the index from the last period (peace) was 9 percent above that of the first (war). *Aguardiente* exports, once again using the average from 1784–96 as base 100 (1,318 arrobas), shows 105 in 1780–83; 195 in 1797–1800; 267 in 1802–4; 94 in 1806–8; and 74 in 1809–10. Although there was a 29 percent decrease between the first and last periods, it should be noted that the greatest average corresponds to a period of peace (1802–4).

In spite of the rises and falls in the indexes from the periods of peace and war, which seem to indicate that war had a considerably positive effect on Cuyo wine and brandy exports, there were strong fluctuations within each period that cannot be automatically attributed to the external situation. The explanation for these variations should be sought more in the supply than in the demand. Wine exports had extreme variations from 119 percent in 1797 to −52 percent in 1783; *aguardiente* exports, from 172 percent in 1783 to −83 in 1791. Even though brandy exports show even deeper varia-

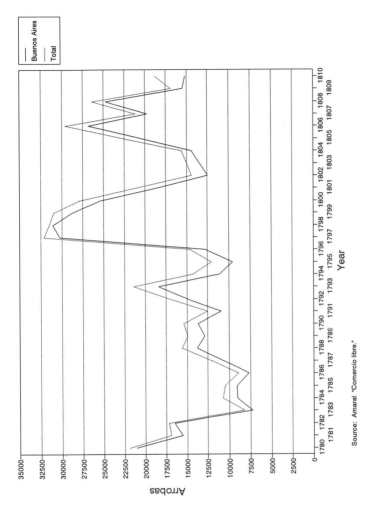

Source: Amaral. "Comercio libre."

Figure 6.3. Mendoza: Wine Exports, 1780–1810.

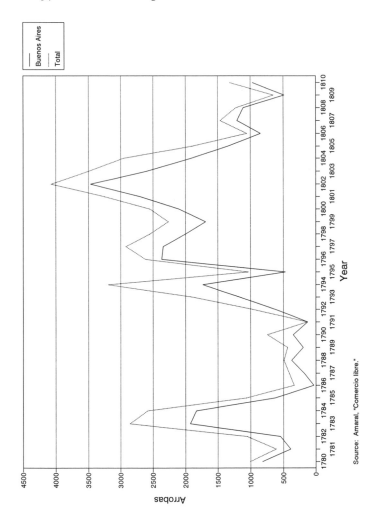

Source: Amaral, "Comercio libre."

Figure 6.4. Mendoza: Brandy Exports, 1780–1810.

tions, the wine export figures also show the instability of grape/ wine production. The regional distribution of Mendozan wine and *aguardiente* shows Buenos Aires as the predominant final destination. Between 1780 and 1810, 89.7 percent of the wine went to Buenos Aires.

After 1810, we have only the information Woodbine Parish provides for 1827, which he apparently took from an official report by the Mendozan government.[18] If it can be believed, the total exports would be 20,020 arrobas of wine, and 13,640 arrobas of *aguardiente*. The regional distribution of these exports followed the same pattern. Nonetheless, the growth in the volume of *aguardiente* exports, compared to the levels known for the period previous to the 1810s, is surprising. In spite of the extension of free trade after 1810, the Mendozan exports of spirits kept on growing. This does not necessarily mean free trade had a positive effect on the Mendozan economy, especially if prices were falling at the same time.

Buenos Aires increased its consumption of Cuyan spirits as it accelerated its population growth at the end of the eighteenth century. However, that is not enough to explain the flow of Cuyan products if the market price was not sufficient, as Godoy Oro claims, to cover production and transport costs. If this had happened over a long period of time, San Juan and Mendoza would have had to decrease the exportation of the products or reorient its exports toward the center and the north. There was no such reorientation, however, and exports of wine from Mendoza and *aguardiente* from San Juan grew. These facts do not sustain the affirmations of Godoy Oro.

On the contrary, from the beginning of the 1780s, Buenos Aires and the other domestic markets in the region seem to have been able to consume as much as Mendoza and San Juan could export. Therefore, the inflexibility of the supply was a bigger limit to exports than Spanish competition. The analysis of the conditions of production (biological, technical, climatic) and marketing (transport) will give us a better idea of the determining factors in the supply of Cuyan wine and spirits.

Production and Marketing Conditions

Production in the Cuyo wine industry was extremely primitive, both in the quality of the grape vines and the techniques used. Even in the main European grape/wine regions at the end of the eighteenth century, no more was known about the cultivation of grapes and the production of wine than previously. At the beginning of the 1770s, the first systematic observations on fermentation were effected, but it was not until the work of Louis Pasteur that the process was totally understood. Traditional cultivators met the technical innovations with much resistance. Only after the Phylloxera crisis in the 1880s did the French viticulturists begin to introduce productive techniques based on scientific discoveries. The first French vines were introduced in Mendoza by Michel Pouget in the middle of the 1850s; previously, only the native variety had been used.[19] In the middle of the nineteenth century, the production methods, from the care of the vine to the making of the wine, were still inadequate: the must (the juice produced from freshly pressed grapes) was not given either the time or the rest needed to clarify, and the majority of the wine was consumed within two or three months after being pressed.[20]

The only detailed description of the cultivation and production methods used in Mendoza and San Juan was written by Damián Hudson and published in 1867. These methods differ very little from those used in Chile in the 1820s and 1830s.[21] After the grape harvest, around the middle of April, the must was fermented and mixed with *cocido*. *Cocido* was fresh must cooked until it was reduced to two-thirds of its volume. One part *cocido* was added to ten parts pure must. If this were not done, the wine would sour because the grapes did not have enough sugar to produce the quantity of alcohol needed. The fermentation took place in *tinajas* (large earthenware jars), which were coated with pitch and covered during fermentation. The wine remained in the *tinajas* until it was sold or until a decision was made to transform it into brandy. The quality of the product depended both on the work done (irrigation, pruning, and other care required by the vines) and on the climate and conditions in which the must was fermented. Weeds that grew around the vines affected the taste. However, no work was done in the vineyards to control growth and improve the quality of the grapes. The grapes also suffered from overwatering, which was to blame for the low sugar content of the fruit.

Beside the soils, climate had the greatest influence on production results. Hail, early frosts, late heat waves, untimely rains, and excessive winds influenced the quantity and quality of the final product, even when the long-term averages for temperature and humid-

Plate 1. Dancing the Minuet in the Home of the Escalada Family
(Pellegrini, c. 1830).

Plate 2. Hussar of General Pueyrredón (Anonymous, c. 1806).

Plate 3. Dress and Sash of Students in Córdoba (Baucke, c. 1760).

Plate 4. Gaucho Cavalry (Morel, c. 1820).

Plate 5. Invasion of the Indians (Pallière, c. 1850).

Plate 6. One Hour before Departure (Morel, c. 1820).

Plate 7. Cattle Branding at the Estancia Rincón de Luna, Corrientes (D'Orbigny, c. 1827).

Plate 8. The Interior of a *Rancho* (Pellegrini, c. 1830).

Plate 9. A Soldier of Rosas (Monvoisin, 1842).

Plate 10. A Sunday Excursion (Palliere, c. 1850).

ity showed stability. A hailstorm that fell on San Juan in November 1806 caused damage estimated at more than 30,000 arrobas of must, reducing that year's production by about 25 percent. Whatever the methods of cultivation and production used, the climate remains even now one of the factors that determines the quality of grape and wine production, not only in Cuyo, but wherever grapevines are cultivated.[22] In the nineteenth century, some methods were utilized to improve grape production: fire and smoke for frost; pruning of unnecessary foliage from the vines; and weeding to combat excess rain and humidity. But these methods were too costly compared to the price of wine.

There was no way (nor is there now) to impede nature's effects. The much-feared hailstorm or even small variations in temperature could disrupt the harvest date. A plague of locusts could affect the whole year's production in an instant. While traveling through Mendoza in March 1835, Charles Darwin saw the sky darken and the earth turn red from a cloud of locusts that flew overhead, advancing at a rate of ten to fifteen miles per hour.[23] One study of nineteenth-century French wine production shows that, in any given decade, natural causes would result in catastrophe in two or three years and in unfavorable conditions in another two or three.[24] There is no reason to believe that it was much different in Cuyo.

San Juan and Mendoza share a dry climate and plenty of sunshine; the former is a bit hotter and the latter more humid. The average annual temperatures between 1870 and 1913 were 16.1 and 17.7 degrees centigrade respectively, with seasonal averages that showed differences of 1.8 degrees centrigrade in summer and 1.4 degrees centrigrade in winter. In the same period, the annual average for rain was 55 millimeters in San Juan and 185 millimeters in Mendoza. The ten-year average for hailstorms was 24 in Mendoza and 5 in San Juan.[25] Both regions benefit from the snow melt in the nearby Andes mountain ranges. The runoff facilitates irrigation, without which this arid land of uncertain summer rains would not be suitable for grape growing. On the irrigation ditches depend (said a petitioner sent by the city of San Juan to the Royal Treasury in Santiago de Chile in 1749) "the cultivation and profitability of the vines, farms and other crops."[26] The irrigation canal that originated in Luján, sixteen miles to the south of Mendoza, carried the water to the city, where it coursed in ditches through the cultivated zone (about fifteen miles in circumference) of *huertas* (truck gardens), the gardens in the city, and the vineyards. This easy access to water prompted growers to overirrigate the vines, producing an increased quantity of grapes of inferior quality.[27] This preference for quantity over quality was not limited to the Cuyan producers. Growers in nineteenth-century Chile also tended to overirrigate their vines; even French producers used varieties that gave an abundant harvest but only mediocre wine.[28] Cuyan and Chilean wines were short-lived and soured easily. Various methods were tried to improve them, some as strange as submerging cats (or at least a piece of meat) in the casks. Because alcohol content remained low due to the climate and excessive irrigation, Mendozan wines likewise passed rapidly into an acidic fermentation.[29]

The poor quality of the vines, the lack of knowledge about the fermentation process, plagues, overirrigation and, above all, the unpredictable climatic influences are factors that determined the quantity and quality of wine production. To attribute the annual fluctuations in production and exports exclusively to demand ignores these supply-side factors. The mediocre wines from Cuyo also suffered from deficient transportation conditions. The wooden casks made in Mendoza were crude, their tops and bottoms covered by leather. They were loaded onto carts pulled by oxen. At least twelve and often up to thirty carts traveled in trains (as protection against Indian attacks); their trip to Buenos Aires took a little more than a month and a half.[30] Wine was also transported from Cuyo on mules: teams of 60 to 80 animals were used, only half of which carried loads at one time. Mule trains serviced the route from San Juan to Buenos Aires, because the unevenness of the terrain made the trip difficult for carts. Each mule carried two casks at a freight charge of seven pesos per two-arroba cask. Each cart carried twenty casks, or forty arrobas of wine, at a cost of approximately four pesos each. The greater expense of using mule trains explains why San Juan distilled the majority of its wine into *aguardiente*, which sold for twice the price of wine in Buenos Aires.[31]

Even though producers from the interior, asking for tax relief, complained of a lack of profits, the sale of domestic wines and brandy in Buenos Aires apparently could be profitable. Transport costs in the 1820s remained lower than production costs, and there was also a demand in Buenos Aires for wine and *aguardiente* that could not be supplied by any other source at such a low cost. John

Miers has pointed out that the sale of bad Mendozan wine produced considerable profit. But improving the quality (and price) would probably not have produced bigger profits, as he believed it would. The additional costs of refining the varieties of grape, improving the wine fermentation process, and adding more men to plow between rows, protecting the vines, and increase the pruning, would not pay off. The cost of putting a cask of Mendozan wine in Buenos Aires around 1780 was 11 pesos 5¼ reales, of which 34.3 percent went to the producer, 8.6 percent for the container, 42.9 percent for freight charges, and 14.2 percent for various taxes, according to a petitioner at the beginning of the 1780s.[32] Although Godoy Oro and other petitioners wanted to eliminate taxes and to demonstrate that the selling price of wine was too close to the cost of transporting it, Cuyan products did compete with Spanish products. The fact that wine and *aguardiente* from Mendoza and San Juan continued to arrive in Buenos Aires would seem to indicate that the profits were not insignificant.

Moreover, Buenos Aires was practically the only large market for Cuyan products, as other large markets in the Southern Cone were supplied by competing grape-growing regions. Alto Perú (Bolivia) had always been supplied with brandy from the valleys of Arequipa and with wine from Cinti. Chile fulfilled its own needs in both products, and Lima was supplied by Pisco, Nazca, and Arequipa. Around 1770, the valleys of Vitor, Mages, and Moquegua jointly produced 550,000 *botijas* of brandy (more than a million arrobas), while Cuyan production did not reach even 20,000 arrobas. At the end of the eighteenth century, the Cuyan spirits supplied less than 1 percent of the Potosí market.[33] Cuyo's main market, Buenos Aires, and its two secondary markets, Córdoba and Santa Fe, were also supplied from imported foreign wines. In 1795, Montevideo and Buenos Aires consumed 6,874 arrobas of Spanish *aguardiente* and 14,480 arrobas of Spanish wine, while the combined exports from Cuyo to Buenos Aires were 6,049 arrobas of brandy and 10,359 arrobas of wine. Cuyan spirits satisfied less than half the demand in Buenos Aires.[34]

To evaluate the impact of free trade on Cuyo, one would have to consider the evolution of prices in order to estimate the income produced by fluctuating exports. There are no price series available, but other Cuyan economic indexes allow us to estimate the income produced by wine and brandy exports.

Regional Economies

The sources most commonly used in the study of Spanish American colonial economies are the tithes (*diezmos*), assessed on production and the sale duties (*alcabalas*) levied on trade. We shall analyze the tithes and sale duties for San Juan and Mendoza, and data from customs duties on their products imported into Buenos Aires.[35]

Tithes are not an index of agrarian production. But even if, in spite of their weaknesses, they are taken as such, one still could not conclude unequivocally that the impact of free trade on the interior provinces was negative. The collection of tithes at San Juan rose from a yearly index of 100 in 1786–90 to 225 in 1808; Mendoza's index rose to 311 during the same time period. Setting aside the fact that the tithe could have expressed the expectation of income more than the volume of production, this increase in tithe collections would indicate growing income for the economies of San Juan and Mendoza. Part of these tithes, however, came from the production of goods for local consumption, such as meat and cereals, whose prices and proportion of the total tithe are not known. For this reason, it is better to disregard the tithes as indexes of any kind.[36]

The impact of the liberal measures can be assessed better through the information supplied by sales taxes, which reflect the expenditures in Mendoza and San Juan for products from other regions. These expenditures were closely related to the income produced by the main exports, wine and *aguardiente*. There are two sales tax series for Mendoza, one covering the period from 1783 to 1820, the other from 1800 to 1831.[37] Between 1783 and 1802 the values are below the average (1800–1803 = 100). Both sources, however, show a marked growth compared to the average in the 1810s: 24 percent in 1816 and 56 percent in 1817. Both series show an abrupt fall after 1823, a consequence of the civil war. After 1821, one of the series shows values below those of the previous decade, but still 66 percent above the base value. The last year for which there are data, 1831, is barely one point below the base. The figures for San Juan for 1786–1810 show a trend that accompanies the growth registered by the Mendozan taxes.[38]

Although we have no information on wine and brandy prices in Mendoza and San Juan, it is possible to measure Buenos Aires imports of wine from the interior. Comparing the five-year averages from 1782–86 (for Mendoza) and 1783–87 (for San Juan) with those of 1817–21, we note that the growth of wine exports from Mendoza to Buenos Aires was 137 percent and that of San Juan 114 percent, with annual growth rates of 2.5 and 2.3 percent respectively. *Aguardiente* exports from San Juan to Buenos Aires grew by 83 percent, and from Mendoza to Buenos Aires by 284 percent. The annual growth rates were 1.8 and 3.9 percent respectively. The curves of the total volume of *aguardiente* imports from San Juan and wine from Mendoza show depressions occurring in 1819–20, when the civil war affected internal trade.[39]

Implicit prices (the value divided by the volume of entries into Buenos Aires) show variations relating less to the origin of the product than to the product itself. Wine prices increased between 1802 and 1808, fell in 1809–10, and held steady until 1821 with slight fluctuations of around five pesos per cask. Overall, wine prices rose 8 percent between 1804 and 1819. Prices of Mendozan *aguardiente* increased by 17 percent and that of San Juan 9.8 percent in those same years.

For Mendoza, the consequences of peace seem more serious than those of the civil war. For San Juan, however, even if the sales declines of 1804–6 and 1809–10 are assigned to peace time, they were less steep than those of 1819–21, when the civil war interrupted internal commerce and reduced the supply of workers in Cuyo. Such a clear demarcation of causes, however, would be imprudent given the natural fluctuations of grape production. The elimination of taxes on land entrances in Buenos Aires in 1821 led to the disappearance of this valuable historical source. There are data on the land entrances in Buenos Aires between 1837 and 1842, but it has been impossible to verify up to what point they reflect total imports.[40] If this information were complete, we might observe the impact of the French naval blockade at Buenos Aires on the wine and *aguardiente* markets, particularly how San Juan and Mendoza responded to the sudden dearth of foreign wine imports.

Cuyo did not capture markets suddenly abandoned by the foreign wines during the blockade of 1838–40. Buenos Aires previously had imported up to 99 percent of its wine and 82 percent of its brandy from abroad. It is not possible to determine in what measure the decreased market shares of Cuyo wines at Buenos Aires was due to competition from foreign imports or to disturbances suffered by domestic production as a consequence of the civil wars. It seems tempting to give greater weight to the presence of French and Spanish wines. However, the decrease in the labor pool, because of the demand for men for armed service in Cuyo, and the consequent abandonment of the vines are not factors to be discounted. Grapevines require great care and recover slowly from production declines. The vines did not produce until they were three years old and only reached full productiveness after eight years.[41] Cuyan production depended on irrigation—and this, in turn, depended on the maintenance of the ditches by available laborers.

The consequences of the civil war can also be seen in the fluctuations of Córdoba's consumption of wine and brandy from San Juan and Mendoza and of wine from La Rioja. Córdoba's wine imports fell in 1829, recovered between 1833 and 1838, and then fell and stagnated during the following years. *Aguardiente* imports fell in 1829 and in 1839–1841, and stagnated from 1843 on. Between 1822 and 1851, the introduction of Mendozan wine into Córdoba fell by 91 percent, that of San Juan by 46 percent, and that of La Rioja by 61 percent. Córdoba's imports of Mendozan *aguardiente* fell by 56 percent, but that of San Juan broadly increased by 6 percent. These decreases could be attributed to the importing of foreign spirits by Buenos Aires, were it not for the fact that the naval blockades of that port in 1826–28, 1838–40, and 1845–47 had no effect on Córdoba's purchase of wine and brandy from Cuyo.[42] It is true that the grape production cannot react to market conditions from one year to the next and that the same climatic factors mentioned above could have limited production during these years. On the other hand, one Mendoza citizen, Damián Hudson, had no doubts as to why the Cuyo wine industry was so decrepit at midcentury. He referred to the "complete annihilation of all the industries to which the civil war and a dark tyranny have carried us." In 1852 the grapevines were "reduced to a level barely adequate for local consumption," he said.[43] If an estimate based on his own figures is correct, Mendoza's people were drinking a lot of wine. In other words, must production was around 100,000 arrobas at that time, or around 75,000 arrobas of wine, 63 percent more than during the peak years of the 1790s.

Conclusion

Yet the image of interior economic crisis in the provinces from the late eighteenth to the mid-nineteenth centuries continues to convince historians. If Mendozan wine exports in the final decades of the colonial period show that there was no shrinkage in production, and San Juan brandy exports actually grew, why does everyone think in terms of depression? If indexes such as the collection of tithes and customs taxes, and Buenos Aires' imports of Cuyan spirits, also indicate no signs of a crisis until the civil wars of 1820 (besides those that naturally affected the wine industry), why do observers still conjure up images of domestic economic disaster stemming from the 1778 free trade law and liberal trade measures after 1810?

Two answers suggest themselves. In the first place, due to the lack of systematic recording of commercial and fiscal statistics during the time period, contemporaries were unable to measure their own economic performance. Second, as Adam Smith suggested, economic privileges are much more attractive than competition. In the colonial economy, privilege was the habitual mark of production and marketing. The Crown regulated the economy and dispensed licenses to produce and trade, to reward loyalty, service, or influence and to raise revenues. The official complaint was the basic instrument used to achieve larger profits or a redistribution of income. Thus, the answer to the liberal measures of the first revolutionary decade was a return to the crudest mercantilism: rather than contenting themselves merely with protective tariffs, Cuyan producers asked Buenos Aires for a complete ban on the import of foreign spirits.[44] The petition that the Cuyan grape growers made in 1817 to the government of the newly independent United Provinces of the Río de la Plata, is an expression of corporate interests. For the sake of gaining a privilege (in this case, a captive market that they could only partially supply), the domestic wine producers did not hesitate to sacrifice the no-less-legitimate interests of the consumers of Buenos Aires.[45] Why did these men suppose that protection could be awarded without any cost? The Economic Commission on Tariffs ruled against the ban. Its commissioners did not believe that absolute protection was enough to stimulate domestic wine production, and foreign spirits were a source of revenue for the state that Cuyan wines could never be.[46] The taxes on imported brandy and wine were six to eight times larger than those imposed on the Cuyan spirits. Moreover, even though the consumption of Cuyan spirits at Buenos Aires fell between 1810 and 1860, the provinces of San Juan and Mendoza meanwhile had diversified their production sufficiently to assure that they were no longer dependent on one product or one market.[47]

Despite the sectorial complaints of the time, it was not free trade but civil war that most damaged the economies of San Juan and Mendoza.[48] In the economy of the first half-century of independence, when regulatory powers became vastly decentralized, local powers erected barriers to the free circulation of people and goods. However, the sparse economic data totally disappears in the 1820s, when the internal civil conflicts began in earnest. The impression remains that the Cuyan grape industry, while not disappearing, did not share in the growth of what were formerly the principal markets for their spirits. The most imprecise of numbers tell us that the Cuyan economic response was, on the one hand, production diversification and, on the other, an expansion of the area cultivated for grapevines.

The Cuyan economy actually was affected less by free trade than by precarious technology, plagues, climate, and, above all, the civil war. There was no golden age prior to the free trade reforms of the late eighteenth century, and free trade did not produce any agony at all. The critical fluctuations were produced mainly by the scourge of a marginal economy, which was dedicated entirely to an especially fragile crop. In any event, all meaningful production came to a definitive end with the civil war. This war did indeed unleash a crisis that took grape production, because of its slower rhythms, a long time to overcome. Until then, Cuyo only knew its golden age and its agony in the writing of those complainants, such as Domingo Sarmiento, who operated within an economic tradition dominated by privilege.

Notes

1. A review of the recent literature on the 1778 free trade regulations appears in Carlos D. Malamud and Pedro Pérez Herrero, "Reglement du commerce libre en Espagne et en Amerique: Principaux problèmes d'interpretation," in *L'Amérique Espagnole a l'époque des Lumières* (Paris, 1987).

2. Eduardo Arcila Farías, *Reformas económicas del siglo XVIII en Nueva España* (Mexico, 1974), 134. The royal decrees are found in the Facultad de Filosofía y Letras, Universidad de Buenos Aires, *Documentos para la Historia Argentina*, vol. 5, *Comercio de Indias: Antecedentes legales, 1713–1778*, introduction by Ricardo Levene (Buenos Aires, 1915).

3. Antonio García Baquero González, *Comercio colonial y guerras revolucionarias* (Sevilla, 1972); Javier Cuenca Esteban, "Statistics of Spain's Colonial Trade," *Hispanic American Historical Review* 61, no. 3 (1981): 381–

428; John Fisher, "Imperial 'Free Trade' and the Hispanic Economy, 1778–1796," *Journal of Latin American Studies* 13, no. 1 (1981): 21–56.

4. See Ricardo Levene, *Investigaciones acerca de la historia económica del virreinato del Plata*, 2 vols. (La Plata, 1928); Pedro Santos Martínez, *Historia económica de Mendoza durante el virreinato, 1776–1810* (Madrid, 1961); Martínez, *Las industrias durante el virreinato (1776–1810)* (Buenos Aires, 1969); Horacio Videla, *Historia de San Juan* (Buenos Aires, 1969), vol. 1.

5. Tulio Halperín Donghi, *Revolución y guerra* (Buenos Aires, 1972), 23. On the survival of the native textiles, see Juan Carlos Garavaglia, "Los textiles de la tierra en el contexto colonial ríoplatense: Una revolución industrial fallida?" *Anuario IEHS* 1 (1986): 45–87; Brooke Larson, "The Cotton Textile Industry of Cochabamba, 1770–1810: The Opportunities and Limits of Growth," in *The Economies of Mexico and Peru during the Late Colonial Period, 1760–1810*, ed. Nils Jacobsen and Hans-Jürgen Puhle (Berlin, 1986), 150–168; and Klaus Müller, "Comercio interno y economía regional en Hispanoamérica colonial. Aproximación cuantitativa a la historia económica de San Miguel de Tucumán, 1784–1809," *Jahrbuch für Geschichte von Staat, Wirtschaft und Gesellschaft Lateinamerikas* 24 (1987): 308.

6. José Torre Revello, *El marqués de Sobremonte, gobernador intendente de Córdoba y virrey del Río de la Plata* (Buenos Aires, 1946); Germán Tjarks, "Un informe comercial sanjuanino para la Secretaría de Balanza de Madrid," *Boletín del Instituto de Historia Argentina y Americana Dr. Emilio Ravignani* 2, nos. 4–6 (1958): 203–37. There are also sources that mention the critical situation in Mendozan grape and wine production. The city's agent in 1781 and a tariffs and excise tax statement in 1782, for example, reported on the decline of the wine trade. See Martínez, *Historia económica de Mendoza*, 292–93.

7. Facultad de Filosofía y Letras, Universidad de Buenos Aires, *Documentos para la Historia Argentina*, vol. 7, *Comercio de negros y de extranjeros (1791–1809)*, introduction by Diego Luis Molinari (Buenos Aires, 1916), 134–35, 157–59, 192–93, 199, 207–8.

8. Edberto Oscar Acevedo, "Los impuestos al comercio cuyano en el siglo XVIII (1700–1750)," *Revista Chilena de Historia y Geografía* 126 (1958): 34–76; Acevedo, "Los impuestos al comercio cuyano en el siglo XVIII (1750–1800)," *Revista Chilena de Historia y Geografía* 131 (1963): 75–120.

9. Thaddaeus Pereginus Haenke, *Descripción del Reyno de Chile*, introduction by Agustín Edwards (Santiago, 1942), 277; Félix de Azara, *Viajes por la América Meridional*, (Madrid, 1969), 95; Emeric Essex Vidal, "Ilustraciones pintorescas de Buenos Aires y Montevideo," in Facultad de Filosofía y Letras, Universidad de Buenos Aires, *Colección de viajeros y memorias geográficas*, trans. Carlos Muzio Sáenz Peña (Buenos Aires, 1923), 226; note by Justo Maeso in Woodbine Parish, *Buenos Aires y las provincias del Río de la Plata*, 2d ed., trans. Maeso (Buenos Aires, 1958), 489.

10. José Godoy Oro reports that each cask contained two arrobas; see Tjarks, "Un informe comercial sanjuanino," 213 n.

11. For the sources and methodology of the reconstruction, see Samuel Amaral, "Comercio libre y las economías regionales: San Juan y Mendoza, 1780–1820," *Jahrbuch für Geschichte von Staat, Wirtschaft und Gesellschaft Lateinamerikas* 27 (1990). I thank Silvia Palomeque for the figures on San Juan's *sisa* for 1796, 1798, and 1803–4 collected at the Archivo Histórico Provincial, Córdoba.

12. The data from 1752–64 come from Archivo Nacional de Chile, Santiago (hereafter cited as ANC), Contaduría Mayor, 1st series, 3523, San Juan. For the sources of other data, see note 11.

13. To define the periods of peace and war, the fluctuations of Spanish imports to America have been taken into account according to the figures of García Baquero González, Cuenca Esteban, and Fisher cited in note 31. The references to the effects of the wars on the production and marketing of wine and *aguardiente* from Catalonia at the end of the eighteenth and beginning of the nineteenth century derive from Emilio Giralt Raventós, "La viticultura y el comercio catalán del siglo XVIII," *Estudios de Historia Moderna* 2 (1952): 173; Jaume Torras Elías, "Aguardiente y crisis rural. Sobre la coyuntura vitícola, 1793–1832," *Historia agraria de la España contemporánea*, vol. 1, *Cambio social y nuevas formas de propiedad (1800–1850)*, ed. Angel García Sanz and Ramón Garrabou (Barcelona, 1985), 163–65. The Spanish wine and *aguardiente* imports in Veracruz derive from Javier Ortíz de la Tabla Ducasse, *Comercio exterior de Veracruz (1778–1821)* (Sevilla, 1978), 248.

14. Miguel Izard, "Comercio libre, guerras coloniales y mercado americano," in *Agricultura, comercio colonial y crecimiento económico en la España contemporánea*, ed. Jordi Nadal and Gabriel Tortella (Barcelona, 1974), 315–16; Carlos D. Malamud, "El comercio de neutrales en el Río de la Plata (1805–1806)," *Cuadernos de Historia Regional* 2, no. 4 (1985): 17–41.

15. Halperín Donghi, *Revolución y guerra*, 26.

16. Hernán Asdrúbal Silva, "El vino y el aguardiente en la Buenos Aires de la primera mitad del siglo XVIII," in Academia Nacional de la Historia, *VI Congreso Internacional de Historia de América*, 4 vols. (Buenos Aires, 1982), 4:247; Carlos S. A. Segreti, "La repercusión en Mendoza de la política comercial porteña en la primera década revolucionaria," *Jarbuch für Geschichte von Staat, Wirtschaft und Gesellschaft Lateinamerikas* 19 (1982): 183–89.

17. Kendall W. Brown, "A evolucão da vinicultura em Arequipa, 1550–1800," *Estudos Ibero-Americanos* 4, no. 1 (1980): 39–52; Brown, *Bourbons and Brandy: Imperial Reform in Eighteenth Century Arequipa* (Albuquerque, 1986).

18. Parish, *Buenos Aires y las provincias*, 489.

19. Leo A. Loubère, *The Red and the White: The History of Wine in France and Italy in the XIXth Century* (Albany, 1978), xviii, 24; Georges Durand, *Vin, vigne et vignerons en Lyonnais et Beaujolais (XVIe.–XVIIIe. siècles)* (Lyon, 1979), 194–98; Eusebio Blanco, *Las viñas y los vinos en Mendoza* (Buenos Aires, 1884), 11.

20. Hermann Burmeister, *Viaje por los estados del Plata*, trans. Carlos and Federico Burmeister, 2 vols. (Buenos Aires, 1943), 1:213–14.

21. Damián Hudson, *La viticultura en Cuyo* (Buenos Aires, 1867), as taken from *Anales de la Sociedad Rural Argentina* 15 (1867): 477–90; John Miers, *Travels in Chile and La Plata*, 2 vols. (London, 1826), 2:298–301; Claudio Gay, *Agricultura chilena*, 2 vols. (Santiago, 1973), 2:189–92.

22. Gay, *Agricultura chilena*, 2:182–83; Loubère, *The Red and the White*, 119; Archivo General de la Nación [hereinafter cited as AGN], Sala IX, 4-6-5, Consulado, San Juan, f. 73; John D. Post, "A Study in Meteorological and Trade Cycle History: The Economic Crisis Following the Napoleonic Wars," *Journal of Economic History* 34, no. 2 (1974): 315–49; Torras Elías, "Aguardiente y crisis rural," 164; Pierre Vilar, *La Catalogne dans l'Espagne moderne*, 3 vols. (Paris, 1962), 3:374–76; Pierre Butel, "Production viticole et rente foncière in Bordelais aux XVIIIe siècle," in *Prestations paysannes, dimes, rente foncière et mouvement de la production agricole a l'époque pre-industrielle*, ed. Joseph Goy and Emmanuel Le Roy Ladurie, 2 vols. (Paris, 1982), 2:512–19; Mariano Zamorano, "El viñedo de Mendoza," *Boletín de Estudios Geográficos* 6, no. 23 (1959): 90.

23. Charles Darwin, *Journal of Researches into the Geology and Natural History of the Various Countries Visited during the Voyage of H.M.S. Beagle Round the World* (London, 1912), 315–16. On the date of the grape harvest and the effects of an early or late harvest, see Argentina, Junta Reguladora de Vinos, *Memoria correspondiente al año 1935* (Buenos Aires, 1936), 410–23; Alfred Angot, "Études sur les vendanges en France," *Annales du Bureau Central Météorologique de France* (1883): B29–B120, cited by Emmanuel Le Roy Ladurie, "Histoire et climat," *Annales E.S.C.* 14 (1959): 16; Juan Llerena, "Cuadros descriptivos estadísticos de las tres provincias de Cuyo," *Revista de Buenos Aires* 11 (1866): 254.

24. Loubère, *The Red and the White*, 77, 122, 363–65.

25. Walter G. Davis, *Historia y organización con un resumen de los resultados* (Buenos Aires, 1914), 174–75; Davis, *Climate of the Argentine Republic* (Buenos Aires, 1910), 83; V. Martin de Moussy, *Déscription géographique et statistique de la Confédération Argentine*, 3 vols. (Paris, 1864), 3:418–19, 452–53.

26. ANC, Contaduría Mayor, 1st series, 3523.

27. Miers, *Travels in Chile and La Plata*, 1:224.

28. Ibid., 2:298; Loubère, *The Red and the White*, 146.

29. Gay, *Agricultura chilena*, 2:198–99. On the traditional methods of

improvement, see Michael R. Best, "The Mystery of Vintners," *Agricultural History* 50, no. 2 (1976): 362–76; Miers, *Travels in Chile*, 1:246.

30. Miers, *Travels in Chile*, 1:52, 243, 245; Miguel Angel Rosal, "Transportes terrestres y circulación de mercancías en el espacio rioplatense, 1781–1811," *Anuario IEHS* 3 (1988): 123–59; Theodorick Bland, "Report of Theodorick Bland, Esq. on South America," in U.S. Congress, House, Documents, 2 vols. 15th Cong., 2d sess., 1818–19, 2:32.

31. Miers, *Travels in Chile*, 1:52, 55; Rosal, "Transportes terrestres"; Edberto Oscar Acevedo, *Investigaciones sobre el comercio cuyano 1800–1830* (Buenos Aires, 1981), 55; AGN, Sala IX, 4-6-5, Consulado, San Juan, ff. 49–50; Haenke, *Descripción de Reyno de Chile*, 277; Tjarks, "Un informe comercial sanjuanino," 213; Guillermo Gallardo, *Joel Roberts Poinsett, agente norteamericano 1810–1814* (Buenos Aires, 1984), 114; Claudia M. Wentzel, "Estadística del comercio interior de Buenos Aires, 1800–1821," unpublished ms., 1988.

32. Archivo Histórico de Mendoza, Colonial, folder 84, doc. 86.

33. Carlos Sempat Assadourian, *El sistema de la economía colonial* (Lima, 1982), 155–60; Brown, "A evolucão da vinicultura," 43; Marcel Haitin, "Prices, the Lima Market, and the Agricultural Crisis of the Late Eighteenth Century in Peru," *Jahrbuch für Geschichte von Staat, Wirtschaft und Gesellschaft Lateinamerikas* 22 (1985): 188; Enrique Tandeter et al., "El mercado de Potosí a fines del siglo XVIII," in *La participación indígena en los mercados surandinos*, ed. Olivia Harris et al. (La Paz, 1987), 415, 419; Joseph Barclay Pentland, *Informe sobre Bolivia (1826)*, trans. Jack Aitken Soux (Potosí, 1975), 60, 104.

34. Pierre Vilar, *La Catalogne dans l'Espagne Moderne*, 3 vols. (Paris, 1962), 3:540; García Baquero González, "Comercio colonial y producción industrial en Cataluña a fines del siglo XVIII," in *Agricultura, comercio colonial y crecimiento económico*, 285; Carlos Manera Erbina, "Producción agraria e infraestructura mercantíl en el comercio mallorquín con América, 1778–1818," in *El comercio libre entre España y América Latina, 1765–1824*, coord. Antonio Miguel Bernal (Madrid, 1987), 237, 245.

35. Marcello Carmagnani, *Les mécanismes de la vie économique dans une société coloniale: Le Chili (1680–1830)* (Paris, 1973); Garavaglia, "Economic Growth and Regional Differentiations," *Hispanic American Historical Review* 65 (February 1985): 15–64; Tandeter et al., "El mercado de Potosí a fines del siglo XVIII."

36. Garavaglia, "Economic Growth and Regional Differentiations," 65 (Graph 4). I thank Juan Carlos Garavaglia for the figures on tithes from 1786 to 1808, which he collected at the Archivo General de Indias.

37. Edberto Oscar Acevedo, *Investigaciones sobre el comercio Cuyano, 1800–1830* (Buenos Aires, 1981), 41–44; and Wentzel, "Los flujos de circula-

ción de Mendoza, 1783–1820," in *VI Jornadas de Historia Económica* (Córdoba, 1984).

38. Ibid. For San Juan's sales tax, see AGN, Sala XIII; those figures were collected by Wentzel, whose unpublished manuscript I have used here.

39. Estimates based upon figures taken from Wentzel, "Estadística del comercio interior."

40. Andrés R. Allende, "Notas sobre la supresión de los derechos de tránsito y nacionalización de las aduanas en las provincias de la Confederación," in Academia Nacional de la Historia, *Primer Congreso de Historia Argentina y Regional* (Buenos Aires, 1973), 305–18; V. Buenos Aires (Provincia), *Registro Oficial*, 1836–40; AGN, Sala X, 42-10-11.

41. Blanco, "Las viñas y los vinos en Mendoza," 7; Gay, *Agricultura chilena*, 2:180.

42. Nora Barrionuevo, "El intercambio comercial de Mendoza, San Juan y La Rioja con la provincia de Córdoba, entre los años 1822–52: Aportes para su estudio," in Academia Nacional de la Historia, *Cuarto Congreso Nacional y Regional de Historia Argentina*, 3 vols. (Buenos Aires, 1979), 1:52, 57–60.

43. Hudson, *Apuntes cronológicos para servir a la historia de la antigua provincia de Cuyo* (Mendoza, 1852), 11; Pedro N. Arata, *Investigación vinícola* (Buenos Aires, 1903).

44. Segreti, "Mendoza y la política porteña (1835–1836)," *Investigaciones y Ensayos* 16 (1974): 177–78; Izard, "Comercio libre, guerras coloniales y mercado americano," 218–20; Segreti, *La economía del interior en la primera mitad del siglo XIX*, vol. 1, Cuyo (Buenos Aires, 1981), 45–63.

45. Vicente G. Quesada, "Representación al Rey de los labradores de Buenos Aires (1793)," *Revista de Buenos Aires* 17, no. 66 (1868): 141–43.

46. José María Mariluz Urquijo, "Aspectos de la política proteccionista durante la década 1810–1820," *Boletín de la Academia Nacional de la Historia* 37 (1965): 151–52; Acevedo, *Investigaciones*, 96–97; Segreti, "La repercusión en Mendoza," 219–20.

47. Llerena, "Cuadros descriptivos estadísticos," 66; William J. Fleming, *Region vs. Nation: Cuyo in the Crosscurrents of Argentine National Development, 1861–1914* (Tempe, Ariz., 1986), 8–18.

48. Hudson, *Apuntes cronológicos*, 11; Arata, *Investigación vinícola*, 184; Ricardo Palencia, "Monografía de la industria viti-vinícola argentina," in Argentina, *Censo agropecuario nacional: La ganadería y la agricultura en 1908*, 3 vols. (Buenos Aires, 1909), 3:336.

Thomas Whigham

Trade and Conflict on the Rivers: Corrientes, 1780–1840

Politics and commerce go hand in hand, so much so that any constraints on the one invariably undermine the other. Even under the worst political conditions, however, merchants can find ways to advance their own interests and rise above the disorder. In the early history of independent Argentina, the northeastern province of Corrientes provided just such a case. The breaking of linkages with Spain did not bring full-fledged nationhood to Argentina. Instead, a lengthy period of political division only gradually gave way to a situation where Buenos Aires could exercise the same level of authority over the hinterlands that it had enjoyed in colonial times. Before this situation could occur, however, the *porteños* had to eliminate rival provincial power bases. Achieving this proved no small matter, since the provinces set their own political and economic agendas and were often unwilling to adopt those of the capital.

This essay will examine how commerce was affected by this process in one region of Argentina, the northeast. The northeastern region is dominated by large rivers, the Paraná and the Uruguay, which crisscross a fertile landscape of broad plains and expansive jungles. These waterways provided the littoral with outlets to the sea and with all of its major external markets. They were the key to the economic integration of the region with the rest of South America. The northeast gravitated between two extremes on the issue of trade, depending on whether unencumbered passage was possible on the rivers. When the rivers were open, the region actively participated in commerce that linked it with most parts of Spanish South America and with Brazil. Though the variety of regional commodities was limited, sufficient demand always existed to promote their export. Likewise, both native-born and foreign merchants were ready to invest and join in the trade. But when the rivers were closed, the northeast became a collection of isolated, self-contained entities that displayed little disposition to trade even with each other. This semi-autarkical arrangement had its partisans within the region, just as open trade had its supporters.

The inhabitants of Corrientes and Misiones were bitterly aware that the flow of commerce beyond their area depended on Buenos Aires. The port city constituted the northeast's most important market, a reality that was as necessary as it was resented, because the location of Buenos Aires at the mouth of the estuary meant that its merchants and fiscal authorities could control commercial access to the littoral provinces. The *porteños* could therefore make or break the external trade of the northeast, and their willingness to apply political pressure on Corrientes spurred no end of enmity. Because these hard feelings colored political relations with Buenos Aires over the years, the issue of access to river routes provided the context for political alliances between the northeast and adjacent powers.

The Economic Dimensions

The commercial development of Corrientes depended squarely on the export of three items—yerba mate, timber, and hides. Since early colonial times, yerba had been gathered wild from the forests of northern Misiones. The leaves of this shrub were toasted and then ground to produce a green tea. In the beginning, the tea was known only in Paraguay, but eventually it became popular throughout the southern half of the continent.[1]

Fine hardwoods also were extracted from the forests of the northeast. Unlike yerba, high-quality timber was available in large quantities all over the region and had never been a Paraguayan or Misionero monopoly. Craftsmen utilized these hardwoods for many purposes, including construction beams, cart axles, furniture, tool handles, and gunstocks. Correntino timber was also important in shipbuilding, so that shipyards sprung up in the late 1700s in the towns of Corrientes, in Itatí, as well as in such out-of-the-way villages as Esquina.

Hides and cattle by-products provided the third major export of the northeast. Though the region never rivaled the southern provinces in cattle production, ranching was a key sector of the economy, especially in southern Corrientes. Misiones, on the other hand,

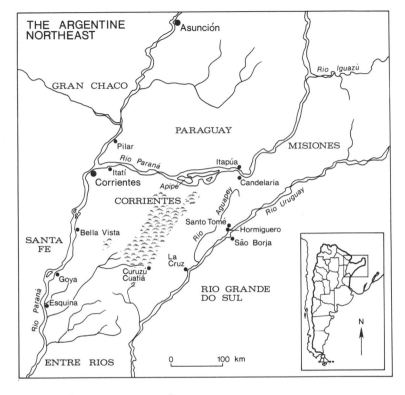

Map 2. The Argentine Northeast.

never possessed abundant herds of wild cattle (*cimarrones*), so stock raising there proved only marginally important after independence.

The Paraná river system runs through the eastern half of a broad, low plain, and cuts across the edge of this plain on its way to the sea. The swampy Gran Chaco region forms the northern part of this plain, the pampa grasslands the southern. During the times of flooding, larger vessels can proceed as far north as the junction of the Río Iguasú, but normally the terminus of river trade was at the port of Corrientes. The Paraná, with its shallow, winding, and island-strewn course, offered no good channel for navigation. Its banks below Corrientes did not lend themselves to the founding of ports, and the right bank was often inundated as far south as Santa Fé. Settlements on the western side of the river were invariably established at some distance from the riverbank. Some stretches of the eastern bank were high and well-defined, but intervening marshes prevented easy contact between the populated centers in Corrientes and the main river channel. As a commercial artery, the Paraná's chief disadvantage lay in the relatively poor access it afforded to the surrounding territory.[2]

The hydrographic features of the Río Uruguay were quite different from those of the Paraná, their only navigational similarity being that each river had a fall barrier. In the case of the Río Paraná, the rapids at Apipé interfered little with downriver trade because the principal ports were all located well below the rapid. The Uruguay, on the other hand, possessed extensive rapids, which constituted a major obstacle to regular river passage, especially during the dry season, when cargo had to be unloaded at one end of the rapids and reloaded aboard another ship at the other end.[3] Moreover, because of the precipitous rise and fall of the Río Uruguay, many of its nominal river ports were in fact founded on tributary streams to offset the effects of the river's regime.[4]

Settlement patterns on the rivers owed little to commercial speculation in the early phases of colonization. Before the eighteenth century, the Spanish Empire regarded the northeast as peripheral, scarcely worth the funds necessary to maintain it. Cracks in the veneer of isolation appeared only in the late 1600s with the development of an external market for yerba mate. The tea provided a sounder base for commercial growth than any of the other regional commodities, since the region constituted the only source. As the demand for yerba grew in the seventeenth century, producers used their monopoly position to overcome high transportation costs. By 1700, yerba was being drunk not only in Buenos Aires but also in Quito and Santiago de Chile. Still, although yerba permitted the northeast to participate in the broader economy of Spanish America, conditions for internal commerce remained poor during most of the eighteenth century, mostly due to shortsighted government policies. The colonial administration in the Río de la Plata, as elsewhere in the New World, was less interested in the promotion of trade than in the generation of revenues for defense.

The Viceregal Period

Few reforms were possible before the creation of the Viceroyalty of the Río de la Plata in 1776. Previously, all Spanish territories in

South America were linked within the massive Viceroyalty of Perú, which had its economic center at the vast silver complex of Potosí in Alto Perú. The work at Potosí involved not just the mining and processing of ore, but also the provisioning of miners, a requirement that brought Potosí into regular contact with Platine suppliers of foodstuffs, mules, and yerba mate. The authorities at Lima could not stem the concomitant flow of smuggled goods. In time, the Crown accepted the inevitable, giving permission for individual shipments of imports from Buenos Aires to Potosí and for the export of silver that had paid the royal taxes. The establishment of the new viceroyalty, which included Potosí within its boundaries, soon followed.

In the meantime, major changes in colonial commerce had transformed Buenos Aires into the principal emporium of southern South America. Chief among these changes was the 1778 adoption of free trade as the linchpin of imperial trade. Not to be confused with the free trade of later years, the policy of *comercio libre* sought to garner revenues for Madrid, both by implementing new taxation and by increasing the volume of transactions with the colonies. The new policy rationalized commerce by streamlining taxation, ending the strict licensing system of the past and allowing direct and open trade between different regions of the empire. This interregional trade was particularly significant for the northeast, making it easier for Correntino and Paraguayan merchants to respond to growing outside demand for their commodities. This increased demand was itself an outcome of *comercio libre*.

Certain commodities—timber, hides, and most notably yerba—responded in dramatic fashion. The quantity of yerba to reach Buenos Aires, for example, amounted to 114,000 arrobas in 1781. Eight years later the figure had risen to 188,215 arrobas.[5] Not only did the traditional sources of yerba production in Paraguay grow to fill the expanded market, but the Guaraní towns of Misiones, under secular rule since the 1767 expulsion of the Jesuits, rapidly abandoned their subsistence economy in favor of an outward-oriented and profitable yerba commerce.

In the late colonial period, the growing trade with Paraguay was largely confined to the ports of Asunción, Corrientes, and Concepción, the latter being important only as a transit point for yerba. Candelaria, the main Jesuit port on the Upper Paraná, lost significance after 1767 and, as the Indian population fell, it became increasingly less vital as the hub of Misiones exports.

Together with Asunción, Corrientes furnished the northeast with its main center of trade during colonial times. In terms of population, the latter town paralleled the patterns of composition seen elsewhere in the region; the total number of inhabitants—Indians, blacks, mestizos, and whites—was 4,500 in 1793.[6] Merchant groups, largely composed of immigrants, congregated in Corrientes, transforming the formerly sleepy backwater into a bustling community. Imports of rarely seen luxury items—wine, perfumes, silver plate, and ready-made clothes—became articles of conspicuous consumption for an emerging elite intimately tied to commerce and the outside world, particularly Buenos Aires. This group had ready capital and access to credit as well as to government patronage. Their political influence derived from their all-important place within the commercial structure, yet, ironically, this proved their greatest weakness. Because the power of the merchants rested on specific patterns of trade with the viceregal capital, they had little to fall back on when that pattern was disrupted. And, because so many of their number were foreign-born, the merchants could claim no long-term commitment to regional interests, only a commitment to their own commercial interests narrowly conceived. This ultimately made them easy targets for their political opponents in the region, the long-established landowners.

The landowners could trace their collective presence in the northeast back to the time of the Conquest, and they generally were more at home speaking Guaraní than Spanish. Even at the end of the eighteenth century, many of them still lived a rustic existence, treating their Indian peons with a combination of paternalism and harsh discipline, much as they had done for centuries. Some members of this traditional elite entered into partnerships with the merchants, though apparently this was not common. More often, the landowners feared the newcomers, suspecting that the latter would undercut their established authority in the region.

The struggle for political ascendancy between merchants and landowners proved counterproductive for both groups. On some issues, such as the desire for open trade, the two groups shared a common outlook, but competition often arose on the question of ultimate political power in the region. The merchants tacitly acknowledged the authority of Buenos Aires in its dealings with the interior provinces, and often regarded the locals as poor cousins. For their part, the northeastern landowners resented the prominence of merchants in the regional economy and particularly their ties to Crown officials. This gap between the different groups assumed critical proportions in the period just after independence and proved to be a significant factor in the subsequent political fragmentation of the region.

In real terms, regional trade boomed. Records indicate that an average of forty merchant ships a year left Corrientes for downriver ports between 1792 and 1797.[7] These vessels carried well-stocked cargoes of hides, cotton, and woods as well as honey and other foodstuffs. Tanbark (*curupay*), a source of tannic acid for use in leather curing, was another major export of Corrientes. It proved so popular in Buenos Aires tanneries that in 1797 alone the province exported nearly 20,000 arrobas to the port city.[8]

Demand for northeastern commodities rose steadily in Buenos Aires during the first decade of the new century, and credit flowed liberally along the rivers to underwrite even bigger ventures. The British invasions of 1806–7 exposed the *porteños* to a de facto free international trade. With Buenos Aires now as much a part of the Atlantic economy as any European port, the commercial integration of the northeast with the rest of the viceroyalty also became a reality. Specie had become an important part of the regional economy, and profits from yerba were so high that smugglers soon entered the picture. At about the same time, Spanish officials first reported contraband dealings in hides and tallow at a small estancia fifty-two leagues below Corrientes at the confluence of the Río Paraná and Riacho de Goya. From these obscure beginnings, the village of Goya rapidly evolved into the principal trade center of southern Corrientes.[9]

All these developments nudged the northeast out of its isolation. The indifference of earlier days had been replaced by a Bourbon administration keenly interested in the expansion of trade. Nevertheless, development carried a price, as the region now entered into a new and unfavorable economic relation with Buenos Aires, a reality that led to no end of resentment. The *porteños* had the viceroy's ear as well as access to capital; and whether it was a question of yerba pricing or the admittance of foreign traders onto the interior rivers, the merchants of Buenos Aires would always carry more weight with the authorities than would their counterparts in the northeast.

Independence and Disruptions in the Paraguay Trade

The events of 1810–11 caught the merchants of Corrientes in the middle of revolutionary disturbances. Their frustration at their own weak position in Platine trade, already much in evidence at the end of the colonial era, now took on the aspect of a panic, especially in that subsector of commerce concerned with transshipments of yerba and tobacco from Paraguay. The military occupation of the entire region by José Gervasio Artigas, which occurred almost immediately thereafter, only increased the despair of the region's mercantile elite. Until the return of some stability on the rivers in the next decade, the traders would have to get by as best they could.

In 1811, Buenos Aires and the northeast got a foretaste of the difficulties that would haunt them for the next forty years. When Buenos Aires renounced the Regency of Cádiz in May and in effect separated from the Spanish Empire, the northeastern provinces responded hesitantly. News of the *porteño* action came in June when emissaries of the new *porteño* government arrived with a plea that the region give recognition to its authority. Corrientes, through its *cabildo* (town council), acquiesced almost immediately, but the Paraguayan *cabildo*, hoping to avoid conflict on all sides, declared both for fidelity to Cádiz and for good relations with Buenos Aires. The *porteños* then began preparations to compel the adherence of the Paraguayans, and a patriot military force under Manuel Belgrano soon crossed into Paraguay in late December. The overconfident Belgrano then met two successive defeats and, in March 1811, had to capitulate and withdraw, leaving the Paraguayans to establish their own independent state a few months later.

These occurrences diminished the natural role of the port of Corrientes as a transit point for Paraguayan exports. Desperately wishing to regain the lost ground, the new Correntino government, composed largely of merchants and estancieros, had to choose between rapprochement with Asunción, which they hoped would restore the old trade linkages, and outright exclusion of Paraguay, which might remove the latter as a competitor. This might encourage local production of tobacco and yerba for export. Both options held dangers. The Correntinos could not long afford to act as agents for Buenos

Aires in the region if they desired a permanent stake for themselves in Platine trade. And it was not wise to offend Paraguay in too direct a fashion. In the end, the Correntino yerba merchants were shunted aside and the province began a loose collaboration with the *porteños*. As with water upon stone, Paraguayan resistance would be worn down.

In pursuing this end, the *porteños* could count on the help of officials in Corrientes and the lower provinces, who were instrumental in interfering with Paraguayan shipping on the Río Paraná. In January 1812, the Junta of Asunción addressed a sharp note to Elías Galván, the popular governor of Corrientes, demanding that he immediately release a number of Paraguayan merchant vessels then being held in the port of Corrientes. The official reason for their detention was the presence of Spanish raiders on the river.[10] Forays by the royalists were a part of the commercial scene in the northeast at this time, and the Paraguayan junta itself had to order ships to port on several occasions to avoid their capture by the Spaniards.[11] But Corrientes also suffered from Paraguayan competition, and Galván, himself a *porteño*, felt he had good reason to harass the Paraguayans and did not hesitate to utilize what leverage he had. The division of the former viceroyalty into separate and mutually antagonistic entities was already making itself felt only two years after independence.

The provincial government of Santa Fé also aggravated the situation for Paraguayan trade. Santafecino authorities wrote the treasury minister of Corrientes in February to inform him that they had detained a shipment of Paraguayan produce because its transporters had not paid the *alcabala* (sales tax) at "the approved [rate] of twelve pesos an arroba."[12] The Santafecinos knew that earlier agreements precluded *alcabala* payments except in the city of final sale, and that the rates, even during emergencies, were to be moderate. Twelve pesos per arroba constituted sheer extortion since the yerba could not be sold for more than four.

Such incidents colored trade relations on the Paraná River. The Paraguayans usually blamed the *porteños* for the contrary attitude of governments in intermediate provinces even when this was not so. The Portuguese, taking advantage of the troubles within the former Spanish possessions, began to push their claims along the frontier, pressuring the Misiones and Corrientes as well as Paraguay.

In an effort to find any friend among so many enemies, the Junta of Paraguay began direct negotiations with José Gervasio Artigas, the Oriental chieftain whose troops had already begun to occupy the right bank of the Uruguay River, Entre Ríos, and the Banda Oriental. Buenos Aires regarded these diplomatic feelers as an affront to its own authority in the anti-Spanish struggle.[13]

To force the issue, in September 1812 the *porteños* decreed a double duty (three pesos per arroba) on Paraguayan tobacco. To make their point clear, they also established a customs post at Corrientes.[14] An 1811 agreement between Buenos Aires and Asunción specifically forbade such elevated duties, but the *porteños* felt justified in employing any means to reestablish their control over the breakaway province. In reply to the Paraguayan objections, the *porteño* officials cynically answered, "You have looked with icy indifference upon our dangers and not only have not attempted to cooperate with the common defense, but have abandoned Buenos Aires to its fate. . . . Who then has the right to complain of an infraction of the Treaty?"[15]

Having lost its prominent role as an entrepôt for Paraguayan yerba, Corrientes contented itself with its own minor export trade in hides and timber. Despite the limited opportunities that this presented, some foreign speculators did start to arrive in the province at this time. Before independence, nearly all regional commerce had been handled by Basque and Creole traders, but now, in a pattern that lasted throughout the century, merchants of other nationalities, especially Genoese and Britons, began to dominate shipping on the rivers. They were always few in number. Nonetheless, with their supplies of cheap woolens and calicoes, iron goods, and luxury items, the foreign merchants constituted a potentially powerful elite. But they were decidedly vulnerable to political disorder, as they were in the northeast during the Artiguista occupation.

Time of Change

Starting in 1821, Artigas had gone into exile in Paraguay, and the situation for commerce in the northeast began to improve. Thereafter, the northeast was free to concentrate on its three main priorities—peace, trade, and open rivers. For one thing, political stability was finally realized in the leadership of Juan José Fernández Blanco, whose governorship of Corrientes (1821–24) combined administrative talent with circumspection and honesty. Fernández Blanco had

had considerable experience in the river trade, having served with his brother, the chief officer of the tobacco monopoly for the port of Corrientes during the last years of the colony. Moreover, he had worked as a hide merchant in Buenos Aires, so that his intimate knowledge of economic conditions made him an excellent spokesman for the *cabildo*, now resurrected as the Honorable Congreso Provincial, and dominated, as always, by merchants and ranchers.[16]

Events outside the region also affected the growth of commerce. Unrest in the interior provinces had prevented the consolidation of a centralist regime, and in most areas, caudillos ruled their fiefdoms with little concern for the authority of Buenos Aires. The *porteños* had been clumsy in trying to replace Spain as the key political force in the Río de la Plata, and their heavy-handedness dashed any hope for peaceful unification with the provinces of the littoral. The subsequent restriction of foreign commerce to the port of Buenos Aires strained relations still further, since to do so meant subordinating national interests to those of the port city (which alone collected duties on such trade). At the same time, as northeastern merchants loudly complained, the lack of direct contact with foreign traders had placed the region at the mercy of Buenos Aires. "Free navigation" on the rivers thus became the rallying cry of the littoral.[17]

Despite this prognosis for continued trouble, the commerce was by no means stagnant in Corrientes. Rural disorder had subsided. *Habilitaciones*, or trade permits, were being issued with greater frequency and supplies of hides from the ranching districts were again filling the wharves at Goya. On a more irregular basis, the *yerbales* in the Misiones were again being worked, with the product haphazardly exported to Montevideo and Buenos Aires via the Uruguay River.

Another positive sign was a quasi-official opening to trade with Paraguay. For some years, Paraguay's ruler, Dr. José Gaspar de Francia, had had trouble in obtaining armaments for his troops, a fact that Fernández Blanco understood. The Correntino governor shrewdly suggested to the dictator in early 1822 that both parties desired commerce. Noting the defeat of the royalists throughout the northeast, he offered to open the river passage that separated Corrientes from the small Paraguayan port of Pilar de Neembucú.[18] Fernández Blanco was as good as his word; on January 30 a Paraguayan vessel arrived at Pilar from downstream with a large cargo of goods.[19]

Francia's acceptance of this commerce was conditional. He no longer permitted foreign ships, from Corrientes or elsewhere, to approach Asunción. Instead, all ships clearing Corrientes for Paraguay were met by a pilot and escort at the first border outpost and guided from there to Pilar, where trade goods were inspected and duties paid. Samples, along with invoices and price lists, were sent on to Asunción for Dr. Francia's perusal. If he approved, stevedores then unloaded the cargo in exchange for yerba and tobacco. In this manner, Paraguay received shipments of arms, munitions, paper, chocolate, cloth, and iron implements.[20] The dictator himself judged the quality of such goods, at times lowering their price arbitrarily.[21]

The Pilar-Corrientes trade connection, although always limited, outlasted both Francia and Fernández Blanco. It proved convenient because it took advantage of a blind spot in *porteño* trade policy. Trafficking with Paraguay, a secessionist province, could not be tolerated officially, but few problems impeded trade between Corrientes and Buenos Aires. The Paraguayans simply loaded their produce onto vessels at Pilar, then ferried the short distance to Corrientes, where the yerba and tobacco were reexported to Buenos Aires under Correntino label. A substantial quantity of imports moved northward in like manner.[22] As long as immediate needs were met, no one in the lower provinces need be the wiser, and Correntino merchants could make profits on both sides of the Paraná.

The Correntinos also produced exports of their own, which the provincial government anxiously tried to move. The governorships of Pedro Ferré (1824–27, 1830–33), Pedro Dionísio Cabral (1827–30), and Rafael Atienza (1833–37) followed the same procommerce stance espoused by Fernández Blanco. All were sophisticated leaders whose careers give the lie to Domingo Sarmiento's famous dichotomy, which equated "civilization" with Buenos Aires and "barbarism" with the countryside.

Pedro Ferré bore no resemblance to the traditional image of the Argentine caudillo. The son of Catalán immigrants, his fair skin stood out in the predominantly mestizo environment of the northeast. Unlike many of his contemporaries, Ferré did not take the usual route to power via the colonial militia. Instead, he rose through the different levels of the local shipbuilding industry, married well, and by the 1820s owned one of the region's largest shipyards. His work as a master shipwright gave him access to the merchant elite of Corrientes, who recognized in him a potential spokesman. The Provincial Congress elected him governor twice. In turn, Ferré well represented the interests of the tradesmen, ranchers, and artisans of his province, and he came to symbolize the littoral's opposition to Buenos Aires. His hopes for the modernization of Corrientes were combined with eloquence, irascibility, and a stubbornness that rivaled that of Dr. Francia.[23]

Ferré's administration was associated with the promotion of protectionism as a remedy for the ills of Argentina's river provinces. As we have seen, if Corrientes was to gain from independence, then it had to eke out an equitable share from overseas trade, hitherto totally controlled by Buenos Aires. This explains the continuing demands for nationalization of the customs revenues and free navigation of the rivers. Ferré's protectionism added a new element. With heavy tariffs placed on certain foreign imports, the Correntino governor hoped to reorient *porteño* demand in the direction of the northeast. This shift in policy, he argued on many occasions, would rejuvenate the production of northeastern cotton, tobacco, and textiles, all of which suffered from foreign competition. Argentines could thus benefit on all sides rather than share their bounty with Britons, Brazilians, and Paraguayans. And to those consumers who might complain of the shortages created by high tariffs, Ferré had a forceful answer:

Yes, without a doubt a small number of men of fortune will suffer, for they will be deprived of drinking luxurious table wines and liquors . . . the less wealthy classes will not find much difference between the liquors they presently drink, except in the price, and will diminish their consumption, which I do not believe to be damaging. Our countrymen will not be able to buy English-made ponchos; they will not carry *bolas* and rope made in England; we will not dress in foreign-made clothing and other products we can produce; but on the other hand the condition of the Argentine people will be less unfortunate, and the consciousness of widespread misery that today is condemned will not haunt us.[24]

This position was not calculated to win support in the lower provinces and, not surprisingly, the merchants and cattle breeders of Buenos Aires rejected it out of hand. These men gained much from their government's policy of free trade and wanted nothing to do with protectionist schemes.[25]

Ferré's polemics in favor of tariffs have received considerable attention from historians, but few have examined the commercial situation of Corrientes during his time. In the main, the export picture was limited but stable, with the same merchants handling the same goods over the same routes as in the time of the Robertson brothers, John P. and William, who in the mid-1820s owned land in the province of Buenos Aires. The commerce with Pilar was still important, and in the late 1820s it brought even greater profits to Correntino merchants. In 1827, yerba sold for twice as much per arroba in Corrientes as in Asunción, and eager tradesmen were ready to barter arms and other goods to obtain the herb.[26] On August 8, 1827, three ships arrived at Pilar from downriver with wine, firearms, and tin, all to be exchanged for yerba and tobacco. A few weeks later, the commandant of the town reported the appearance of four more ships, noting that "all those coming from Corrientes now want only yerba."[27] Even as this profitable trade proceeded in the west, however, in the east, in the most isolated area of the northeast, a territorial argument with the Paraguayans began to ruin commerce on the Uruguay River.

Border Tensions along the Uruguay

Though possession remained in dispute until the late 1860s, the missions still supported a measure of commerce, even during the worst of times. Artigas and the Portuguese had ravaged the mission communities; now they served only as way stations for trade caravans linking the Río Uruguay ports with the Paraguayan settlement of Itapúa. Corrientes never recognized Dr. Francia's control over this route.

Both Paraguay and Corrientes benefited from the Río Uruguay commerce, but in unequal measure. The Paraguayans were chiefly interested in keeping the line open with the Brazilian town of São Borja because Francia needed the arms that merchants could supply through this corridor. Correntino markets, on the other hand, were relatively remote, with the main centers of population laying on the western side of the Yberá marshlands, a nearly impassable zone described as "a wasteland of wild horses and jaguars."[28] Merchants bound from Brazil to Corrientes had to take a circuitous route to the south, passing the customs station (*receptoría*) of Curuzú Cuatiá and working their way around the swamps to finally reach Goya and Bella Vista. From there they loaded their goods aboard vessels for shipment northward to Corrientes.

Because of the close proximity of Itapúa, the Paraguayans were in a somewhat better position than the Correntinos in the Río Uruguay trade. Political aspirations, however, did not always yield to geography, and the process of Correntino expansion in the east ultimately challenged Paraguayan authority in the 1820s. Since the defeat of Artigas, a tiny remnant of his Indian troops had gathered west of Candelaria, where they hoped to avoid clashes with both Paraguayans and Correntinos.[29] Hoping to strengthen their weak hold over the area, these Indians appealed to the distant province of Entre Ríos, with which they actually signed an alliance.[30] These actions infuriated Dr. Francia, who responded by seizing most of the missions. This action prompted Corrientes to bolster its own position in the west, but war did not break out in 1823 because the Correntinos obtained no material support from their allies in the lower provinces. Three years later, during the Cisplatine War against Brazil, the government in Buenos Aires urged Corrientes to expel the Paraguayans, but again it offered no support.[31]

Hostilities finally did occur in the early 1830s, at roughly the same time that rumors spread about a curious scheme conceived by the *porteño* leadership: to sell Misiones land to certain British investors for settlement. When informed of the plan, Dr. Francia left no room for doubt as to his position:

> The lands between the Aguapey and Uruguay belong to Paraguay and not to Buenos Aires which for the past twenty years has not even thought about them. It is now clear that [Buenos Aires] has conspired to appropriate this [territory] and feign its sale to these Englishmen only to impede and cut the Brazilian trade with Paraguay.[32]

Although the British colonization never materialized, the Paraguayans were now increasingly on guard against possible incursions from the outside.

Meanwhile, the government of Corrientes had concluded a treaty with the tiny Río Uruguay port of La Cruz, whereby the latter village was incorporated into *la familia correntina*.[33] Although this move could have been interpreted as a provocative flanking maneuver to the south, on this one occasion Dr. Francia showed flexibility. Noting that La Cruz did not constitute a link in the São Borja-Itapúa trade, the dictator offered to sell the former reduction to Corrientes together with all territories to the south.[34] Pedro Ferré chose to regard this offer as an insult and an act of aggression, and he attacked Paraguay.[35]

The 1832–34 conflict never went beyond a few skirmishes. Ferré apparently exaggerated the Paraguayan threat to obtain political and material aid in the lower provinces for other ends.[36] In fact, Paraguayan troop movements proved totally ineffectual. After a brief resistance, the Correntinos occupied the settlements of Tranquera and Candelaria in September 1832.[37]

The Correntino hold over Misiones lasted less than two years, but in that time Ferré sought to bring the area under the fiscal sway of his government. On November 9, 1832, he established an official yerba industry, inviting citizens to exploit the virgin stands (*yerbales*) while reserving the plantations of the ruined pueblos for the Correntino state.[38] Ferré also created a *receptoría* at Tranquera, hoping to tax merchants traveling to and from Itapúa. The customs agent at this remote outpost received a high 10-percent commission on all yerba imported. This made the importation of Paraguayan yerba expensive and protected the Correntino industry while possibly keeping the *receptor* honest.[39] The yerba traffic from Paraguay, though it did continue, was extremely light; between October 1833 and the end of that year, Correntino customs officials noted the passage of only 144 arrobas through Tranquera.[40]

Given Correntino weakness, it was only a matter of time before a reinforced Paraguayan military expedition crossed into Misiones. In January 1834, a disillusioned Correntino military commander begged Ferré for artillery to halt the advancing Paraguayans: "If you are disposed that we march to the [front], I shall be the first one into the fray, but not for the sake of any advantage that we might gain, as you cannot doubt that it would be quixotic."[41] By mid-1834, the Correntinos had abandoned the greater part of Misiones, including Santo Tomé and Hormiguero, but they retained control over La Cruz. The main linkages in the trans-Misiones commerce were thus reestablished, the violence soon dissipated, and trade between Itapúa and Brazil began again.

Neither side relinquished claims over Misiones, but with the growth of the Río Paraná trade in the 1840s, the Uruguay route was increasingly ignored, with some predictable results. For instance, while the Paraguayans had earlier provided military escorts for merchant caravans, they now let the traders fend for themselves on the overland journey. Assaults by Indians or gaucho brigands occurred frequently. One band of highwaymen, led by a notorious cacique named Carabí, was responsible for a series of major thefts in the late

1830s and early 1840s. On one occasion in 1840, Carabí captured two Brazilian merchants coming from Itapúa, stripped them naked, and allowed them to return on foot to the Paraguayan outpost. Seeking redress from the local commandant, the outraged merchants were told to refer instead to Correntino officials, in whose territory the incident supposedly had taken place.[42] In refusing to be held accountable, the commandant admitted that he could no longer police adequately the disputed area.

Adjustments and Limitations: The Río Paraná Trade

Historically, Corrientes did not possess enough manpower to generate a wide-scale commerce of its own. Instead, as we have seen, the province acted as an entrepôt in the Paraguay trade. Independence and Dr. Francia altered this structure, and it took some time before Corrientes carved out a new role within Platine commerce. The long spate of relative calm on the rivers between 1821 and 1838, broken only by the brief Cisplatine conflict, allowed a stable commerce to develop on the Río Paraná.

As Figure 7.1 indicates, much of this trade centered on pastoral products. Ranching in Corrientes expanded under Ferré and his successors Pedro Dionísio Cabral and Rafael Atienza, both of whom had large estancias. Part of this growth was due to increased demands from downriver for Correntino hides and cattle by-products. Government intervention also proved a factor. Temporary prohibitions on the slaughter of cattle were enacted in 1829 and 1834, as well as new laws regulating brands and roundups in 1838.[43] The government also facilitated the importation of salt for licks through the abolition of appropriate tariffs.[44] The provincial authorities even contemplated the establishment of salting plants (*saladeros*) to take advantage of the large market for salted beef in the slaveholding regions of Brazil and Cuba.[45] These various promotional measures had a positive effect on the number of hides exported from Corrientes, as the statistics demonstrate.

What the figures do not show is the amount of smuggling that took place. These activities centered in the south of the province not far from the town of Goya, where the writ of the government extended only to the port itself and not to the rangelands. In these areas, every bend in the river could serve as an improvised port where cattlemen might load contraband hides onto schooners

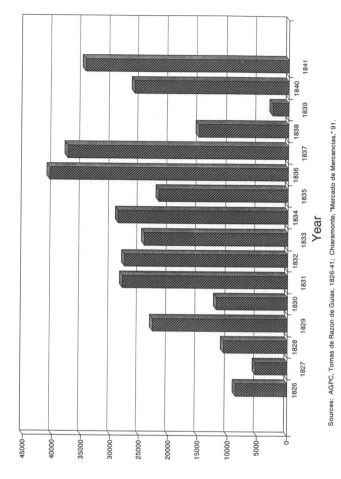

Sources: AGPC, Tomas de Razon de Guias, 1826-41; Chiaramonte, "Mercado de Mercancias," 91.

Figure 7.1. Correntino Hide Exports, 1826–41.

bound for Buenos Aires, pocketing the profit without bothering to pay duties. Goya itself maintained a *receptoría* that did an active business in the 1820s and 1830s, again mostly in hides. Exact figures on these exports are somewhat fragmentary, but to give one instance, on April 3, 1834, the Italian merchant Juan Moises loaded his sloop with 477 hides, 1,940 cow horns, 1,050 cheeses, and small quantities of tobacco, starch, and bamboo, all to be shipped to Buenos Aires.[46] This one presumably typical example shows how Goya's role in the Río Paraná trade was shaped fundamentally by the pastoral economy.

This was only partly the case for the port of Corrientes. Aside from citrus fruit, maize, nutria skins, and the inevitable cowhides, the provincial capital also exported timber. Figure 7.2 records the quantities involved in this trade. We know relatively little about Correntino lumbering. Fine hardwoods such as *lapacho, petereby,* and *urundey* had been exported from the Northeast since colonial days, and by the 1830s sizable logging camps had sprung up in many spots. Foreign entrepreneurs invested heavily in this sector of the export economy, and the provincial government, always concerned with benefiting the exchequer, lent its approval to their efforts.[47] The region continued to ship finished wooden products and rafts (*jangadas*) formed of sawn timber down the Río Paraná well into the twentieth century.

Between the 1820s and 1840s, Corrientes enjoyed a steady, if rather small, export trade along the rivers. This commerce helped the province maintain its long-established links with trading houses in Buenos Aires while at the same time permitting the operation of an avowedly anti-*porteño* regime—a contradiction that served merchants and regional politicians alike.

Northeastern commerce had limited appeal to outsiders, but foreign merchants continued to evince an interest in the region. The relatively peaceful conditions in the northern part of the littoral contrasted greatly with the anarchy in such interior provinces as La Rioja and San Luis and in the Banda Oriental. When the Robertson brothers lived in Goya in the late 1810s, their presence attracted considerable attention throughout the province.[48] Two decades later, however, foreign merchants (including North Americans) appeared on the census rolls of even the smallest country villages of Corrientes.[49] In 1830, the government of Pedro Dionísio Cabral, anxious to "increase the number of merchants" in towns along the

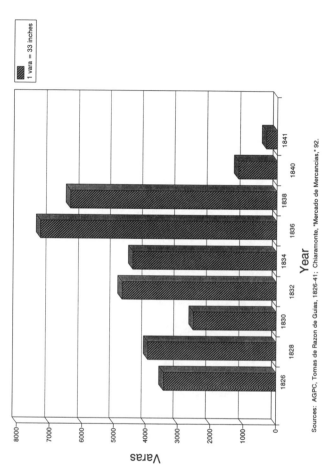

Figure 7.2. Correntino Timber Exports, 1826–41.

Río Paraná, authorized the settlement of foreigners in several of those locations, including the port of Bella Vista, which only three years earlier still retained its colonial status as a *pueblo de indios*.[50] Despite legislation restricting imports, conditions for foreign businessmen clearly remained good in Corrientes, so much so that by the mid-1830s some began to see Argentine citizenship.[51]

The trade situation remained promising only while Correntino politics remained quiet, which they never did for long. Under Ferré, Corrientes had initially espoused the federalist cause, but it was a federalism that stressed provincial autonomy rather than the narrow class interest of the federalist party of Buenos Aires and its estanciero leader Juan Manuel de Rosas. The latter came to regard Corrientes as an enemy. Nevertheless, his opposition was muted so long as the Provincial Congress of Corrientes was in the hands of merchant elites, whose anti-*porteño* rhetoric was often shrill but who did little other than talk. Rosas had more pressing concerns in other parts of the Río de la Plata and therefore contented himself with some minor cajoling in the northeast. He obtained some concessions from the Correntinos, including the election as governor of Cabral, a nominal Rosista.

Even so, as time went by, provincial sympathies increasingly came to rest with the centralists (the "salvajes unitarios"), the group Rosas feared most. The shift owed much to Ferré, whose inconsistency in interprovincial relations some regarded as a strength in the Machiavellian sense. In late 1837, however, Genaro Berón de Estrada became governor, having gained the support of the militia and of some of the southern ranchers. Berón de Estrada proved far less shrewd than his predecessors. He declared openly against Rosas, allowing the centralists to use Corrientes as a base of operation, and thus brought down on the province the unrestrained fury of (as Ferré termed it) "the carnivorous tyrant of Buenos Aires."[52] The Battle of Pago Largo in March 1839, fought near Curuzú Cuatiá, was a complete victory for the Rosista armies under Pascual Echagüe and Justo José de Urquiza. The latter officer ordered the massacre of hundreds of Correntino prisoners, including the sons of key merchants and ranchers of the province. This bloody act ushered in a decade of violence, only periodically broken by short periods of calm. Although these events lie beyond the scope of this essay, to make a broad generalization, we can say that trade conditions in the northeast did not improve much until an Anglo-French intervention forced open the Río Paraná in the late 1840s. Unconditional freedom of navigation of the inland rivers came only with the fall of Rosas in 1852.

Conclusion

Our summary of commerce and politics in the Argentine northeast points out certain trends generally unexpected of a revolutionary era. Rather than the anarchic, "every-man-for-himself" environment, in Corrientes a dominant elite of merchants and ranchers imposed an order within the disorder of independence. Creoles who had been prominent in Correntino society during the late colonial era retained that status in the new circumstances, even on occasion extending their bounty through contacts with foreign traders like the Robertsons. Exceptions existed to this rule, but in general the elites proved flexible, carving out a striking role for themselves in Platine trade. They adapted to the loss of the yerba linkages of the old Carrera del Paraguay by maintaining a quasi-official presence at Pilar and by marketing the acquired Paraguayan produce as their own. The Correntinos consistently strove to increase the volume of provincial exports. Their innovations in this regard smacked of mercantilism and were not well received in the south, where isolated ranchers and smugglers set their own commercial agenda. Nonetheless, the Correntino elites did define their ultimate goal broadly: to bring the littoral into direct contact with the North Atlantic trade and thus make Argentine commerce more "national" in focus. Ferré and others did not hesitate to confront Buenos Aires. Their truculence resulted in deficit spending and in cash-poor economy, but the Correntinos succeeded for years in resisting the *porteños,* all the while continuing their trade with Buenos Aires.

The provincial government did embark on some questionable adventures, such as the struggle with Paraguay in the 1830s over the arguably peripheral Misiones. In practice, however, the Correntino elites usually followed a cautious political line, defended their own vested interests, and abjured the risky notion of expansionism. The merchants probably would have preferred a businesslike authoritarian order in the northeast, something like that of Portalian Chile, but Corrientes was a weak province that had to hedge its bets in the Argentine political arena. The same motives of prudence that led the Correntinos to support Artigas later led them to abandon him, and they did the same with Ramírez, Rosas, and eventually Urquiza. The dominant groups in the province kept their power and cohesiveness throughout this period. The trade routes remained operable, if not always open. Given the limited range of possibilities for commerce in the Argentine northeast, this surely constituted a measure of success.

Notes

1. Temiscocles Linhares, *História Económica do Mate* (Rio de Janeiro, 1969), passim.

2. Clifton B. Kroeber, *The Growth of the Shipping Industry in the Río de la Plata Region, 1794–1860* (Madison, Wis., 1957), 10–12.

3. Regarding the problem of rapids on the Río Uruguay, see Gabriel Carrasco, *Cartas de viaje por el Paraguay, los territorios nacionales del Chaco, Formosa y Misiones y las provincias de Corrientes y Entre Ríos* (Buenos Aires, 1889), 191–93; Domingos de Araujo e Silva, *Diccionario histórico e geográphico da provincia de São Pedro do Rio Grande do Sul* (Rio de Janeiro, 1865), 13. The southernmost of the two formations of rapids today has been converted into the massive binational hydroelectric facility of Salto Grande.

4. Kroeber, *The Growth of the Shipping Industry*, 12.

5. Libros de aduana de Buenos Aires, Archivo General de la Nación de Argentina (hereafter cited as AGN), XIII-35-3-1, 35-3-5, 35-4-1, 35-5-4, and 35-11-5.

6. Félix de Azara, *Descripción e historia del Paraguay y del Río de la Plata*, 2 vols. (Madrid, 1847), 1:335, 344.

7. Ernesto J. A. Maeder, *Historia económica de Corrientes en el período virreinal, 1776–1810* (Buenos Aires, 1981), 297.

8. Ibid., 274.

9. Hernán Félix Gómez, *La ciudad de Goya* (Buenos Aires, 1942), 31.

10. John Hoyt Williams, "Dr. Francia and the Creation of the Republic of Paraguay, 1810–1814" (Ph.D. diss., University of Florida, 1969), 192.

11. Junta of Paraguay to Juez Consular de Comercio, Francisco Díaz de Bedoya, Asunción, 6 February 1812, Archivo Nacional de Asunción, Sección Histórica (hereafter cited as ANA-SH) 217; Junta of Paraguay to Comandante of Neembucú, Asunción, 10 May 1912, Archivo Nacional de Asunción, Sección Nueva Encuadernación (hereafter cited as ANA-NE) 3407.

12. Williams, "Dr. Francia," 193. An arroba is a twenty-five-pound measure of weight.

13. Triumvirate of Buenos Aires to the Junta of Paraguay, Buenos Aires, 24 March 1812, AGN, X-1-9-13.

14. Julio César Cháves, *Historia de las relaciones entre Buenos Aires y el*

Paraguay, 1810–1813 (Buenos Aires, 1959), 192; Jerry W. Cooney, "The Rival of Doctor Francia: Fernando de la Mora and the Paraguayan Revolution," *Revista de Historia de América* 100 (July–December 1985): 222.

15. Williams, "Dr. Francia," 203.

16. Jorge Carlos Chiaramonte, "Organización del estado y construcción del orden social: La política económica de la provincia de Corrientes hacia 1821–1840" *Anuario* [Escuela de Historia, Facultad de Humanidades y Artes, U. N. de Rosario] 11 (1985): 229–50; Maeder, "La estructura demográfica y ocupacional de Corrientes y Entre Ríos en 1820," *Trabajos y Communicaciones* 12 (1964): 111–38.

17. Horacio Pereyra, "Notas sobre la economía del litoral Argentino, (1820–1836)," *Humanidades* 35 (1960): 123–59; Ernesto J. Fitte, "Apuntamientos para una historia de la navegación en el Río de la Plata," *Investigaciones y Ensayos* 13 (July–December 1972): 211–66; Higinio Arbo, *Libre navegación de los ríos. Régimen jurídico de los ríos de la Plata, Paraná, y Paraguay* (Buenos Aires, 1939).

18. Cited in John Hoyt Williams, *Rise and Fall of the Paraguayan Republic, 1800–1870* (Austin, 1979), 72.

19. Pedro Nolasco Torres to Francia, Pilar de Neembucú, 30 January 1822, ANA-SH 383.

20. See, for example, Francia to José Tomás Gill, commandant of Pilar, Asunción, 12 December 1825, ANA-NE 708; Francia to Gill, Asunción, 24 January 1827, ANA-NE 3411.

21. Francia frequently went into minute detail on these matters. On one occasion in 1825, for example, he noted that a recently arrived shipment of flour, "is passable, though it has already taken on a bad odor" (Francia to Gill, Asunción, 22 December 1825, ANA-NE 708).

22. Williams, *Rise and Fall of the Paraguayan Republic*, 72.

23. Manuel Florencio Mantilla, *Estudios biográficos sobre patriotas correntinos* (Buenos Aires, 1884; reprint Corrientes, 1986), 32–47; Ernesto Hilario González, *Pedro Ferré, sus luchas para el federalismo* (Corrientes, 1964); Pedro Ferré, *Memoria del brigadier general Pedro Ferré, octubre de 1821 a diciembre de 1842*, 2 vols. (Buenos Aires, 1921).

24. Ferré to José María Rojas y Patrón, Santa Fé, 25 July 1830, cited in Ferré, *Memoria*, 1:374.

25. Ferré to Government of Buenos Aires, Corrientes, 3 March 1825, AGN, X-5-7-2. Also see Miron Burgin, *The Economic Aspects of Argentine Federalism, 1820–1852* (Cambridge, 1946), 148–51, 228–37, and John Lynch, *Argentine Dictator: Juan Manuel de Rosas, 1829–1852* (Oxford, 1981), 138–40.

26. Gill to Francia, Pilar, 20 February 1827, ANA-SH 394 No. 1.

27. Cited in Williams, "Paraguayan Isolation under Dr. Francia: A Reevaluation," *Hispanic American Historical Review* 52 (February 1972): 108.

28. It was so described on a 1771 map commissioned by the Marqués de Avila (Maeder, "La formación territorial y económica de Corrientes entre 1588 y 1750," *Folia Histórica del Nordeste* 1 [November 1974]: 61). Little had changed as late as 1846 when the Belgian traveler Alexandre Baguet passed by the district (Baguet, *Rio Grande do Sul et le Paraguay. Souvenirs de Voyage* [Anvers, 1873], 48–50).

29. Arsenio Isabelle, *Viaje a la Argentina, Uruguay y Brasil en 1830* (Buenos Aires, 1943), 438.

30. Convention of 12 May 1823, Pueblo of San Miguel, Archivo Histórico y Administrativo de Entre Ríos, Paraná (hereafter cited as AHAER), Gob. serie 3, carpeta 1, legajo 2, no. 21.

31. Marcos Becarce, Minister of War of the United Provinces, to Governor of Misiones, 6 February 1826, Archivo Nacional de Asunción, Coleçáo Rio Branco I-30, 5, no. 6.

32. Francia to Commandant of Itapúa, 22 December 1831, ANA-SH 241, no. 7; see also Francia to Commandant of Concepción, 18 August 1832, ANA-NE 3412.

33. Treaty of La Cruz, 28 May 1830, AHAER, Gob. serie 3, carpeta 1, legajo 9, nos. 70–71.

34. See Francia to Delegado of Pilar, 11 August 1832, ANA-SH 241, no. 12.

35. Marco Tulio Centeno, "San Juan de Hormiguero. Crónica de su orígen y desarrollo. Antecedentes de la refundación de Santo Tomé (Corrientes)," *Primer encuentro de geohistoria regional. Exposiciones* (1980): 98–103; Williams, "La guerra no-declarada entre el Paraguay y Corrientes," *Estudios Paraguayos* 1, no. 1 (November 1973): 35–43.

36. In a letter to the governor of Santa Fé, Ferré stressed the pernicious effect of the São Borja-Itapúa connection "through which passes all news of our political affairs and through which Francia obtains all manner of armaments and munitions . . . this can only mean that the Dictator thinks big, that he wishes to take advantage of our domestic quarrels." See Ferré to Domingo Cullen, Corrientes, 1 September 1832, cited in Ferré, *Memoria*, 1:422–23. The *porteños* initially promised help, which was never forthcoming. See José Viamonte and Tomás Guido to Ferré, Buenos Aires, 30 January 1832, Archivo General de la Provincia de Corrientes, Expedientes Administrativos (hereafter cited as AGPC-EA) 1834, legajo 41.

37. Francia to Subdelegado José León Ramírez, 8 September 1832, ANA-SH 241, no. 12.

38. Decree of Pedro Ferré, Corrientes, 9 October 1832, cited in *Registro oficial de la provincia de Corrientes (1821–1849)*, 8 vols. (1850; reprint Corrientes, 1929–31), 3:140–43 [hereafter cited as *ROPC*].

39. See "Instrucciones provisorias que se dan al nuevo Receptor de la frontera de las Antiguas Misiones," Corrientes, 15 January 1833, AGPC-EA 1834, legajo 43.

40. See "Cuaderno de la receptoría de la Tranquera de Loreto, cuarto trimestre de 1833," Tranquera, 31 December 1833, AGPC-EA 1833, legajo 40. Ferré tried to be flexible in his dealings with the Brazilian merchants and, as long as they paid the proper duties, he left them to trade "at their own discretion" (Ferré to Amaro José Vieira, Corrientes, 26 January 1833, AGPC-EA 1833, legajo 37).

41. Genaro Berón de Estrada to Rafael Atienza, Tranquera, 19 January 1834, cited in Federico Palma, "Un momento en la historia de Misiones, 1832–1882," *Boletín de la Academia Nacional de la Historia* 38 (1965): 5.

42. Blas José Márquez to Pedro Ferré, Santo Tomé, 9 November 1840, Archivo General de la Provincea de Corrientes, Correspondencia Oficial 1840, legajo 71. A similar incident in 1833 found Dr. Francia willing to indemnify a merchant whose goods had been stolen by Indians in an area close to Tranquera (Francia to Delegado of Itapúa, Asunción, 15 February 1833, ANA-SH 242, no. 7).

43. Law of 23 December 1829 in *ROPC*, 2:330, which nonetheless permitted the export of bulls and oxen; law of 31 October 1835 in ibid., 3:229–30; decree of 26 July 1838 in ibid., 4:76–77, 80–83; and decree of 11 May 1838 in 4:42–43.

44. Law of 27 January 1835 in ibid., 3:268.

45. Ibid. See also Law of 31 October 1834 in ibid., 3:119–230, and Jonathan Brown, *A Socioeconomic History of Argentina 1776–1860* (Cambridge, 1979), 110–11.

46. Comprobantes, Receptoría de Goya, 3 April 1834, AGPC-EA 1834, legajo, 42.

47. Decree of 9 June 1831, *ROPC*, 3:68–69. Regarding the promotion of Correntino timber in the foreign community press of Buenos Aires, see *British Packet`and Argentine News*, 16 February 1839.

48. J. P. Robertson and W. P. Robertson, *Letters on South America: Compromising Travels on the Banks of the Paraná and the Río de la Plata*, 3 vols. (London, 1843), 1:140–73, 247–64.

49. Razones de efectos of the Englishman Diego Davison (vecino of Goya), 13 Jan. 1830, AGPC-EA 1830, legajo 28; of the North American John Hayes (vecino of Esquina), 17 May 1831, and of the Englishman John King (also of Esquina), 28 June 1831, AGPC-EA 1831, legajo 32. Four Frenchmen were living in tiny Saladas in 1832 and another three in even tinier Mburucuyá. These two hamlets boasted foreign communities that included Portuguese, Catalans, Paraguayans, Santafecinos, Englishmen, and *porteños*. See Lista de extranjeros residentes, Mburucuyá, 23 July 1832; Saladas, 27 July 1832, AGPC-EA 1832, legajo 35.

50. Law of 22 January 1830, *ROPC*, 2:359–60. In regard to the transformation of the Indian community at Santa Lucía (Bella Vista), see David Bush-

nell, *Reform and Reaction in the Platine Provinces, 1810–1852* (Gainesville, Fla., 1983), 38, 137–38.

51. See petition of Juan Achinelli, Italian, November 1832, AGPC-EA 1832, legajo 36, and José Lopetegui, Basque, 17 June 1834, AGPC-EA 1834, legajo 43.

52. Cited in Bushnell, *Reform and Reaction in the Platine Provinces,* 76.

Pilar González Bernaldo
Translated by Patricia Jepsen and
Mark D. Szuchman
Edited by Mark D. Szuchman

Social Imagery and Its Political Implications in a Rural Conflict: The Uprising of 1828–29

Background to the Rebellion

The complex matrix of factors that telescoped into the political crisis *porteños* (residents of the port city of Buenos Aires) experienced in 1828–29 affords historians an opportunity to analyze the fundamental differences that plagued that city's ruling classes. The resulting struggles also reflected irresolvable disputes among the various provinces and their economic and political interests. Despite the centrality of this problematic, however, no satisfactory treatment yet exists that assesses the rural mobilization that took place in southern Buenos Aires province.

The uprising that spread across the province in 1828 centered in the rural estates to the city's south. It represented the culmination of a series of political crises involving regional, interregional, and international dimensions. In mid-1827, the United Provinces of South America, as its overly optimistic framers referred to the fragile web of a regional entente, was at the point of dissolution. Important interior provinces had failed to ratify the 1826 constitution that had created the government; Brazil had occupied and annexed the lands east of the Río de la Plata while its navy blockaded the port of Buenos Aires; and British support for President Bernardino Rivadavia was weakening in response to an apparently imminent financial collapse. Finally, Rivadavia resigned the presidency in July of 1827.

In order to appease the caudillos who had opposed the liberal and unitarian bent of the previous administration, Manuel Dorrego, Rivadavia's successor in Buenos Aires, dismantled much of the previous government's apparatus and instituted a series of policies designed to provide a federalist political structure. A peace accord was signed with the Brazilians, and in 1828 Uruguay was created as an independent buffer state between Brazil and Argentina, guaranteed by the British.

The restoration of international peace, however, allowed for the return of thousands of troops from the former military theaters, headed by military chieftains committed to the restoration of unitarianism. Among these caudillos was General Juan Lavalle, whose troops reentered the province of Buenos Aires from Uruguay to wage war against the new government. In a skirmish, Governor Dorrego was captured by Lavalle's men and subsequently shot. With Dorrego out of the way, Lavalle was free to occupy the seat of government in the city of Buenos Aires.

However, as the news of Dorrego's death spread throughout the countryside, the rural militia, consisting primarily of gauchos loyal to their estanciero bosses, rallied in rebellion under the leadership of General Juan Manuel de Rosas, one of the province's most influential estancieros. After a series of strategic alliances weaving together the disparate antagonisms against the unitarians of Buenos Aires and several military clashes, Lavalle was dealt a significant blow in April of 1829. By year's end, Rosas had gained the upper hand, forcing Lavalle and his troops out of the province to fight another day. In December, the federalists entered the city of Buenos Aires in triumph. They would remain in power, led by Rosas, until 1852.

According to the conventional thesis, Rosas, commander-general of the militia, was the intellectual author of the uprising against the Buenos Aires government late in 1828 while the actual rebellion was carried out by his troops in alliance with friendly Indian tribes. In the end, the rebels overthrew the *porteño* unitarian leader, Juan Lavalle. This widely accepted thesis thus reduces events to the level of a conflict between Lavalle and Rosas.[1] Indeed, this historiographical tradition is so strongly rooted that, until now, the events of 1828–29 have received virtually no attention.

This work will analyze the context that surrounded the uprising. The questions raised were inspired by Tulio Halperín Donghi's summary of the events that eventually brought Rosas to power in late 1829: this was a "rural uprising" by "rural people, sick of war," who were signaling "a major change in the countryside's mode of political expression." Halperín Donghi bases his thesis on two conditions: the humble social origins of the revolt's leaders, and the landowners' aversion toward acts of protest made by such men of "*chiripá y chuza.*"[2] His thesis is appealing insofar as it raises long-dormant issues.[3]

If we accept the notion that the rebellion of the "anarchist" squads, as the unitarians called their enemies, was carried out with a certain degree of independence, we then must explain how it became possible to coordinate the actions of this rural population, given the isolation that characterized it. The accomplishments of the uprising did not depend on any preexisting organizational structure; instead, a network of relationships and communications was developed to coordinate the activities of the various parties that succeeded in transforming general discontent into effective action. Thus we are led to inquire into the existence and nature of organizational networks in this "isolated habitat." At the same time, if we accept the notion that the mobilization of the rural population was responsible for carrying Rosas to power, we then are compelled to explain why this population failed to impose its own sense of the revolt, leaving it to Rosas. In the process, Rosas came to embody the meaning of this popular rebellion, thereby allowing him to appropriate the principle of its legitimacy and the instruments of power.[4]

The Buenos Aires Countryside at the Beginning of the Nineteenth Century

The coastal region of the Río de la Plata had remained of marginal interest within an economy oriented toward silver production in highland Peru. After the middle of the eighteenth century, however, it experienced significant demographic and economic transformations. Worldwide circumstances favorable to the development of the cattle industry in the last two decades of the eighteenth century were responsible for the economic takeoff of the coastal area. Nevertheless, the coast's links with the world economy remained subordinated to a colonial framework based on the export of silver from Peru until the revolutionary crisis of the 1810s.

This picture of economic expansion and regional renovation arising from the colonial economy was replicated in the social spheres, although the changes appear to have been less obvious there than in economic matters. For example, a social structure based on estates and inequality persisted, in spite of the attempts the Bourbon reforms had made at renovation toward the end of the eighteenth century. Still, the development of the cattle industry and the mercantile boom in the port city of Buenos Aires would indirectly produce modifications in the colonial social order.

First, subtle changes in the system of estates promoted the coexistence of principles of stratification based on bloodlines with those of social prestige afforded by wealth. Second, the expansion of the cattle industry extended the demographic growth that had begun in the middle of the eighteenth century: a stream of men came to this coastal region from the interior, which had retained its economic bases of agriculture and artisanry. This process, which was developing both in the older zone of colonization and in the newer areas of settlement south of the defensive line of forts, formed one of the sources of renewal within rural society. While in the areas of old settlement a roving population had to become integrated into long-standing social structures, in the new lands the weakness or inexistence of social and economic models permitted the establishment of new social relationships, whose own primitive nature turned out to have provided the area with its most modern attributes.

When the Viceroyalty of the Río de la Plata began the process of breaking away from the Iberian Empire in 1810, the revolutionary government tried to restructure the crisis-ridden colonial order according to new economic, military, political, and ideological needs. One of its objectives was to assure the development of a capital economy by promoting territorial expansion for production and greater discipline in the work force. However, the revolutionary process created unforeseen effects that conspired against the attempts to consolidate a new social order. Specifically, the war for independence removed workers and capital from the productive sphere, thereby aggravating the long-standing problem of labor shortage.[5] At the same time, it led to the militarization of society, one of the most important and least expected changes created by the process of independence from Spain. Militarization resulted in the growing political power of the army and its leaders on the one hand, and, on the other, the massive recruitment of the lower classes, which provided a means of redistributing power and wealth from the highest social groups to the lower classes. While the professionalization of the army and the increasingly authoritarian policy of its leaders neutralized any positive aspects, the process of militarization brought to a halt the separation of civil society from the state.

This caused not only a transference of power within society but also the creation of a communications channel between the society and the state. This linkage was initially founded on consensus, but would increasingly come to depend on coercion. Both the dependence of military leaders on the state and the intensification of military conscriptions generated an environment of social and political instability that—as was demonstrated by the December Revolution of 1828—could eventually degrade into armed confrontation.

The revolt broke out in the southern countryside of Buenos Aires. This region, which was geographically circumscribed by a perimeter that extended from the suburban zone of the port city to the new frontier line, had been the scene of important transformations in the structure of production. These transformations were already discernible, as we have noted, by the end of the eighteenth century and became crystallized around 1820, when the commercial elite of the city of Buenos Aires turned its attention to the land. These efforts took place after the first failed attempt (in 1819) to fashion a national entity out of the former Viceroyalty of the Río de la Plata.

Four spaces of production and social relations coexisted within this territory experiencing significant expansion of pastoral activities, each containing a distinct society.[6] One part of the rural society was composed of agriculturalists and cattle ranchers on small and medium-sized properties. This social segment, which had begun to define itself during colonial times, became fully developed as a result of the changes that took place in the port city near the end of the eighteenth century. It consisted of a rural sector, characterized by the links between family-owned small farms and meat-salting plants, representing the beginning of industrialization. Although cattle raising was the principal activity near the Salado River, agriculture was still preponderant in some districts.[7] In this area, which extended southward from the old line of military forts, two types of human settlements—towns and ranches—coexisted.[8]

To the south of the Salado River, the large ranch was the norm, not only as the main economic unit but also as the center of political and social power. This is the agrarian society that would control the region toward the end of the nineteenth century. Further to the south we find yet another social configuration, which, although little studied, merits further study. We are referring to the fringe space, a scene of intense interchanges between the white and the Indian societies. While commerce represented the axis of the rela-

tionship, the marginality of the area gave this zone a hybrid character, enabling it to mediate the social, political, and cultural relationships that developed between the two societies.

Finally, on the other side of this fluid border, one would encounter
the indigenous society of the pampas, an area largely neglected by
Argentine historiography and only now becoming an object of systematic study.[9] Raúl Mandrini points out that here commercial
routes were already established and well organized by the 1820s.
Cattle sales to Chile constituted the main source of wealth. In this
space, one can only imagine the difficulties in expanding the cattle
industry and the urgent need of ranchers to control a society whose
economic system was based on rustling.

Rural Rage

Background of the Rebellion

The coexistence of these four spaces within the process of the region's integration into the world economy gave rise to structural
tensions that, when added to a politically explosive set of circumstances, formed the backdrop to the rebellion. The chronic need for
land and the shortage of workers figured prominently among the
causes of these structural tensions.[10] To this we must add the unfavorable circumstances posed by war and drought, which took their
toll on the population of the countryside from 1825 to 1829. The
most disastrous dislocations came in the form of the war against
Brazil, which lasted from 1825 to 1828 and became one of the causes
of the inflation that lasted from 1826 to 1830. The Buenos Aires
government covered the deficit caused by the war by accepting a
loan from England and issuing paper currency, resulting in a decline
in real wages.[11] Furthermore, the Brazilian blockade of the port of
Buenos Aires from December 1825 until August 1828 had especially
dire consequences, since the state derived most of its income from
customs tariffs.[12] Inflation surged; exports declined significantly
as did production in the meat-salting plants. While the large landowners could muddle through the crisis by limiting supplies and
stock according to their own needs, the situation was critical for
small ranchers, workers in the meat-salting plants, and the urban
population in general, who suffered from shortages of bread and

meat. At the same time, the economic recession caused by the blockade resulted in a significant decline in the demand for workers. The labor market conditions worsened with the return of troops from the Banda Oriental (Uruguay) in 1828, causing an unpredictable imbalance in the job market. All of these factors telescoped into the rural mobilization of 1829.

The war also occasioned stricter applications of the 1823 law governing the militia and of regulations dealing with "vagrants and loiterers." The urgent need for soldiers meant that the public—already "sick of war," as Halperín Donghi reminds us—experienced greater abuse in the form of increased conscriptions. This heightened resentment among both the conscripts and the landowners, who lost workers from their already depleted labor force.[13] Governor Manuel Dorrego tried to ease the situation by enacting the law of August 1827, which was designed to put an end to the excesses that the law of the previous January 2 had unleashed. That law had authorized the government to recruit men "by any available means."[14] Once in the government, and pressured by the provincial legislators, exporters, and landowners, Dorrego adhered to a policy of peacemaking designed to end the crisis unleashed by the military conflict. However, the return of the national army from the Uruguayan front in November of 1828 provoked new disturbances in the countryside.[15]

In addition, the province of Buenos Aires was suffering from its worst drought, which, according to Charles Darwin, lasted from December 1828 until April 1835.[16] Cattle and crop losses were staggering, a catastrophe for all those whose livelihood depended on wild cattle, including independent gauchos and Indians. The desolation and anguish caused by this natural disaster, together with the difficulties in merely subsisting under the threat of the military *leva*, played a fundamental role in shaping the actions of an enraged rural population.

Collective Action: Summer of 1829

One may suppose that the rural mobilization of 1828–29 reflected the inhabitants' response to the threats posed to their way of life by changes in the structure of production. When we test this hypothesis against the sources, however, a series of events remain unexplained. In particular, empirical findings suggest that several rebellions occurred simultaneously, each triggered by different reasons and articulated by an explosive conjunction of forces. Weaving throughout these crises we can identify three distinct phenomena: the Indian aggression, the propaganda war, and the acts of "anarchists."

In the summer of 1828, the population of the northeastern and southern parts of the province of Buenos Aires suffered a series of raids perpetrated by Indian tribes led by "Christians." According to the *porteño* press, these acts of aggression were directed by Rosas, who was accused of mobilizing friendly Indians in order to press Lavalle to divide his forces. In spite of the logic of these arguments, documents suggest that the Indian attacks on the towns of Pergamino, Bahía Blanca, and Patagones were relatively independent of the conflict north of the Indian frontier. The sources tell us that the attacks were led by the Indian chieftain Pincheira.[17] This frontier chief, originally from Chile, had established himself in Argentine territory around 1827. He quickly became a serious menace to the ranchers, whose properties were raided with increasing frequency. Rosas's response to these acts of aggression consisted of establishing alliances with chiefs who were Pincheira's enemies.[18] This policy offered numerous benefits: militarily, these alliances, established along the border, represented a first line of defense, useful for observing the movements of hostile Indians and containing their attacks; at the same time, these friendly tribes constituted a reserve force capable of quelling internal conflicts that might develop among the region's whites. In exchange for the friendship of the authorities in Buenos Aires, these tribes received "gifts" in the form of food and clothing. Through such means, Rosas hoped to give friendly Indians the minimal resources they needed to subsist, which would serve as an alternative to banditry. Finally, this policy would allow for the integration of the Indian into the labor market (once the doors to illegal enterprises were closed), thereby solving the problem of manpower shortage.[19]

However, the difficult circumstances faced by the province of Buenos Aires undid the politics of peaceful understanding with the indigenous society. A terrible drought, which wrought havoc on the roaming cattle, added to the economic difficulties that the state of Buenos Aires suffered as a consequence of its policy of subsidizing friendly Indian tribes. Those same Indians allied themselves with enemy tribes who were involved in raids. Although the intensification of Indian attacks contributed to the undoing of Lavalle's government, they continued well after his fall. Indeed, once in power, Rosas would have grave difficulties suppressing these forces.

At the time of the Indians' attacks, a "war of public opinion"—in the words of the press—broke out. It was waged mainly in the *pulperías* (general goods stores) and small villages. The weapon of choice in this war was the word or, as the press characterized it, the "inflammatory rumor." The principal broadcasters were the *pulpería* owners and their "anarchist" regular patrons, men of the countryside who used these establishments as their primary places to socialize and keep up with current events.[20] In the villages, store owners were joined by residents, including parish priests who also "incited rebellion" through their homilies.[21]

As was the case with Indian attacks, rumors of the uprising were spread prior to the event. This raised the level of uncertainty in the already difficult situation that Manuel Dorrego, governor of Buenos Aires, faced toward the end of 1828. The December Revolution and the governor's assassination aggravated the crisis. If rumor spreading was a fast and efficient process (by the middle of January 1829, the police officers of Quilmes, Matanza, and Lobos were already complaining of this "harmful propagation"), it was because such rumors responded to the fears of the people.[22] Independent of the calculations of those who spread the rumors (accusations were directed mainly against Rosas), the effectiveness of the rumors depended on popular credulity. To be credible, rumors must share certain elements of truth, and they must address the core of the anguish and fears of the collective mentality.[23] The propagation of rumors can also be explained by the scarcity of concrete news or by the lack of trust in the veracity of news reports.[24]

After February 1829, the war of words was also fought in the city of Buenos Aires, where both pasquinades and rumors were used for communication. Although political pasquinades had been used during colonial times, by the beginning of the nineteenth century the press had become the principal means of information dispersal and an important instrument in political struggles. During the conflict, pasquinades provided the opposition with a tool of political combat capable of undermining the monopoly on information that had been enjoyed briefly by the participants in the December coup. Posters were used to mobilize the vast sector of the urban population that had not been drawn in by the press. Moreover, they confirmed the rumors, corroborating in writing what everyone already knew through conversation.

This war, which the press characterized as "more dangerous than an armed conflict," generated a feeling of insecurity, to which different segments of the population responded in different ways.[25] There were those who allied themselves with the "anarchists," while others acted on their own, turning to robbery—in some cases, stealing from the same ranches where they worked; the majority silently condemned the new government for being the cause of so much disorder.[26]

At the time of the Indians' attacks, the Buenos Aires government had to deal with armed bands of gauchos. Sources tell us of "anarchist meetings" and "mounted rebels," peons from the militia or army deserters organized and directed by caudillos (local chieftains). The rebels' main purpose was to steal cattle and arms, and, in some cases, to take part in overtly political operations.[27] The acts of the "anarchists" can be broken down into three different periods within the seven-month span of disturbances, lasting from December of 1828 to July of 1829.

The first period began with Dorrego's assassination on December 13, 1828, following his defeat in the Battle of Navarro, and continued until the federalists' defeat at Las Palmeritas on February 7, 1829. Colonel Prudencio Arnold, who participated in the events of the era, wrote in his memoirs that armed parties were organized soon after learning of Dorrego's death by firing squad on December 14; they "resolved to recognize no authority but that of Rosas," then commander-general of the militia. Their forces, which consisted of some thirty militiamen and three lieutenants, marched south. Along the way, "they were joined by local men and friendly Indians under the command of [Rosas's overseer], Molina."

Police reports provide greater details of the course of events during the first phase of hostilities. They noted that the acts of aggression were the work of men who followed Molina, by now a caudillo at the head of about five hundred "Christians" and a similar number of Indians. Their actions were coordinated with forces under the command of officers loyal to Rosas, such as Major M. Meza and Antonio Ugarte.[28] Meza had been under the command of Rosas before Dorrego's defeat at Navarro, while Ugarte had received "gifts" granted by Rosas for his role as mediator between the Indian tribes and the government of Buenos Aires. These forces operated in the

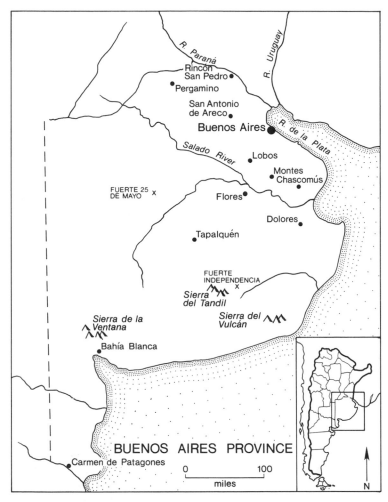

Map 3. Buenos Aires Province.

Salado region of the province during December 1828 and part of January 1829, and then headed south, probably to avoid confronting Lavalle's troops and to seek new alliances with the Indians. On January 21, Lavalle's troops successfully charged "a division of 450 Indians in Chapaleofú."[29] Similarly, federalist forces, under the leadeship of Molina, who was reportedly stationed nearby with a troop of five hundred "Christians," were defeated when they engaged the unitarian army under Lavalle's command in Pergamino on February 7, 1829. Molina managed to flee toward Santa Fé, where he joined Rosas's troops. Other "anarchist" leaders, such as Manuel Céspedes and José Montes, were taken prisoner, along with 121 of their men. Of these, 73 percent were militiamen or army deserters; 25 percent were classified as "rural countrymen" and 2 percent merely as suspicious. These data reflect the importance of the militia in the organization of the revolt. As for the "rural countrymen," their participation points out, although to a lesser degree, the nature of a revolt that was involving the general rural population.

The second period of "anarchist" acts began with these federalist defeats and lasted until the beginning of March 1829, when the district experienced a tense truce. At that time, a series of armed gangs sprang up in the region of Montes and Lobos. Their leaders consisted of army junior officers, such as Basualdo and Arnold; frontier caudillos, as in the case of Miguel Miranda; or Indian chiefs, such as Ventura Miñaña or Benancio. These gangs stepped up their activities in March, at the end of which they achieved an important victory over government troops in Vizcacheras.

We need to distinguish between these "anarchist" actions and those that took place during the previous stage. First, more actions occurred during the second phase, the result, in part, of proliferating armed gangs under caudillo leadership. Second, because of the relative autonomy of each of these bands, the leaders had to demonstrate extraordinary creativity and capacity for self-organization in order to achieve systematic action.[30] Finally, different recruitment mechanisms were employed at each stage. During the first stage, leaders generally were integrated with their own men; by the end, the armed parties were composed of a relatively "loose" population, including "locals, vagrants and scoundrels." Those who served as leaders of these groups—store owners, priests, and the district's civil authorities, for example—also acted as political and cultural intermediaries. Their actions would be facilitated by the climate of general discontent, which had been aggravated by the rumormongers.

In the third and last period, which lasted from the federalist triumph at Vizcacheras until the end of July 1829, new forms of collective action may be discerned. Some of the groups would become integrated into Prudencio Rosas's troops, who would later join with the forces of Juan Manuel de Rosas. Once Rosas was in power, most of these men would, in turn, become incorporated into the regular army; the rest were promptly dispersed throughout the district, where they formed small, roving gangs of about ten men each.[31] Because these armed bands became involved in the general plunder, they may be distinguished from the armed bands that operated during the first two months of the revolt.

The Nature of the Revolt

Can these events be said to have constituted a "popular revolt"?[32] The uprising incorporated a disparate membership that included Indians who circulated beyond white society, seminomadic gauchos along the frontier, and the soldier-gauchos drafted into the army. Such diversity shaped the horizontal ties that would enable self-organization among the inhabitants of southern Buenos Aires. In effect, despite the isolation that characterized these different groups, they all had certain traits in common. For example, gauchos working as peons on estancias or independently, deserters or vagrants, and Indians were all horsemen. In addition, they were all highly vulnerable before the law merely because they lived in a subsistence economy, a feature the men in power considered to be an inherently subversive trait. They were also the main targets of the army: the Indians as enemies and the gauchos as human resources. In fact, the army became the institutional medium that united the gauchos; that is, the gaucho would forge horizontal ties as a soldier. With the intensification of conscriptions, the process of militarization, which had enabled the consolidation of vertical ties at the time of independence, no longer served to integrate the soldiers and their superior officers either socially or politically.[33] Conscriptions broke down vertical ties, providing the gauchos with relationships that corresponded more closely to their own habits as horsemen and allowing them to recognize the injustice and inequality of the law. This explains why the rebellion found the army's men and its organizational structure so useful.

Although the mobilization was carried out on the basis of the lines and structures of authority within the military, a deeper reading of the events reveals additional means of waging combat, including Indian aggression and the propaganda war, thereby lifting the rebellion above the status of a mere military conflict. In sum, the awakening of the masses represented a clash of views and sentiments rooted more deeply than merely in the institutions associated with the army: it represented the opposition by the rural lower classes to the notion of central government.

Identity in the Rebellion

How can we explain that this "popular revolt" failed to formulate any popular claims of redress? Indeed, interpretation of this movement is all the more challenging when we note that these men fought in the name of Rosas, one of the principal promoters of legislation designed to contain the lower classes. Should we conclude, as John Lynch does, that, insofar as the mobilized masses were retained as the estancieros' troops, the uprising ultimately represented an armed confrontation between the estancieros and the military? We cannot agree with this view. The fact that Rosas was an authority recognized by all does not preclude our giving further consideration to the causes of the revolt itself. Here contemporary sources prove useful. Furthermore, the existence of clientelist ties provided the insurrectionists with only one form of shared identity. In other words, the mere fact of participation in the revolt expressed much more than obvious enmity toward opponents. Beyond their military deeds, the rebels' identity was manifested in rhetoric and symbolic representation, speaking to the explosive social imagery found deeply within the rural population.

In effect, participation in the rebellion generated a common identity that, because of the unusually tense circumstances, acquired the sense of social protest. In spite of the efforts by *porteño* authorities and the local press to represent the insurgents as a danger to "honest citizens," the rural population seemed to see these raids through different eyes. Differences in the way these events were interpreted are evident in the sources. While the press presented the insurgents as individuals isolated from the population, which fell victim to their acts, police officials denounced the inhabitants' complicity. Thus, for example, when Police Commissioner Del Monte described the scene at the time of the anarchists' entrance into the town of Lobos, he noted the behavior of the constables who refused to confront the mounted forces (*montoneras*) "because they had come from Buenos Aires only to apprehend thieves."[34] Is it not possible that, behind the crimes perpetrated against the large landowners by men who belonged to the worlds of the large estancia and frontier society, a protest against misery and oppression was taking place? In the eyes of the Buenos Aires press, the reason for the conflict was very clear. In an editorial published on March 26, 1829, the newspaper *El Pampero* proposed that the estancieros increase their ranch hands' wages by 150 percent in order to calm the insurrection. The article ends by saying, "The anarchy in the countryside has corrupted everything, it has broken the ties between the landowner and the workers, and even between the master and the slave; we must once again forge these basic links." It would thus appear that the consequences brought about by the region's integration into the world economy remained incomprehensible to its principal proponents.

The same newspaper had previously denounced the danger of that uprising, alerting the public to the risk of its escalating into a war between the poor and the rich, the ignorant against the educated.[35] The newspaper *El Tiempo* asked how Rosas could convince the gauchos, once peace was restored, to return to work as peons on the ranches that they had recently raided.[36] In a letter dated March 23, 1829, J. M. Díaz Vélez wrote to General Lavalle, expressing his fears about the situation in the Buenos Aires countryside. He pointed out the similarity of symptoms there and in the Banda Oriental (Uruguay): "this region will descend into chaos if abandoned. Do not disregard my opinion. This is to me as clear as water. In each party there is a gang of thieves getting together to kill and loot and then they disperse. This is how it all started in the Banda Oriental."[37]

The existence of a common message that generally identified the rural population with a "war of words" merits our attention, even if we know little about the exact content of such "false news." The *porteño* press presented the news that spread through the countryside as "rumors," a word used to depict all rebel verbiage as false information. What bothered the authorities most was not the content of the "rumors," but the fact that the information remained beyond their control. In addition to alerting the population to the danger, rumors also shaped popular thinking. The transmission of news thus developed consensus within the rural population: the inhabitants identified themselves with the group opinion, creating a collective belief system that functioned as an instrument of social cohesion.

The information networks played an important role in developing this cohesion. The messages were spread principally in the *pulperías*, where social activity depended on various components and

relationships found in the countryside. The basic form of this sociability was free-flowing and masculine, an accurate representation of the basic characteristics of rural existence: a masculine
world conditioned by nomadism.[38] The objectives of encounters
in the *pulpería* were sociability and the subsistence provided by
trade between gauchos and store owners, whose relationship was
egalitarian, just as relations among the gauchos themselves were.
The *pulpería* also manifested an oral culture, such as that of the
minstrel-gauchos who propagated a relationship in which the horsemen's needs were implicitly defined: mobility, freedom, and survival. The network of *pulperías* served to space and widen the
meanings carried by these horsemen. An image of the rebellion's
meaning and the insurgents' world was created and re-created at
these meeting places through the messages that circulated within
them.

Collective action also instituted collective identity among the
rebels by producing symbols: General Dorrego's lithographs, the red
sashes that identified them as federalists, and the lances decorated
with feathers. Thus, we contend that the 1829 uprising, far from
being a simple conflict between Lavalle and Rosas or a crisis of
leadership in the army, carried the sense of a popular rebellion.

And yet, despite popular agitation and the fears the uprising generated among the propertied classes, the movement did not display
modern characteristics of class conflict. The mobilization of the
countryside's men did not start a revolt aimed at undermining the
ranchers' power; rather, it encouraged a type of banditry. While such
banditry may have contained a hint of social protest, it was more
akin to the primitive revolts described by Eric Hobsbawm.[39] The
protest against injustices represented an attempt to vindicate a traditional world searching for greater fairness rather than for new
social relations. It was not a revolt against society or its foundations, but rather against its excesses.

The Role of Rosas in the Mobilization

This analysis brings us to the problem of Rosas's role in the out-
break of this rural fury. That Rosas participated in the uprising is
not in doubt, but, as we have shown, his role went beyond merely
leading his militia troops. In fact, the revolt provided Rosas with a
different political persona than his previous one in the early 1820s.

At first the authorities in the countryside and the *porteño* press hesitated to attribute responsibility for the disturbances directly to Rosas. They regarded the disturbances as a consequence of the flight of Dorrego's men following their defeat at Navarro. Yet, we have indications that the rural population was already loyal to Rosas. On December 30, 1828, Molina, Rosas's overseer, appeared before a committee of estancieros sent to negotiate with the "anarchists" and declared that he was acting on Rosas's orders.[40] Regardless of the veracity of such statements (according to Colonel Arnold, the armed parties made the decision themselves without consulting Rosas), once a connection with Rosas had been asserted by someone perceived to be in a position to represent him, Rosas was viewed as the only individual responsible for the acts of the insurgents, both in the minds of the region's inhabitants and of the authorities in the city of Buenos Aires. This gave him a twofold power: on the one hand, the raw power given to him by the "anarchist" bands; on the other, the authority that accrued to him merely as the result of instability among the Buenos Aires authorities, who recognized him to be the only person capable of resolving the conflict. It would seem that the unitarians were placed in a quandary. Furthermore, the social climate at the beginning of 1829 reflected the anguish felt by virtually the whole rural population. In this climate, the political benefits to Rosas, who appeared to be the only salvation from chaos, were considerable.

As the commander general of the militia, Rosas was not only the recognized authority for all the armed rebels but also the symbol that unified and gave meaning to the rebellion. In the end, he was called "a hero who never engaged in battle."[41] How can this be explained? The climate of tension, rage, rumor, and ascription contributed much, perhaps too much, and Rosas may have been overtaken by events.[42] Yet, while the overwhelming display of support for Rosas consecrated him as the charismatic leader of the population at arms, it does not explain his ultimate achievement; after all, Rosas had long been anointed as the rural population's leader, because he had served as its spokesman well before the rebellion. In this leadership role, we can see how it was that, despite the intensity of the rebellion, Rosas did not become a revolutionary. Thus, even though Rosas implemented coercive policies designed to destroy every illegal means of subsistence—becoming, thereby, the enemy of the rural population, much in the same way as had the state of Buenos Aires previously—he continued to respect the cultural values and meanings of the countryside's inhabitants.

In this fashion, the political imagery of the rural population would become crystallized around the figure of Rosas. This stemmed from an objective desire: they wanted protection from the upheavals caused by economic and political changes. Insofar as Rosas represented rural traditions, he was awarded the role of supreme protector of this society at risk. To achieve this, Rosas the militia commander and Rosas the rancher had to share a common cultural style with the rural population.[43] Here, then, we find one of the essential differences between Rosas and the urban elite: the actions of each were propelled and conditioned by very different conceptions of nature and man's relationship to it.[44] Rosas and the countryside folk shared a similar relationship with nature, which the latter humanized and, in certain cases, deified. In fact, the period's sources indicate that Rosas's most admired features were his physical abilities, his extreme courage, and his sense of justice. Thus, it is not only great wealth that made Rosas an almost mythical figure but also his reputation as a "super-gaucho." Rosas embodied perfection as it was understood by the gaucho culture: "He is a gaucho-god," said the men of the countryside.

Rosas's absence from the scenes of the rebellion contributed to the construction of his symbolic role; in fact, his invisibility was one of the necessary conditions for that role. According to Marc Augé, a leader's power is enhanced when his relationship with the group is reduced to a minimum, allowing symbolic representations to be maximized.[45] Rosas's physical absence from the revolt left a certain space richly seeded in representations and imagery, among which Dorrego's fate represented a good example. Leader of the *porteño* popular party yet totally abandoned by these same people, Dorrego became, only after his death, a symbol of the victims of the aggressions that the army was inflicting upon the people. Rosas was thus placed in a position of redeemer and avenger of circumstances from which he was perceived to have been totally absent and thus completely untainted. Having apparently taken no sides, he could be called upon to restore the legal order.

In addition to his physical absence, Rosas's silence during the period of crisis contrasted with a propaganda campaign consisting of speeches filled with imagery. In effect, the people who were articulating his words multiplied during the rebellion's critical phases at the cost of the insurgents' own discourse. In this fashion, an uprising that had shown an extraordinary capacity for creating meanings became incapable of reifying them in or through their social institutions, whether in the form of language, political institutions, or social relations. By appropriating the sense of the rebellion, Rosas became its embodiment. His rise to power would be seen as the realization of the sense of the rebellion and the consecration of popular power, which would explain the acceptance of the measures he took to reestablish order, even when they were being directed against the instigators of the revolt.[46] Here, then, we find the origins of the imagery put at the service of Rosas's federation.

The Uprising in the Context of "Politics"

The policies of Lavalle and the liberal elite who supported him were designed to associate the rebels with "barbarian Indians" in order to discredit the revolt and to sensitize the urban public to the dangers posed by the "rural masses." The unitarians used the term "barbarians" to legitimate their military coup of December 1828 and thus their side of the resulting conflict. The newspaper *El Pampero* thus justified Dorrego's execution for his "brutal crime," which he had committed by enlisting the help of savages.[47] In this manner, current events were translated into a conflict between city and countryside, which was subsequently developed as the struggle between civilization and barbarism.[48] However, this opposition surpassed the rural-urban cultural cleavage and entered a fundamentally political area. As Lavalle stated, it was a conflict between "the people" and "the armed populations," which demonstrated the antagonism between legitimate democracy and the "colonial-monarchic reaction."[49] It was thus that Lavalle compared Rosas to a conquistador, and the yoke of the viceroy to the "rancher's whip." For Lavalle, the uprising in the countryside was equivalent to the reactionary conduct of the people of the Vendée against revolution; he used the French and Argentine cases as examples of the people struggling for sovereignty against the privileges of nobles and conquerors.[50] The conflict between the traditional and barbarous worlds on the one hand, and democracy and civilization on the other, were the most prevalent images used in the contemporary sources and the ones that meander throughout Argentine historiography down to our day.[51] This perspective must be examined first.

In designating the rural hordes the enemies of the people, the unitarians came to the notion that redeeming democratic legitimacy from the unreliable and barbarian forces required the entrustment of such legitimacy to the military. Yet this enmity represented only one aspect of the imagery of democratic power, and certainly did not reflect empirical reality. Arbitrary force, insofar as it was cast negatively, became equated with the antithesis of democratic power.[52] According to this view of reality, the struggle against the Spanish royalists was followed by the struggle against reactionary barbarism; both battles served to justify the liberal elites, whose power represented democratic values. Such was the liberals' political schema and discursive logic.

As for the actions of the rural population, we had defined them as forming a set of rebellions through which a common identity became materialized within a traditional world. When the city of Buenos Aires appeared papered over with pasquinades proclaiming "Better Indian than Unitarian," reference was being made to a rural identity that implied a rejection of "Unitarian policies" and of political matters in general.[53] Was the rebellion used as a vehicle to redeem a traditional form of power that would permit the survival of this "holistic" society?[54] Everything—the nature of the rebellion, the role of Rosas, and the unitarians' political discourse—points in this direction.

However, the propaganda war that accompanied the mobilization deviated from tradition. To be sure, the virtually eschatological nature of the messages and their origins in the churches and *pulperías* bespeak the traditional world in which the revolt was deeply steeped. Yet by shaking the general population out of its passivity and giving it agency through the spread of rumors, the war of words symbolized the principle of popular sovereignty and expressed the general will. If the instrument of this war was the word, which took the form of rumors and fiery tracts read to the people, the *pulpería* was its best forum. The role the *pulpería* played as a cultural instrument for collective action has already been discussed. A perception of the world and its political implications was inscribed within the war of words heard inside the *pulperías*. The sociability found in the *pulpería* was of a traditional type to the extent of its implied affinities and their political repercussions.[55] Despite a type of sociability based on open-ended relationships lacking in form, specific objectives, or strength of ties, preexistent bonds made cooperative action possible nonetheless. *Pulperías* established within the confines of estancias, or accompanying troops on their way to the frontier, acted as the fundamental venues for these bonds. They reinforced ties between "boss and peon" or among armed men.[56] The characteristics of the pampas inhabitants made this specific form of sociability unique even within traditional sociability. The instability of work, living arrangements, and forms of family life made it difficult to establish lasting bonds. The weakness of social ties made the situation of the rural population more akin to that of the individual in modern society than to that faced by a member of colonial society. The type of egalitarian relationships that flourished in the *pulperías* was yet another characteristic that distinguished these social encounters from those found in a traditionally hierarchical society.

Moreover, since the *pulpería* was the only meeting place for an isolated and heterogeneous population, it was not only a center for spreading the news—a necessary condition for any modern political culture—but also a place to sing folk songs and recite poetry, the cultural forms in which gauchos' sorrows and joys were expressed. In other words, it was a forum for "gaucho discourse," instituted on the basis of the traditional sense of liberty and equality. The fundamental role of the *pulperías* in the 1829 uprising was not to create cells for political participation or challenge to the norms (the *pulperías* were not associations or clubs, despite such depictions by Domingo Sarmiento), but rather to generate and disseminate opinions that, by symbolizing popular will, legitimated political power.[57] Rosas's power cannot be understood without taking into consideration this aspect of the uprising. As Halperín Donghi has shown, Rosas achieved a completely depoliticized society within twenty years of the great mobilization of 1828–29 by using a brutal political style that had been made possible by the transfer of power from a popular will, defined by action, to himself, the man who embodied its sense and symbolized its values.[58]

Conclusion

We have shown the existence of a movement that cannot be reduced to a conflict within the ruling classes in their quest for power. We have also pointed out the inadequacy of the classical thesis, which claims that the mobilization was based on clientage ties. Instead, the 1829 rebellion poses new questions that are altogether ignored by interpretations founded on either elite fragmentation or patron-client relations.

Rural sedition is presented, above all else, as a symptom of social tensions in the countryside, a consequence of the changes in the structures of production, which were aggravated by explosive circumstances. By combining coordinated armed activities, which resembled social banditry more than political combat, with Indian aggression and the psychological dispositions shaped by disseminated rumors, the revolt assumed a sense of social protest. Still, the question remains: how can we account for the fact that, despite an extraordinary capacity for organization and the creation of symbols, the rebels failed to formulate any claims of collective redress. The answer can be derived from the empirical evidence analyzed here, which points to the rebels' desire to maintain traditional social habits and forms of exchange. Rather than taking sides with one political personality or another, the rebels were moved to act by fears emanating from changes in the structure of the production that were aggravated by the growing isolation of traditional society and that impelled the rural population to fight for an authoritative power which would afford them the protection needed for their survival.

Although we agree that the 1829 uprising cannot be explained without accounting for the figure of Rosas, it should be clear that it was the result neither of the actions of Rosas's militiamen nor of the calling up of gaucho troops belonging to his allies among the estancieros, as John Lynch suggests. Instead, the rebellion stands as a charge placed upon Rosas by collective representations. Thus, we propose to invert Lynch's analysis of the social bases of Rosas's power: that is, Lynch places at the start of Rosas's government what we present instead as the culmination of almost twenty years (1810–29) of a specific type of power—a power in which Rosas's domination was reinforced through a continuous appeal to imagery and symbolism.

Finally, we must not ignore the destabilizing consequences of the mobilization for the authorities in the city of Buenos Aires. The sedition by "vagrants, scoundrels and Indians," in addition to having provoked panic among the "majority of the local people," was ample proof of the ruling classes' limited control over the countryside. Furthermore, the rural mobilization not only militarily destabilized Lavalle's government but also legitimated Rosas's authority. We are dealing with a traditional society that invoked an equally traditional form of authority; that authority would become integrated into the field of politics by being cast as the general will. Rosas will, in the end, be the greatest beneficiary of the contradiction embedded in a society whose mentality is traditional yet whose general will implies the a priori existence of the modern individual. Rosas will achieve his goal of absolute leadership by using traditional bonds in order to integrate the sector of civil society that had been excluded from politics for having represented unacceptable "popular opinion," to fasten himself to a form of power that required such "democratic fiction."[59]

Notes

1. The most recent analysis was made by John Lynch, *Juan Manuel de Rosas* (Buenos Aires, 1985), 44–45. For a more detailed examination, see Pilar González Bernaldo, "El Levantamiento de 1829," *Anuario IEHS* 2 (1987): 137–76.

2. *Chiripá* was the clothing gauchos used as leg coverings; the *chuza* was the lance used in military actions. The term *chiripá y chuza*, which expressed both contempt and fear, referred to men of the countryside, who were ready to ride and fight, and thereby to threaten the social order. *Ed.*

3. See Nicolás de Anchorena's letter to his lawyer, Lezica, dated March 16, 1829, in Tulio Halperín Donghi, *Argentina, de la revolución de independencia a la federación rosista* (Buenos Aires, 1972), 262–64.

4. In order to study the uprising, I have utilized materials from the police archive found in the Archivo General de la Nación, Buenos Aires (hereafter cited as AGN). I also relied on the press of the period, travelers' accounts, and political correspondence by the French chargé d'affaires in Buenos Aires. It is necessary to point out the limits of this work, which does not involve a complete treatment of the subject. Although my research has yielded a series of unpublished data, we are still missing a study of prices and wages. The dearth of research dealing with the structures of production in the Buenos Aires countryside as well as the absence of exhaustive studies of demographic and social structures places us in uncertain territory and thus limits our analyses. Despite these gaps, however, the data remain significant, for they permit a first level of analysis. By using this material, we wish to raise for discussion the problematics of the preconsolidation era in the province of Buenos Aires, within which Rosas's government occupied a central role.

5. On the problem of labor shortage for the exploitation of cattle, see Carlos Mayo, "Estancia y peonaje en la región pampeana en la segunda mitad

del siglo XVIII," *Desarrollo Económico* 23, no. 92 (January–March 1984): 609–16; Samuel Amaral, "Producción y mano de obra en la estancia colonial 'Magdalena,' 1785–1795," in *Actas de las VI Jornadas de Historia Económica*, (Córdoba, 1984), vol. 1. See also the debate among Carlos Mayo, Samuel Amaral, Juan Carlos Garavaglia, and Jorge Gelman in *Anuario IEHS* 2 (1987).

6. Few works do justice to these differences. If they do acknowledge such distinctions, they are presented as mere variations of the same structure. Lynch, for example, defines the social structure of the countryside as bipolar: "the estancieros and the others." This analysis is correct only when we refer to the rural society that begins to be reinforced as of the 1820s (see Lynch, *Juan Manuel de Rosas*, chap. 2). Halperín Donghi traces suggestive lines of thought in "La expansión ganadera de la frontera de Buenos Aires, 1820–1852," in *El régimen oligárquico. Materiales para el estudio de la realidad argentina (hasta 1930)*, comp. Marcos Giménez Zapiola (Buenos Aires, 1975), 57–110.

7. This observation is of considerable importance, not because of the magnitude of production levels, but because of the implications that this type of production carries for the demographic structure. In comparing the population data for the *partido* of Lobos, a primarily agricultural region, to those of San Vicente, a region dominated by cattle, we note that Lobos had a lower percentage of non-natives and single men. This difference leads us to consider the important differences in familial stability within the Buenos Aires countryside. See *Buenos Aires. Su gente, 1800–1830*, comp. César García Belsunce (Buenos Aires, 1976), appendix 2.

8. For references to the various types of settlement in the countryside, see Parchappes, *Expedición fundadora del Fuerte 25 de Mayo en Cruz de Guerra. Año 1828* (Buenos Aires, 1977).

9. See Raúl Mandrini, "La sociedad indígena de las pampas en el siglo XIX," in *Antropología*, comp. Mirta Lischetti (Buenos Aires, 1985); Lischetti, "Notas sobre el desarrollo de la economía pastoril entre los indígenas del suroeste bonaerense (fines del siglo XVIII y comienzos del siglo XIX)," paper presented at the VII Jornadas de Historia Económica, Tandil, 1986; Lischetti, "Desarrollo de una sociedad indígena pastoril en el área interserrana bonaerense," *Anuario IEHS* 2 (1988): 71–98.

10. For a detailed study of the problem regarding the structural tensions of the social relations in the countryside, see González Bernaldo, "El levantamiento de 1829."

11. Halperín Donghi, *Guerra y finanzas en los orígenes del Estado Argentino (1791–1850)* (Buenos Aires, 1982); Amaral, "El Banco Nacional y las finanzas de Buenos Aires: El curso forzoso y la inconvertibilidad en 1826," in *VI Congreso Internacional de Historia de América*, 6 vols. (Buenos Aires, 1982), 5:415–29.

12. In the years between 1825 and 1828, taxes on imports account for only

20.53 percent of the state's total resources, while in 1821 customs receipts comprised more than 58.51 percent.

13. On the excesses of these laws, see José M. Beruti, *Memorias curiosas, Biblioteca de Mayo,* vol. 4, p. 3990, and Archives du Ministère des Relations Exterieures, Paris, Correspondence Politique Argentine (hereafter cited as AMRE, CPA), No. 4.

14. See Ricardo Rodríguez Molas, *Historia social del gaucho* (Buenos Aires, 1982), 136–57.

15. Mendeville to the Ministre des Affaires Etrangeres, 19-6-1829, AMRE, CPA, No. 4.

16. Charles Darwin, *Viajes de un naturalista alrededor del mundo.* . . . (Buenos Aires, 1942), 173–75. Other references appear in Martin de Moussy, *Descriptions geographique et statistique de la Confederation Argentine,* 2 vols. (Paris, 1860–61), 2:127. According to the English scientists, the regions most affected were the northern parts of the province of Buenos Aires and southern Santa Fe. Nevertheless, the drought appears to have affected the pampean region as a whole. Thus, in a letter dated August 8, 1830, sent to Governor Juan Balcarce, Colonel Estomba refers to the deprivations suffered by his troops in Bahía Blanca, the result of "the shocking drought that has been experienced since we arrived" (AGN, V-16-10-5). See references to this in Parchappes, *Expedición fundadora,* 51, 56, 88.

17. On the subject of attacks in the northwestern frontier, see references in *La Gaceta Mercantil,* 27 and 28 October, 3 November 1828; El Tiempo, 3 November 1828. The narrative of the events of Bahía Blanca is given in *El Tiempo,* 9 and 20 March 1829. On the presence of Pincheira in Patagones, see José Biedma, *Crónicas históricas del Río Negro de Patagones (1774–1834)* (Buenos Aires, 1905), 664–69. Other references can be found in a letter from J. M. Paz to Lavalle of 9 February 1829, in AGN, VII-1-3-6, f. 118, and complaints by the people of Patagones (in which Rosas is accused of perpetrating the attacks) published in *El Tiempo,* 13 February 1829. On the life of the Pincheira brothers in Argentina, see Alicia Doval, "Los hermanos Pincheira," in Comando General del Ejército, *Política seguida con el aborígen,* 2 vols. (Buenos Aires, 1973–74), 2:189–252.

18. The enmities among Chileans could well be the expression of their struggle for the dominance of commercial ties with Chile. Rosas astutely exploited such rivalries. See Rosas's letter to J. M. Paz of 9 February 1829, in AGN, VII-1-3-6.

19. These are the terms Rosas employed in a letter he wrote to Tomás Guido from San Miguel del Monte on 29 September 1829, in AGN, VII-16-1-10. On the policy of peaceful integration of the Indians, which Rosas defended, see "Segunda memoria del Coronel Juan Manuel de Rosas," in Adolfo Saldías, *Historia,* 3 vols. *Historia de la Confederación Argentina, Rosas y su época,* 5 vols. (Buenos Aires, 1911), 1:347–56.

20. See, among others, the narrative of Colonel Prudencio Arnold, *Un soldado argentino* (Buenos Aires, 1970), 26–28.

21. The priests' power to mobilize is highlighted in a letter written by J. M. Díaz Vélez to Lavalle, dated 21 December 1828, in which he advises the firing of Father Vilar and replacing him with Father Illescar: "Do not tell me, my friend, that priests are not important, for they very much are, my General." He then points to the benefits of the recommended change, writing, "We would be taking a more popular step, we would be grabbing the notion of all the poor people who are saying that priests are for Dorrego" (AGN, VII-1-3-6, ff. 80–81). The priests' participation in the insurrection appears to have been significant in the area north of the Salado River, where towns had been established for a longer time and the power of the Church was more deeply rooted. References to the priests' role in the rebellion can be found in AGN, X-15-1-5; *El Pampero*, 17 March 1829; and *El Tiempo*, 17 March 1829.

22. Note written by police officer of Quilmes on 13 January 1829; note written by police officer of Matanza on 16 January 1829 (AGN, X-15-1-5). In an attempt to eradicate rumors, Guillermo Brown and José M. Paz enacted a decree against disturbances, where they stipulated that "the commanders-in-chief are authorized to pursue wherever necessary and with every means available all those who gather crowds and disseminate seditious news." See *Gaceta Mercantil*, 26 January 1829.

23. In a letter to General Lavalle, dated 18 December 1828, Gregorio Araóz de la Madrid points to the fear generated by rumors as the cause of the rebellion: "In sum, I have well-founded hopes that Mesa and the rest will also come, and put all this to rest, because what really abounds is fear caused by the lies that are circulating" (AGN, VII-1-3-6). Although accurate, de la Madrid's observation is a half-truth, because, although the proliferation of rumors creates a climate of insecurity, their dissemination must, in turn, reflect the response to fears that vex society. Gabriel García Márquez provides an excellent literary analysis of this theme in *La mala hora* (Buenos Aires, 1982). On the belief in rumors, see J. Delumeau, *La peur en occident* (Paris, 1978); Jean Nöel Kapferer, "Porquoi croyons nous les rumeurs?" in *Rumeurs, le plus vieux mediat du monde* (Paris, 1987), 79–103; S. Kaplan, *Le complot de la famine: Historire d'un rumeur au XVIII siècle* (Paris, 1982).

24. The considerable decrease in the number of publications—only two publications in Spanish survived the December coup, *La Gaceta Mercantil* (1823–52) and *El Tiempo* (April 1828–August 1829); the newer *El Pampero* (January–August 1829) lasted only a few months—and the unconditional support two of them gave to the government can explain the speedy propagation of rumors and their role as an alternative communications medium for the large sector of the population that did not identify with the views of the unitarian press. According to the United States commercial attaché, the absence of concrete or verifiable news was the cause for the spreading of

rumors. See John Murray Forbes, *Once años en Buenos Aires* (Buenos Aires, 1956), 519. On the periodicals of this period, see Antonio Zinny, "Bibliografía periodística de Buenos Aires hasta la caída del gobierno de Rosas," *La Revista de Buenos Aires* 10–13 (1866–67).

25. *El Tiempo*, 11 March 1829; *El Pampero*, 19 March 1829. On the assumed intent of the unitarians to pursue the conflict with Brazil, see *El Pampero*, 22 January 1829.

26. *El Pampero*, 17 January and 26 March 1829.

27. On January 3, a party of three hundred men attacked the estancia of Zenón Videla, member of the Unitarian Council, taking him away as a prisoner (*El Tiempo*, 1 July 1829). In Quilmes, the appointment of the alcalde of ward number 5 could not proceed because the anarchists entered the town and took him away (AGN, X-31-11-6).

28. Molina is a good example of the type of caudillo who lived in the frontier society. A longtime foreman of Francisco Ramos Mejía at the time of the latter's imprisonment in 1821, Molina sought refuge among the Indians. There he formed a gang of Indians and deserters for the purpose of raiding. The national government incorporated him into the frontier garrisons in 1826. Rosas also sought him in 1827 to sign peace treaties with several Indian tribes. See Jacinto R. Yaben, *Biografías históricas argentinas* (Buenos Aires, 1952–54); Woodbine Parish to Lord Aberdeen, 12 December 1829, in Lynch, *Juan Manuel de Rosas*, 43.

29. *El Tiempo*, 27 January 1829.

30. See, for example, the elections that precede the battle in Monte in March 1829. See Arnold, *Un soldado argentino*, 30.

31. Once in the army, José González, Miguel Miranda, Pedro Lorea, and Leandro Ibáñes held the rank of lieutenant colonel; Francisco Sosa and the Indian cacique Ventura Miñaña were colonels. See Fernando Baldrich, "Lista de oficiales superiores y jefes que revistaron en las fuerzas armadas de la Confederación Argentina u ofrecieron sus servicios durante parte o toda la época del gobierno de Rosas," in Arnold, *Un soldado argentino*, 199–207.

32. By "popular revolt" we mean individuals or groups who rise in open or covert rebellion against the institutions that control them. We use the concept of "popular" to allude to a movement that excludes the "powerful" elements, that is, estancieros or military chiefs.

33. Halperín Donghi has treated the important and complex question of the possible relationship between militarization and social and political democratization on several occasions. See his "Militarización revolucionaria en Buenos Aires, 1806–1815," in *El ocaso del orden colonial en Hispanoamérica* (Buenos Aires, 1978), 121–58; "El surgimiento de los caudillos en el cuadro de la sociedad ríoplatense post-revolucionaria," *Estudios de Historia Social* 1, no. 1 (1965): 121–49; *Revolución y guerra. Formación de una élite dirigente en la Argentina criolla* (Buenos Aires, 1972); *Guerra y finanzas*.

34. AGN, X-32-11-6.

35. *El Pampero*, 16 March 1829.

36. *El Tiempo*, 20 May 1829.

37. AGN, VII-1-3-6.

38. In the city of Buenos Aires, the *pulpería* is a social form belonging to the lowest urban sectors. The elites attend other centers of sociability, such as cafés, literary salons, and circles. In the countryside, the *pulpería* is a cross-class and interracial center. See Pilar González Bernaldo, *Sociabilité démocratique et idéologie nationale* (Paris, 1985).

39. Similarities to Eric Hobsbawm's model can be found in the characteristics of the actors involved in these rebellions, in the type of acts they committed, and in the historical process within which these types of movements can be located. However, because of its organizational capacity, the 1829 rebellion presents a peculiarity for which Hobsbawm's model cannot account. Moreover, Hobsbawm's model stresses the absence of ideology, leading him to characterize such revolutionary movements as prepolitical, a conclusion with which we disagree. See Hobsbawm, *Primitive Rebels: Studies in Archaic Forms of Social Movement in the Nineteenth and Twentieth Centuries* (New York, 1963), and *Bandits* (Barcelona, 1976).

40. *El Tiempo*, 30 December 1828 and 7 January 1829.

41. John A. King, *Twenty-Four Years in the Argentine Republic* (Buenos Aires, 1846), 231.

42. Lavalle to Rosas, 27 June 1829, in *Contribución histórica y documental*, ed. Gregorio Rodríguez, 2 vols. (Buenos Aires, 1921–22), 2:410. See also Arnold, *Un soldado argentino*, and AMRE, CPA, No. 4. The *porteño* press used this argument to oppose the peace treaty with Rosas; see *El Tiempo*, 20 and 22 May 1829.

43. Perhaps it would be convenient at this point to remember the oft-cited letter from Rosas to Santiago Vázquez, since it was written on December 8, 1829, when Rosas was taking measures to contain the population that had risen up in arms.

I noted this since its beginning and it appeared to me that in the throes of the revolution, the very parties gave cause for this class to impose itself and cause the greatest damages, since you know the constant tendency for those who have nothing to be against the rich and their superiors. It thus seemed very important to me, from that moment, that I should gain a dominant influence over that class in order to contain it, or to lead it; and I planned to acquire this influence at whatever cost. In order to carry this out, it was necessary for me to work with great consistency, at the cost of great personal and financial sacrifices, to become a gaucho like them, to speak like them, and to do whatever they did, to protect them, to make myself their representative, to care for their interests, in sum, to spare no amount of labor or means to gain their trust.

In Arturo E. Sampay, *Las ideas políticas de Juan Manuel de Rosas* (Buenos Aires, 1972), appendix 6, 131–32. On Rosas as a social articulator, see Arnold Strickon, "Estancieros y gauchos: clase, cultura, y articulación social," in *Procesos de articulación social,* comp. L. Bartolomé (Buenos Aires, 1977).

44. For a greater development of these issues, see González Bernaldo, "Idéologie de la conquête de désert" (Memoire de Maitrise, Université de Paris I, 1984).

45. Marc Augé, *Theorie des pouvoirs et idéologie* (Paris, 1975). See also Bronislaw Baczko, *Les imaginaires sociaux. Memoires et espoire collectifs* (Paris, 1984).

46. The decrees of October 31 and December 12, 1829, were designed to subordinate the leaders who had participated in the uprising. See Buenos Aires (Province), *de las leyes y decretos promulgados en Buenos Aires des de el 25 de mayo de 1810 nasta el fin de diciembre de 1840,* 4 vols. (Buenos Aires (Province), *De las leyes y decretos promulgados en Buenos Aires desde el 25 de mayo de 1810 hasta el fin de diciembre de 1840,* 4 vols. (Buenos found in private hands; see Buenos Aires (Province), *Registro oficial* (Buenos Aires, 1821–), vol. 2. In 1830, other measures were taken "against an excited crowd claiming to be federalist" (AMRE CPA, No. 4).

47. *El Pampero,* 17 January 1829.

48. Domingo Sarmiento's paradigm of the struggle between civilization and barbarism is already present in the way the press of the era interpreted the facts of the rebellion. For example, *El Tiempo* of January 27, 1829, speaks of the "struggle of anarchy against order, of ignorance against civilization." *La Gaceta Mercantil,* a newspaper of federalist tendency, also makes use of this language of dichotomy. If it accepts the confrontation between unitarians and federalists, it rejects the intervention of the "habitual criminals," denouncing the danger posed by the participation of the brutish sector of the population. *El Tiempo* of September 14, 1829, speaks of the confrontation between the cause of the people and the horde of vandals; *El Tiempo* of March 11, 1829, defines the civil war as "the war of barbarism against enlightenment." The same newspaper concludes, on April 8, 1829, that it is all a conflict between civilization and barbarism.

49. Juan Lavalle, *Exposición.*

50. "Let us ask the history of today, in the event we wish to know our future luck, if such a catastrophe were to take place. The chiefs of the Vendée also proposed to themselves the reestablishment of everything that the revolution had destroyed; they attempted to roll back France to the time of the meeting of the Estates General and to the quiet listening of the decrees written by a crowned law maker. What would have France's fate been if the Vendée had triumphed over the Directory?" Ibid.

51. Lucio V. López, "La revolución argentina," *Revista del Río de la Plata* 13 (1877); Ricardo Levene, "La Subleración del 1 de diciembre de 1828 y los

gobiernos de Lavalle y Viamonte," in *Historia de la nación argentina desde los orígenes hasta la organización definitiva en 1862*, 7 vols. (Buenos Aires, 1949), 7:1:277–344; Lynch, *Juan Manuel de Rosas*, 113. Juan Alvarez suggests this even without studying the uprising in *Las guerras civiles argentinas y el problema de Buenos Aires en la República* (Buenos Aires, 1936), 67–80.

52. François Furet traces the first lines of a study of the imagery of democratic power by analyzing the French aristocrats' designs and their role in creating revolutionary ideology. According to Furet, the birth of democratic politics is inseparable from a value system that defines the general or national will as a new collective identity that legitimates power. This new legitimacy is conceived as an indivisible whole and cannot tolerate opponents from within. See Furet, *Penser la revolution française* (Paris, 1978), 76–79. One of the most complete conceptualizations of this imagined position in Argentine political culture is found in Sarmiento's model of civilization and barbarism.

53. "Better to be an Indian than a Unitarian, on the day that the Federation arrived." "Indian yes, foreigner no." These are posters that appeared on the streets in Buenos Aires in support of the rebels. See *El Tiempo*, 4 April 1829.

54. Louis Dumont's concept of "holistic society" is designed to differentiate the concept of the "individual" in traditional societies from the concept of the individual in modern society. Dumont points out that in the holistic society, the stress is placed on society as a whole, in undifferentiated fashion. The ideal is thus of society consisting of Collective Man. By contrast, in modern society, the ideal is defined through the realization of each human being as a unique biological entity and as a thinking subject. See Dumont, *Homo hierarchicus. Le système de castes et ses implications* (Paris, 1966).

55. Traditional sociability is situated within a framework of secular and unvarying solidarities—the family, the parish, the corporation, the order. These bonds are both natural and instinctive. This view has been developed for France by Maurice Agulhon, *Penitens et franc-maçons dans l'ancienne province* (Paris, 1968), and for Latin American history by François X. Guerra, *Le Mexique: De la societe d'ancien régime a la revolution* (Paris, 1983).

56. A study of the linkages between patron and peon is found in Lynch, *Juan Manuel de Rosas*.

57. Domingo F. Sarmiento, *Facundo* (Madrid, 1975), 108–10. A distinction needs to be made between the two principal meanings of the word "club." While in France "club" refers to a political association, in England it alludes to that typical form of bourgeois sociability—the association for the sake of amusement. Both meanings imply a certain organization and the existence of semiclosed networks, constructed either on the basis of political convictions or as the result of a recruitment process that converts individuals into members of the same network. Neither of the two meanings can

be applied to the *pulpería,* which is an occasional gathering, even though, as Sarmiento pointed out, "by repeating this ritual [of sporadic association], it comes to form a closer-knit society."

58. Halperín Donghi, *Una nación para el desierto argentino* (Buenos Aires, 1982), 60.

59. As François X. Guerra has pointed out, popular sovereignty, as a principle of legitimacy among young Latin American republics, carried the fiction of democracy, a consequence of the contradictions and conflicts between modern elites and traditional societies. See Guerra, "Le peuple souverain: Fondements et logique d'une fiction (Pays Hispaniques au XIX siècles)," in *L'avenir de la démocratie en Amérique Latine* (Toulouse, 1988), 19–54.

Kevin Kelly

Rosas and the Restoration
of Order through Populism

In the early nineteenth century, the Río de la Plata regions wavered
on the brink of anarchy. Pampean Indians continued their relentless
siege of frontier areas; bandits roamed rural cart trails, rendering
hazardous the trade between the port and the interior. War with
Brazil was diverting valuable resources, human and economic, away
from national development and toward military endeavors. Inter-
nally, Argentine public opinion was divided between the political
faction favoring a centralist, unified nation built along liberal, secular, and free-trade lines and that advocating a federal form of government respecting traditional values and provincial autonomy. Juan
Manuel de Rosas, who was to dominate the period between 1829
and 1852, entered this political, economic, and social scenario determined to bring order out of chaos and to restructure society according to older customs. How could anyone accomplish such a
task given the enormous obstacles involved?

The present study specifically advances the thesis that Juan Manuel de Rosas did not represent some anomalous political aberration.
He was, rather, a primitive populist who arose from and responded
to popular demands. Striding confidently into a seething cauldron of
political chaos, the charismatic Rosas, rooted in the rural gaucho
culture, boasted the support of large, multiclass segments of society.

"Populism," of course, requires conceptual precision if it is to
be utilized with any degree of meaning. As described by Michael
Conniff, populism, or people's movement, is a multiclass, expansive, "popular," and generally, although not always, urban-based
phenomenon led by a charismatic figure.[1] Broadly speaking, populist movements involve political participation of the masses in a
kind of multiclass coalition. The leader's promise of political and

economic benefits for faithful followers expedites the "massifica-tion" or consolidation of this amorphous collectivity.

Periods of hegemonic crisis, or moments of political and eco-nomic instability, give rise to unusual opportunities in which re-sourceful leaders may manipulate coalitions of the socially and politically disadvantaged. The populace, meanwhile, confers leader-ship authority on selected individuals, in no small measure because it perceives them to exhibit distinguishing, extraordinary personal qualities. The person who rises to the top possesses exceptional powers—is regarded by ordinary people as exemplary, possibly of divine origin, and inaccessible. A sense of mission and a capacity to inspire devotion, loyalty, and absolute trust characterize the char-ismatic leader. Finally, Conniff proposes that charismatic legiti-macy can be both democratic and authoritarian in nature. Thus, the masses may "democratically" elect and depose their heads through popular uprising.[2] When in power, the populist leader may rule in an authoritarian manner.

The model of populism reads like a biography of the political life of Juan Manuel de Rosas. His regime was multiclass, expansive, popular, driven by charisma, and both urban and rural based. Au-thoritarian and democratic in nature, the Rosas state emanated from the political turmoil of the early Argentine national period and survived for twenty years by virtue of its popular legitimacy.[3]

The Political Scenario

Independence from Spanish colonial rule, formally declared in Ar-gentina in 1816, precipitated a protracted political struggle among Argentine regions of varying cultural and economic profiles. These divisions pitted advocates of a strong central government based in Buenos Aires, the so-called *unitarios*, against the proponents of a loose confederation of provinces, the *federalistas*. Anarchy seemed imminent in the early nineteenth century as Argentina, then known as the United Provinces of the River Plate, grappled with the question of political organization. In 1826, the *unitarios* convened a national constituent congress in Buenos Aires, drafted a constitution, and named centralist Bernardino Rivadavia president of the young republic.[4] However, the mere existence of a constitu-tion and an executive remained insufficient to create a consensus of opinion or action among the population of the new nation.

Rivadavia came to the office equipped with a modernization program designed to expedite the entry of the United Provinces into the industrialized world. His cosmopolitan orientation sought cultural, political, and economic alignment with Europe while his liberal nationalism promoted economic growth through free trade, foreign investment, and European immigration.[5]

Federalists opposed the liberal program as undemocratic and as calculated to reduce provincial autonomy. Such prominent estancieros as Juan Manuel de Rosas and his wealthy cousins, the Anchorena brothers, typified the reactionary, federalist xenophobia which denounced foreign influences in all areas of Argentine life.[6] This stance appealed to many chieftains of the interior, the caudillos, who vehemently objected to a constitutional framework that would force them into a unified and centralized Argentina. Naturally, any centralization of authority would reduce their own regionally based powers.[7] Several other points provoked strident, and finally armed, opposition to Rivadavia's "magnificent" vision of Argentina. Rosas assailed the government's refusal to allocate more resources to subdue the southern Indians plaguing the frontier. Immigration, the federalists believed, was expensive and unnecessary at best, and subversive at worst because competition for land and labor would raise the best of both. The regime's religious policies, which curtailed the power of the Catholic Church and extended religious freedom, brought together priests, federalists, estancieros, and other conservatives for whom anticlericalism was anathema.

The impediments faced by President Rivadavia were insuperable, and on June 27, 1827, he bowed to the conservative movement. His resignation symbolized the triumph of the strong estanciero sector against the intellectuals, bureaucrats, merchants, and professional politicians.[8] The rivalries between *unitarios* and *federalistas* and between Buenos Aires and the interior continued unabated, however, with the interim federalist regimes of Vicente López y Planes and Manuel Dorrego. When Dorrego was overthrown and executed by the unitarian *porteño* (Buenos Aires resident) Juan Lavalle in December of 1828, Rosas felt compelled to respond. Now acting as Comandante General de Las Milicias de la Campaña (General Commandant of the Rural Militias) in Buenos Aires province, he defeated Lavalle in pitched battle. On December 26, 1829, Juan Manuel de Rosas, self-proclaimed protector of regional autonomy, became elected governor of Buenos Aires.[9]

The political and economic stage was thus set for the dramatic ascension of Rosas as virtual dictator of Buenos Aires. He inherited a volatile situation of political instability and regional and sectorial economic disparity. He confronted multiple and interdependent problems demanding immediate solutions: geographic and ideological divisions led to seemingly incessant civil wars; Indian raids on the frontier threatened the security of settlements and cattle operations; the Catholic Church adamantly protested unitarian secularism; and the viability of promoting national economic growth and development through livestock remained in question. The estanciero and *saladero* (meat-salter) class had begun to exert its economic might. It would now turn to Rosas to champion its political cause. He, in turn, would successfully utilize a populist program to balance and satisfy lower-sector and estanciero claims while building a solid personal political base.

The Gauchos

Contemporary accounts testify to the irrefutable popularity of Juan Manuel de Rosas upon his ascension to the governorship of Buenos Aires in 1829. As early as 1828, the United States chargé d'affaires in Buenos Aires, John Forbes, remarked that Rosas, called "King of the Gauchos," exercised a supreme influence over all the peasants of the country.[10] Forbes proffered this tentative biographical description of the new, unanimously installed governor: he was a man of moderate education but one who owed his great popularity among the gauchos to his having assimilated their singular modes of life, their dress, their labors, and even their sports—at which Rosas reputedly excelled. Forbes maintained that the high moral authority Rosas enjoyed emanated from his providing the gauchos with an example of courage, patience, and constancy.[11]

The roots of Rosas's popularity among the gauchos can be traced with reasonable clarity. Born into auspicious circumstances in Buenos Aires on March 30, 1793, Juan Manuel Ortiz de Rozas (as his name was then often spelled) suffered from no absence of wealth or prestige.[12] As the eldest child, young Juan's rudimentary education consisted of home tutoring in reading and writing and one year of private school at age eight. Dismissing the possibility of honing professional skills, he made the estancia his classroom, learning the ways and language of the inhabitants of the plains, including Indians.[13] From 1811 to 1815, Rosas administered his parents' estate without taking a salary, utilizing the opportunity to learn about the profits to be garnered in the exportation of Argentine hides and dried beef. In 1813, in spite of the protestations of his mother, he wed Encarnación Escurra y Arguibel, a woman also born into wealth and privilege. Two years later, Rosas took permanent leave of his parents, turning over to his brother Prudencio the operation of his parents' property.

Rosas wasted little time in forging a new land company, in partnership with Juan Nepomuceno Terrero and Luis Dorrego. Buying up land in the district of Guardia del Monte astride the Salado River, the entrepreneurial triumvirate established what would later become Rosas's most powerful estancia, Los Cerrillos.[14] Colonizing empty territory and encroaching upon Indian dominions, Rosas and his partners constructed a vast complex of land, power, thousands of head of cattle, innumerable peons, and Indian tribes.[15] Rosas also entered into business association with his second cousins Juan José and Nicolás de Anchorena, who, together with a third brother, Tomás Manuel, constituted one of the most affluent merchant families in Buenos Aires. Throughout the 1820s, Rosas managed their estates as well.

A patrician by birth and a gentleman of some refinement, Juan Manuel de Rosas nevertheless considered the *campo* his element. He learned the ways of gauchos and Indians in his youth and stood as the first among equals in adulthood. He preferred to participate in their brutal diversions rather than to don the symbolic accoutrements of urbanity. His unmatched ability to lasso, break a horse, and identify neighboring ranches by the taste of their grasses contributed to his legendary reputation and status.[16] Even his critic, Domingo F. Sarmiento, with reluctant admiration placed his despised enemy among the pathfinding gauchos, who "know every span of twenty thousand square leagues of plain, wood, and mountain!"[17]

Rosas also possessed a crude and at times obscene sense of humor, which was at odds with his elite background. His notion of a joke might involve lassoing a man around the neck, jerking him off his horse, and dragging him for a considerable distance. By conforming to the habits and dress of the gauchos, noted biologist Charles Darwin, Rosas obtained the unbounded popularity of the rural masses.[18]

With the peons of his estates, Rosas acted like a fellow worker, ostensibly evincing a profound social egalitarianism. Sharing their austere living circumstances, he demanded order, discipline, and hard work. In return, he proferred subsistence, protection from marauding Indians, and evenhanded justice.[19]

The law of honesty and discipline Rosas applied universally and unswervingly. Violation of prescribed rules met with swift reprisal, even when the culpability fell upon the very promulgator of these decrees. Those who carelessly forgot to carry lasso and lariat to work could expect fifty lashes. Once, when pouncing upon a rabbit, Rosas left his lasso and ordered his black servant Matías to give him twenty lashes for being a bad gaucho. When Matías balked before other peons, Rosas commanded him to strike hard or risk being whipped five hundred times.[20] The effect of these actions, beyond the immediate preservation of rigid order, lay with the creation of charismatic, almost suprahuman appeal among the rural population. Rosas, an intelligent pragmatist, recognized the value of the lower-class rural bloc:

Previous governments had acted very well towards educated people, but they despised the lower classes. . . . So . . . I thought it very important to gain a decisive influence over this class in order to control it and direct it . . . I had to work at it relentlessly, sacrificing my comfort and fortune, in order to become a *gaucho* like them, to speak like them, to do everything they did. I had to protect them, represent them . . . to secure their allegiance.[21]

The federalist party meanwhile, with its demand for popular government based upon universal male suffrage, proved extremely attractive to the politically inarticulate lower classes. The program of Europeanization introduced by the unitarians, specifically the Rivadavia government, also helped to fan the flames of fear of foreign invasion.[22] Under the leadership of the popular caudillo Rosas, regarded as the guardian and patriarch of folk traditions, the masses felt more identification with local government than with the imported political solutions advocated by the urban intellectuals.[23]

Rosas enjoyed the best of several political worlds: as an estanciero he inherited a subservient peonage; as a popular caudillo he earned the respect and devotion of the rural folk. Opportunistically identifying the direction of political winds, he succeeded in cultivating the conviction among the masses of his natural right to exercise authority.[24] Writing to another caudillo, Facundo Quiroga, in 1832, Rosas manifested his desire to accommodate ideology to public opinion: "I am a federalist . . . but alas . . . I would subordinate my-self to being a unitarian; if the vote of the masses favored Unity."[25]

Rosas, perhaps more than other caudillos, understood the magical power of the word over the multitudes; he made the term "federa-tion" the symbol of his politics, completely enveloping himself in it.[26] When the people called him "Restaurador de las Leyes" (Re-storer of the Laws), they referred more to his zealous defense of folk traditions that seemed condemned to extinction than to his protec-tion of legal norms. José Romero suggests that the masses, proud of their "Americanism," their superior pastoral virtues of courage and manual dexterity, intransigently opposed economic progress and found in Rosas their champion. Along these lines, he built the indisputably popular basis for his policies.[27]

If the center of Rosas's prestige lay in the country, it also became the political stage from which he ultimately would become master of the province.[28] Rosas seized control of the United Provinces of the River Plate by means of his adept use of gaucho militias. While in a general sense most estancieros defended their properties against Indians and outlaws with militias composed of their own gaucho workers, Rosas cut a more imposing military and political presence. Not only did he recruit and mobilize the denizens of his own es-tates, but he exercised charismatic authority over peons everywhere in the countryside.

The year 1820 foreshadowed the moment when an amorphous popular collectivity would propel Rosas to virtual omnipotence. Chaos had prevailed. Buenos Aires was struggling to subdue the independent republics (Paraguay, Uruguay, and Bolivia) that had proliferated among the interior provinces of the former Spanish viceroyalty. Provincial caudillos, led by Estanislao Ramírez of Entre Ríos, had succeeded in razing all vestiges of the central government and seemed poised to force upon Buenos Aires a provincial govern-ment of their choosing. Rosas would not stand idly by as an alien *montonero* (gaucho rabble) dictated the course of the future of Bue-nos Aires; neither would he tolerate the kind of disorder that could prove calamitous to his haciendas. Thus, clad in red, well-mounted and disciplined, the original five hundred "Colorados del Monte" under Rosas joined the army of Buenos Aires as the Fifth Regiment of Militia.[29] As a result, Rosas's favored politician, Martín Rodrí-guez, assumed the governorship of Buenos Aires. Rosas received the commission of colonel of cavalry, an estancia of 36,000 acres called

El Rey, a tract of land measuring 192,000 acres in Santa Fe province, and 37,500 silver pesos.[30] More significantly, Rosas had entered the political arena and had made the full weight of a gaucho militia felt throughout the confederation.

The December (1828) Revolution of Juan Lavalle once again found Rosas turning to the rural populace for military help. As an estanciero, he enjoyed sufficient resources to control the countryside. As chief of the military force organized at his own expense, the Colorados or Red Rangers, he wielded decisive influence over the events precipitated by Lavalle's usurpation of power. And as commandant of the province, he was unmatched in his ability to recruit, train, and direct multitudinous troops.[31] Rosas entered the fracas with the intention of mobilizing the lower sectors and avoiding open, pitched battle with the enemy.

The execution of Dorrego on 13 December precipitated a crisis that paved the way for Rosas's emergence as savior of Buenos Aires. Bolstered by estanciero and Indian support, Rosas and his gauchos succeeded in waging guerrilla warfare against Lavalle's more experienced but underpaid professional army. On November 3, 1829, the commandant rode triumphantly into Buenos Aires, not only as the victorious military servant of the government but also, despite the appointment of interim governor Juan José Viamonte, as the undisputed leader of the federalist party.[32]

Rosas's reputation grew to idolatrous proportions. Throngs gathered to meet the avenger of Dorrego's execution, the defender of law and order, the conqueror of anarchy, the representative of the gauchos and the pampa.[33] Rosas was cheered by the plebeian crowds on his way to the Plaza de Victoria amid arches of triumph, music, red banners, bell chimes, and red silk steamers.[34] Affectionately called "El Viejo" (old man) at the age of thirty-six, Rosas exhibited the kind of strong hand, intolerance for crime and immorality, and austere style of living that enhanced his image as the man of the masses.[35]

Determining that the unitarian threat still posed a danger to the government, the deputies voted on December 6, 1829, to allow the new governor dictatorial powers until May 1, 1830.[36] Rosas took the oath of office before the legislature and cheering crowds. He promised to respect the federal system and to restore Catholicism; he also spoke of the sacrifices he had endured, of his lack of inclination for power, and of the painful destiny that had been thrust upon him.[37] This feigned reluctance to serve in the capacity of supreme ruler, a common tactic employed by populists to justify perpetuation of sovereignty, became a recurring motif throughout the Rosas era. In the end, Rosas voluntarily returned the extraordinary powers and completed his first stint as governor on December 5, 1832.[38]

Out of office, his formidable reputation acquired greater prestige. He was appointed Commander General of the Countryside and Chief of the Left Division of the National Army for operations against the Indians. Governor Juan Balcarce assigned to Rosas the commission that came to be known as the Desert Campaign, an expedition against the pampean Indians of the south. In a little over a year, Rosas and his cavalrymen managed to secure the frontier and sign peace treaties with most of the Indian tribes. Although definitive conquest of the desert would elude the Argentine government until Julio Roca's campaign in 1879, Rosas had added to Buenos Aires two hundred square leagues (one league equaling three statute miles) west to the Andes and south beyond the Río Negro.[39] As "Conquistador del Desierto" (Conqueror of the Desert), he received as compensation freehold of the inhospitable island of Choele-Choel, which he later exchanged for sixty square leagues of pasture land in Buenos Aires province. The Desert Campaign also established a precedent to which Rosas would conform throughout his political career: rewarding loyal soldiers with gifts, principally of land. The regime decreed a grant of seven leagues to General Angel Pacheco, forty-three leagues to eleven colonels, and sixteen leagues to the soldiers of the Andes regiment.[40]

Although Rosas had claimed, upon relinquishing the extraordinary powers with which he was endowed, that there were those who "judged me erroneously to harbor ambitious ideas and desires," evidence suggests that *rosistas* in Buenos Aires—including his own wife Encarnación—deliberately undermined the Balcarce and Viamonte governments for the purpose of reinstalling the former governor.[41] American consul Eben Dorr cogently summarized prevailing political conditions through consular communiqués. On March 6, 1835, he noted that Rosas resigned the command of the country forces, apparently to avail himself of the soon-to-be-vacated governor's seat. Dorr observed that "it has, for some time, been the intention of General Rosas to invest himself with the power of [a] dictator."[42] "His great influence and popularity in the country are sufficient to place the province wholly at his will," continued the consul, "and all attempts are being made to excite the people in favor of [his] coming in . . . and some to influence the public against individuals thought to be opposed to the views of the *Restau-radores.*" Two days later Dorr reported that the resignation of Interim Governor Manuel Vicente de Maza was placed before the House, which thereupon acted to confer on Rosas an unlimited dictatorship.[43]

Rosas undoubtedly viewed the rural *gauchaje* as a political and military clientele. The governor also had targeted urban and rural working classes as a potentially valuable pool of political adherents. Expanding urban enterprises, particularly the *saladero* operations in Buenos Aires, which salted Argentine beef for export, required ever-increasing labor forces that European immigration could not satisfy. The large standing army diverted human resources from the productive economy. While the continued demand for unskilled labor attracted rural migrants to the city, the reception they received was far from cordial. European immigrants devoured the prime artisanal jobs.[44] It also seems reasonable to conclude that rural migrants were, in the main, of mixed race, which only exacerbated the problems of racial condescension prevalent in a society that prized the whiteness of skin.[45] Creole workers certainly resented the arrogance and exemption from military service of the foreigners. Rosas asked his wife to favor these unemployed and underemployed Argentine-born migrants with gifts and attention.

The popularity of the gauchocracy, as Sarmiento pejoratively called the new regime, facilitated long-term, centralized, authoritarian rule. Rosas appeared as an element of moderation and order during an anarchical epoch distinctly lacking in modern principles of liberty.[46] Regarded by urban and rural inhabitants as the only man capable of restoring traditional ways of life to the Río de la Plata, the charismatic governor elicited idolatrous respect from his adherents. Indeed, the "mysterious" origin of his power provoked people to sing:

> He, with his talent and his science,
> Keeps the country secure,
> and that is why he gets his help
> from Divine Providence.[47]

The perceived possession of supernatural or extraordinary qualities is another important characteristic of the populist leader. Blind obedience to the elected one foments in the collective imagination a mythical political leader, who in turn finds himself obligated to think and labor for all. Rosas found no difficulty conforming to this despotic development.

Indians and Blacks

The populist multiclass coalition supporting Juan Manuel de Rosas included the previously neglected, and in some instances persecuted, lower sectors of society. Beyond courting the Argentine *gauchaje*, the governor also relied to a great extent upon amicable relations with Indians and blacks. While Rosas never considered them his racial or social peers, he nevertheless became fully cognizant of their value to the crystallization of his power. To Rosas, skillful manipulation of the lower sectors of society did not presuppose egalitarian ideals.

As noted earlier, Indians posed a constant threat to the security of estancias on the pampa frontier. During the late eighteenth and early nineteenth centuries, Indians controlled much of the territory now forming the province of Buenos Aires. The predatory incursions launched from their modest *tolderías* (camps) revealed a marked ferocity that oppugned Rousseau's romanticized concept of the noble savage. The expansion of the cattle economy from 1815 onward drew Creole settlers to south of the Salado River, creating conditions of inevitable conflict. The Indians naturally resented the uninvited occupation of lands they had always considered their own. To this unwarranted intrusion, the Pampas, Ranqueles, and other migratory Indians responded with intensified retributive raids.[48]

As early as 1821, the future governor adamantly disapproved of extirpative military expeditions, proposing instead a line of frontier forts and a deterring militia presence. His plan advocated depriving Indians of the training that warfare afforded them, attracting them to civilization, and utilizing their labor to compensate for the short rural supply.[49] Rosas the rancher did, in fact, employ many Indian peons, to whom he introduced the rudiments of white civilization. Many of his Indians received Christian baptism and moral instruction; in particular, they were taught about the sanctity of private property. Frequent contact with the fearsome Pampas allowed Rosas the opportunity to learn their language and to cultivate trust, which led the Indians to regard him as a man who delivered on promises and protected their interests.[50] Through tributes of cattle, sheep, horses, and other supplies, Rosas managed to offset their impressive war machine of long cane lances, cudgels, *bolas,* and supreme horsemanship.[51]

During the years 1825 and 1826, Governor Juan Gregorio de las Heras made pacification of the interior a priority, particularly since the war with Brazil threatened to drive the Indians toward an alliance with Buenos Aires's foe. Under the auspices of a delegation led by Rosas, the government procured a preliminary peace agreement with southern Indians based on trade and mutual restraint. On October 31, 1825, the governor also organized a commission, composed of Rosas and others, charged with the responsibility of establishing the frontier south of the Salado and of studying the placement of three new forts and a cavalry garrison.[52] Completing its work by January of the following year, the commission found, much to its chagrin, that the new Rivadavia government was unwilling to implement the proposals.

Rosas indefatigably continued to bring the Indians and whites into peaceful coexistence. In January of 1826, he visited the Pampas and Tehuelche encampments in ambassadorial fashion, concluding a peace settlement called the Treaty of Laguna del Guanaco. The treaty procured Indian nonaggression in exchange for various articles of tribute.[53] Offers of friendship, gifts (principally of mares), hospitality, and patience seduced wary Indian tribes. In 1828, Rosas procured a pact with the Pampas whereby the Indians relinquished claim to some of their land and promised to cooperate in defending the territory against the hostile Ranqueles and their allies. Rosas's role in dealing with the Indian problem even prompted him to complain that the numerous Indians who came to the city and the thousands who lived on the haciendas he administered had become a real burden on his time.[54]

The unitarian revolt of 1829 provided further testimony that, by courting the Indians, Rosas had added a formidable weapon to his populist political arsenal. Rosas commanded the support of most tribes taking sides in the political dispute. Sizable contingents of Indian *montoneros* defeated the unitarian commandants Francisco Morel and Federico Rauch and moved toward Buenos Aires.[55] A hastily gathered militia of unitarians and foreign—mostly French—nationals proved no match for Rosas's hordes. Federalists stirred nationalistic zeal with the placards of "Indios sí, extranjeros

no" (Indians yes, foreigners no), and "Valen más indios que unitarios" (Indians are worth more than unitarians).[56] As a result of
these machinations, Lavalle's army could boast virtually no support
among the pampean Indians, rendering his military and political
station highly pregnable.

Seeking viable solutions to practical difficulties, Rosas subscribed
to no theory of social egalitarianism. As with the gauchos, he recognized the Indians' potential worth to his multiclass coalition of
adherents. However, Rosas did not squander the opportunity to take
the land of Indians who betrayed his trust. Rosas the estanciero
sought more territory for cattle expansion; Rosas the militia commander distinguished between friendly allies and enemy Indians,
whose aggression necessitated a swift military response. In 1833,
when the Pampas launched a series of attacks across the southern
border of Buenos Aires province and plundered upwards of 12,000
head of cattle (much of it belonging to Rosas himself), the consum-
mate negotiator felt his hand forced.[57] Rosas then undertook the
Desert Campaign.

Rosas's bellicose tactics, however, constituted an attempt only to
bring incorrigible Indians into line, not to exterminate them. Despite acquiring the title Conquistador del Desierto (Conqueror of
the Desert) for his military victories, the commander never abandoned his preferred option of alliance. Confidently explaining the
credo that motivated him, Rosas endeavored to persuade Cacique
Caninquín from Tapalque of the advantages accruing to friendship:

you will see that my friendship is very valuable to you and should be preserved at all costs. . . . And just as I am a fine and true friend, so too do I
pursue those who become unfaithful or treacherous.[58]

As his diary indicates, the shrewd Rosas enlisted the military aid of
partisan tribes in the Desert Campaign.[59]

Throughout his subsequent relations with Indians, Rosas balanced a strong hand with a willingness to arrive at a negotiated
peace. But against what he regarded as "theft" his crusade never wavered. Writing to Estanislao López in 1835, Rosas restated his guiding philosophy about rewarding friends and smiting enemies. He
determined to continue assaulting the *tolderías* of the Ranqueles,
whose feigned acts of contrition and amity, he said, could not disguise their unflagging proclivity to steal.[60] As an estanciero, he had
to consider Indian raids on the cattle herds as a form of "theft."

The successful conclusion of the Desert Campaign one and a half years after its commencement broadened Rosas's already impressive political base. Compacts of peace bound some 10,000 Indians to keep to their own territory, to refrain from crossing the frontier, to provide military service when called upon, and to act as peaceful citizens. In exchange, each cacique received regular specified tributes of cattle, sheep, horses (mares), yerba, tobacco, and salt.[61] While this liberality may have been tantamount to bribery, Rosas had undeniably struck a bargain from which both parties reaped tangible gains. The Indians felt a certain degree of affection and respect for the man who demonstrated a volition to substitute mutual collaboration for traditional policies of obliteration.

As a popular movement, *rosismo* deliberately recruited nonelites into provincial politics. The manner in which Rosas dealt with the gauchos and Indians defied past practices. Also somewhat iconoclastic was his treatment of the Afro-Argentines, whom he identified as another potential pillar of manipulated support.

The history of blacks in the Río de la Plata begins with the blight of slavery. African slaves were imported into the labor-scarce Río de la Plata region throughout the colonial period. The expanding livestock economy of the 1820s, chronically short of labor, provided the rationale for continuing the bondage of those slaves who had not yet secured their freedom by joining the militias. As administrator for the Anchorena estates, Rosas himself began buying slaves in 1822.[62] In 1831, Governor Rosas reopened the trade in domestic servants brought into Buenos Aires by foreigners, making it legal for them to be sold to Argentines as slaves. Despite these legal shackles, however, the twenty years of Rosas's administration transformed Afro-Argentines into a potent instrument for federalism and populism.

As with the gauchos and Indians, Rosas's initial contact with blacks resulted largely from their participation in his estancia operations. The 1836 census of the ranches he managed or owned showed that fifty-four of the 154 peons in the Monte and twenty-nine of forty-six in Los Cerrillos were black.[63] Recognizing the advantages to be gained by organizing the masses on his behalf, the ever-astute Rosas nurtured a mutually, although by no means equally, beneficial relationship with blacks. In fashioning a political coalition, he did not begin from ground zero. Dorrego, too, enjoyed the unqualified support of Afro-Argentines. Rosas inherited Dorrego's following.

The year 1831 seemed to augur the dramatic events of a century later, when Juan Domingo Perón utilized the services of his wife, Evita Duarte de Perón, to garner the support of the lower classes. In that year, Doña Encarnación had the pleasure of reporting to her husband the success of her efforts to organize workers in his favor. "I have called together the *paisanos* [countrymen]," she proudly recounted. "I have spoken to them, as well as to the presidents of all the black nations [mutual aid societies composed of slaves and free blacks born in Africa]."[64] In 1833, when ex-governor Rosas had embarked upon the Desert Campaign, Encarnación received explicit instructions from her spouse that left no doubt as to the importance Rosas placed upon urban and black support.

You have already seen . . . how important it is to nurture it [friendship of the poor] and not miss ways to attract and cultivate their allegiance. . . . Write them frequently, send them gifts. . . . I say the same concerning . . . the *pardos* [mulattoes] and *morenos* [coloreds] who are faithful. I repeat, do not fail to visit those who merit it and to invite them to your parties, as well as to help them in their misfortunes.[65]

As a result of these directives and of her own fierce devotion to the commandant, Encarnación as the agent and purveyor of *rosismo* earned the title of "heroine of the federation." Calling in black women to receive her favor and sending them out as clients, she transformed her patio into a club for the populace.[66]

Rosas's daughter Manuelita provided another—and in the view of unitarians, scandalous and offensive—link with Afro-Argentines. Particularly unpalatable in their eyes was her habit of attending the dances of the African nations and of swinging in the arms of black men. The government newspaper, *La Gaceta Mercantil*, defended the ruling Rosas family, commenting in 1843 that the governor considered *pardos* and mulattoes to be valiant defenders of liberty against would-be foreign usurpers and savage unitarians. The women of the Congo nation reaffirmed their loyalty to father and daughter by composing a "Hymn to Doña Manuela Rosas" on the occasion of her birthday in 1848.[67]

Afro-Argentine dances, particularly the *candombé* (the most representative of the first half of the nineteenth century), constituted a powerful means of winning black trust and affection. The immediate postindependence ruling class banned black street dancing in 1822 and all public forms of dance in 1825. Rosas lifted the prohibition and, under his auspices, the *candombé* enjoyed its pinnacle of popularity.[68] As a result of the governor's patronage, dances unfailingly began with verses in his honor, penned either by blacks themselves or by *rosista* propagandists.

> You all see how at the *candombé*
> The black people shout and call
> "Long live our Father Rosas
> The best governor of them all."[69]

After each federalist victory, bands of black musicians paraded through the streets. On at least one occasion, when the provincial treasury once again found itself hard-pressed to meet mounting military expenses, forty-two Afro-Argentine "nations" made special contributions.[70]

Although greatly aided by the efforts of Encarnación and Manuela, Rosas himself procured black support through flattery, propaganda, and genuine concessions. Naming his suburban mansion after the black saint Benito de Palermo, for instance, proved of considerable symbolic value. Rosas also instructed teams of propagandists to write literature in Afro-Argentine dialects for distribution to the populace. The irregularly published newspaper *La Negrita* exemplified the public relations strategy. Sprinkled throughout its pages were condemnations of the nefarious influence of the ambitious unitarian politicos.

The most reasonable explanation for the fact that blacks remained steadfastly loyal to the governor lies with the principle of reciprocal advantage. It is true that Rosas renewed a limited slave trade in 1831, that he relied in large measure upon black males to fuel his war machine, and that in 1834 he instituted a policy of automatic conscription of all foreign-born *libertos*, or liberated slaves.[71] Tulio Halperín Donghi suggests, however, that a redistribution of wealth may have mitigated somewhat the injustice of herding blacks into the army. Maintenance of large military forces in fact may have met with the approval of the chronically underemployed lower classes, as some 900,000 pesos in salaries passed into the hands of the lower sectors.[72] As has already been seen, General Rosas also deliberately lavished gifts and attention, often through the intercession of Encarnación and Manuela, upon poor Afro-Argentines. Urban blacks, forming a strong populist base in Buenos Aires, responded by displaying the red federalist insignias that came to mark the epoch. Rosas did, however, move beyond what might be construed as an enormous payoff. In 1836, he abrogated earlier legislation mandating a universal draft of *libertos* over the age of fifteen. Three years later, possibly as the result of British abolitionist pressure, the governor finally terminated the slave trade. Demonstrations of appreciation ensued. Rosas also promoted carefully selected blacks to relatively high military ranks and took others as personal retainers. Prominent among the latter group were Domiciano, a much-feared executioner, and Zabalia, a Mazorca (secret police) member.[73]

Afro-Argentines unequivocally demonstrated their political potency as a collective agent for the propagation of federalism or, in the unitarian lexicon, barbarism. Detractors of the administration would later contend that Rosas manipulated blacks to advance his own ambitious cause. José Wilde inveighed against the indispensable role they performed in the dictator's elaborate urban espionage network. Domestics presumably reported on their employers to Rosas or the secret police, usually with catastrophic consequences for the accused family.[74]

As has been observed, Rosas also relied to a notable extent upon black soldiers to acquire and preserve power. During 1830 and 1831, he created a regiment of free blacks called the "Defenders of Buenos Aires," and the fourth battalion of the active militia. Blacks formed the greater part of the Argentine infantry, with thousands dying in the almost incessant warfare of the early nineteenth century.[75] On September 14, 1840, Rosas decreed that all slaves of unitarians be drafted into military service. The draft swelled the ranks of his own troops and denied much-needed labor and military service to the enemy.[76]

Urban Support

If Rosas succeeded in radicalizing and mobilizing the rural populace, he also unified politically militant sectors of the city and the countryside.[77] The general's second grand entry into Buenos Aires in 1835 led American Consul Eben Dorr to remark that only the higher socioeconomic classes refrained from participating in the seemingly ubiquitous rejoicings. He observed that the populace, both rural and urban, was wholly in his favor.[78]

Early on in the organization of his state, the "Restorer" implemented concrete measures to win public affection. Capitalizing on the animosity produced by ubiquitous wartime despoliations, he issued several edicts of restitution. The first law granted land to those dispossessed citizens who were willing to populate the frontier. A second decree ordered that all those who lent goods to the Restoration army justify their claims to justices of the peace, after which valid claims would be paid out of the public treasury. Since the justices were federalist adherents of Rosas, the poor received viable protection of their donations to the war effort. The claim period lasted one year and fueled the hope of the less fortunate that one day they would recover some of their lost meager wealth. By 1831, the executive had not yet paid all debts, but the mere act of accepting as public responsibility the onerous financial burden led "everyone [to be] happy . . . and confident of the religiosity of payment."[79] Rosas knew that by giving the urban populace a vested interest in the perpetuation of his rule, *porteños* would be unlikely to back an opposition faction that might repudiate the war debts.[80] He further consolidated his position among the poor by occasionally awarding confiscated houses of "savage unitarians" to urban squatters by lowering the rents charged by suspected unitarian landlords. The urban working class also appreciated the regime's fixing of beef prices.[81]

The city of Buenos Aires experienced no industrial revolution during the first half of the nineteenth century. Traditional artisans did, however, survive the transition to independence and the ensuing escalation of foreign competition. Hat and chair makers, carpenters, forgers, smiths, saddlers, tapestry makers, tailors, and coopers lent an industrial hue to the urban landscape. The state of constant military preparedness promoted by Rosas met with the unqualified support of this sector, which profited from the extraordinary demand for arms, equipment, uniforms, and hardware. Rosas recruited his urban militia principally from among this group of artisans: the *primer tercio cívico* (first civic third) consisted of retail traders and shopkeepers; the *segundo tercio* (second third) encompassed the youth of the middle sector, craftsmen, employees, carters, and small property owners; and blacks and mulattoes fitted out the *tercera brigada* (third brigade).[82] It is noteworthy that the different social sectors served in separate military units.

Economic policy served a particularly prominent political role in 1835 with the passage of a significantly higher tariff. As an estanciero involved in extensive export trade, Rosas believed in the free play of market mechanisms to achieve economic progress and max-imum personal profits. Nevertheless, throughout the 1820s artisans pressed for state intervention in the form of protective legislation. They sought to minimize external competitive advantage by im-porting duty-free raw materials requisite for manufacture and by protecting goods processed from local products. These economic nationalists pled their cause more insistently in 1835, when Rosas bowed to the protectionist pressure. As with the issue of his party affiliation, Rosas once again demonstrated at this juncture a con-cern for pragmatism over ideological fidelity.

Beyond its economic significance, the year 1835 also marked a moment of enormous *porteño* support for the returning governor.[83] Having created the widespread conviction of his singular ability to restore orderliness to the traditional Argentine way of life, Rosas demanded that a plebiscite be held on the issue of dictatorial pow-ers. In employing this typically populist tactic, he recognized the paramount importance of preserving at least the veneer of hege-monic legitimacy. Thus, on March 26, 27, and 28, the government of Buenos Aires registered voters in the churches of the several munic-ipal precincts.[84] That the people would ratify the conferral of un-limited faculties to the revered Restorer was a foregone conclusion. An impressive 9,320 people cast affirmative votes; there were only four dissenting ballots.[85]

Future renunciations of honors and dramatic acts of abdication could not disguise the governor's intent to preserve and even aug-ment his political capital. On a less passive level, Rosas set in mo-tion a rather elaborate propaganda machine designed to preclude the political deviation of his followers and to silence critics. He unapol-ogetically controlled the press and all other organs of public infor-mation. Always the astute populist, the chief executive employed competent journalists and propagandists to argue his case before the Argentine people and the rest of the world. Rosas and his al-lies were portrayed as the bastions of morality battling insidious elements, appearing alternately as Frenchmen, foreigners, North Americans, liberals, monarchists, old Spaniards, and certain Indian tribes. While dangerous and numerous, these "criminals" were de-picted as infinitely less debased than the putatively treacherous, murderous, pernicious, and savage unitarians who sought to disrupt the sanctity of the Christian community and to oppress the humble urban and rural working classes.[86] However overstated, the diatribes encouraged a sense of common purpose among a people weary of civil anomie.

Beyond the dexterous use of propaganda, Rosas also culled and expressed popular consensus through other devices. The infamous Mazorca, the secret police organization pejoratively known as *más horca* (more hanging), took its name from the cornstalk, symbolizing strength through union. The liberal tradition of Sarmiento has passed to history the image of a bloodthirsty collectivity of thugs roaming the streets of Buenos Aires in search of thousands of innocent, arbitrarily chosen, and defenseless victims. Evidence does suggest that paramilitary squads engaged in some assassination and persecution schemes. However, the targets were precisely chosen and carefully identified unitarians, real or alleged, and federalists of dubious loyalty, who were considered security risks. Mass murders did not occur, as the ensuing horror might have provoked a large-scale counterreaction. Estimates of the number of political executions over the twenty-year period of Rosas's hegemony approached two thousand victims.[87]

Rosas resorted to tactics of terror during moments of economic stagnation and political tension, such as those that existed during the French blockade of 1838 and the Anglo-French quarantine of 1845. He succeeded in eliminating incipient anarchy, assuring ordinary citizens that they had nothing to fear if they remained faithful to the political line. He wanted to wear down the opposition through irresistible force.[88] Disputing widely circulated accounts of the prevalence of an atmosphere of fear, even the most skeptical contemporary observers conceded that urban inhabitants enjoyed and appreciated a heretofore unknown environmental security. In 1844, American Consul Amory Edwards concluded that Rosas alone possessed the ability and determination to keep his countrymen in order.[89]

Besides ferreting out potential subversives, the Mazorca also assumed the responsibility of stimulating mass urban enthusiasm for the regime. It perfected the device of popular (not official) reprisal for violation of the implicit obligation to wear the crimson color of the Rosas party.[90] The bearing of a red badge and *cintas de punzó* (ribbons) produced a conformity that bound the population into a rather rigidly defined community of federalist supporters.[91] Red apparel identified adherents to the cause (on whatever sincere, apathetic, or feigned level of commitment) and possible opponents.

Political orthodoxy expressed through federal symbolism brought the support of the lower and middle classes to the forefront of Argentine politics. Carried to an absurd degree, it required a federalist physiognomy of men: true advocates sported a luxuriant moustache and sideburns.[92] The blue color of unitarianism vanished from all parts of the Argentine landscape, and red became the incontrovertible means of allaying any suspicion the Mazorca might harbor of individual disloyalty. Rosas achieved unity.

Religion constituted another instrument by which Rosas further ingratiated himself to the urban and rural masses. Rivadavia's anticlerical policy of curtailing the temporal power of the Catholic Church and extending religious freedom were anathema to the clergy and to all those with conservative values.[93] Rosas wasted no time in recognizing the utility of championing the Catholic cause. Arising out of the same antiliberal tradition as Quiroga, he adopted the latter's appealing motto of *religión o muerte* (religion or death) as a guiding principle. During the period in which Rosas was engaged in the Desert Campaign, he instructed the ultramontane party, known as the *apostólicos* (apostolics), to wave the banner of religion as a vehicle through which to attract the kind of popular support needed for his political return. He was thus honored as the "Great Protector of the Catholic faith."[94]

Rosas viewed the Church as a bulwark against the spread of liberalism. In 1831, Woodbine Parish reported that the governor relentlessly pursued a policy of paying priests, erecting new parishes, building new churches, and renovating old ones. One British minister complained acrimoniously of the medieval mentality that seemed to pervade the administration. According to him, Rosas created a climate of intellectual prostration by reviving the bullfight and reopening the Dominican convent.[95] The Church's association with its patron became unmistakably obvious: a political liturgy urged staunch support of the regime; during the French blockade, a portrait of Rosas mounted among floral decorations was idolatrously paraded from church to church and revered as a sacred icon; in 1842, the governor ordered that six effigies (customarily of Judas) be made in the form of notorious unitarians and burned on Holy Saturday; such higher clergymen as Bishop Mariano Medrano wore federal vestments and extolled the "Holy Federal Cause"; and the lower clergy, often of Creole heritage, fanatically exhorted their congregations to exterminate unitarian insurgents.[96]

Rosas simultaneously courted and dominated the Church. He assumed the right of patronage, appointing only federalist priests. He also rendered null and void any papal bulls or ecclesiastical appointments introduced to the Río de la Plata since 1810. Authorizing the return of the Society of Jesus (Jesuits) in 1836, he quickly became concerned with their growing influence and their political neutrality. In 1843, he expelled them from the province of Buenos Aires.[97] In a mutually advantageous relationship, the governor exchanged protection for ideological backing. In practical terms, not only did the governor recruit the Church as an ideological agent, lending a measure of legitimacy, respectability, and increased popularity to the regime, but he also won the affection of the urban and rural populace through his unswerving defense of the faith.

Estanciero Support

This study has thus far concerned itself principally with the lower-class support curried by Rosas. However, the Argentine landed elite also benefited from Rosas's rise to power in very tangible ways. While achieving a sense of identification with the *gauchaje*, the chief executive could not escape the reality of his social and economic class. No matter how effectively he cultivated the image of "Protector of Gauchos," he was first and foremost an estanciero. Naturally, therefore, he actively promoted the interests of the cattle economy, although not necessarily to the exclusion of farming and artisanry.

Rosas's qualifications as an estanciero were unquestionable. In the exclusive group of seventeen landowners with property over fifty square leagues (roughly 300,000 acres), he occupied tenth place with seventy square leagues (approximately 420,000 acres) in 1830.[98] Even before being elected governor of the province, Rosas enhanced his reputation among his wealthy peers. In a move that presaged his future political concern with the livestock industry, he pushed for a land distribution directive (September 1829) ostensibly designed to ameliorate the squalor in which rural families languished. State lands were to be divided among poor farmers willing to settle the inhospitable frontier territory south of Azul. This colonization was to provide estancieros of the interior with a buffer zone of security against marauding Indians. The government charged Rosas, at that time militia commander, with the responsibility of selecting the recipients as well as the sites to be allocated.[99] As administrator of the decree, he wielded an important instrument of patronage with which to reward victorious federalists. Rosas also successfully lobbied for a resolution of September 22, 1829, which, "because of the harmful effects of the civil war on capital employed in land, cattle-raising, and farming," exempted these enterprises from the *contribución directa* (direct tax on property and capital) for that year. Another measure favorable to the landed elite and passed at the commander's insistence (October 12, 1829) established two public cattle-holding pens in Buenos Aires for livestock driven to the city.[100] If Rosas provided tangible rewards to his lower-class flock, they were nothing compared to the benefits garnered by the estancieros. The upper rural and urban strata in the legislature repaid their political/economic debt by electing Rosas governor in both 1829 and 1835.

Of immediate and paramount gubernatorial concern was the improvement in the status and security of landholding. The livestock economy of the early nineteenth century required the conquest of Indian territory in order to expand. Rosas combined sporadic acts of retribution against hostile Indians with a law of June 9, 1832, setting aside 360 square leagues for distribution to drought-stricken ranchers and militia veterans. The federalist party in some ways represented the political expression of a major portion of the estancieros of the province.[101] As the federalist standard-bearer, therefore, Rosas countenanced no delay in the execution of a plan projected to rid the estancieros of the Indian menace forever. In the 1820s, Indians still controlled the southern two-thirds of what is now Buenos Aires province.[102] As noted earlier, Rosas preferred negotiation to extermination, as peaceful coexistence could augment his clientele. Indian aggression grew so acute in 1833, however, that the now ex-governor determined to undertake the punitive and expansive Desert Campaign.

Contracts to provision the expeditionary force yielded sizable profits for the estanciero suppliers, particularly Rosas's friends. As has been seen, the commander of the campaign brought to fruition the military subjugation of recalcitrantly bellicose tribes and the diplomatic settlement with those more peaceably disposed. One year's effort had added approximately two hundred leagues of territory west to the Andes and south beyond the Río Negro. Rosas judged that one hundred estancias, supporting one million horned cattle and yielding for export 300,000 hides, 365,000 quintals of salted meat, and 600,000 arrobas of tallow, would be established.[103] By extending the frontier and making more land available, particularly although not exclusively to estancieros, Rosas achieved a state of border security for which his social and economic peers had long clamored.[104] His popularity and respect among this distinguished group grew commensurately. Just as urban and rural inhabitants had come to conceive of Rosas as the only man with sufficient charisma and strength to end the civil wars, so, too, did the hacendados begin to tie their hopes for continued frontier peace to the governor's continued tenure.

Rosas also brought about legal modifications in landholding that favored the rural elite. The system of emphyteusis (rentals on government-owned land), in which a few individuals held vast tracts of land, generated little revenue for the state—some 152,000 pesos in 1835 and 198,000 in 1836. When the original leases expired in 1837, most tenants seized the opportunity to purchase their land outright, thus curtailing even further the already meager government income. Rosas doubled the rent on the remaining holdings (3,500 square leagues) in 1838, but managed to collect only the relatively insignificant sum of 196,000 pesos.[105] Rather than attempt to salvage the obsolete and obviously flawed system of emphyteusis, the administration preferred to sell land outright, thereby raising considerable funds for use in moments of national crisis. The first large-scale land sale was sanctioned by a law of May 10, 1836, authorizing the governor to dispose of 1,500 square leagues (part of which was held in emphyteusis) at very inexpensive rates.[106] Emphyteusists were given priority to purchase the land they already held. While not obligated to buy, they felt the pressure of a doubling rent upon the expiration of the lease period.[107] A decree of July 27, 1837, stipulated that lands forfeited to the state because of the nonpayment of rent would be offered at public action.[108] In 1839 the regime's land policy netted 1,062,000 pesos; in 1840, only 101,000 pesos. Thereafter the treasury reported no income from this source.[109]

While the sales proceedings may have availed the small estancieros of some land tied up by the magnates, the early results seemed to increase the power of the large cattlemen. In 1840, an estimated 3,436 square leagues of land had fallen into the hands of 293 individuals, the overwhelming majority of whom were former emphyteusis barons.[110] A mere 825 men accumulated 8,000,000 hectares (19,768,000 acres) of rich pampean pasturage.[111] The governor encouraged this acquisition of land by permitting payment in installments, in treasury bills, and even up to 50 percent in cattle.[112] The French blockade of Buenos Aires caused a decline in the demand for land by creating a cash shortage and by severing the outlet for estancia exports. The administration responded by carrying to its logical conclusion the initial favoritism applied to large landholders: Rosas gave away vast tracts to supporters.[113]

Land grants in the form of *boletos de premios en tierra* (certificates of land rewards) abounded during the Rosas era. Exemplary military conduct, outstanding contributions to specific campaigns, or reliable civil service elicited these official acts of patronage. Issuing upwards of 8,500 certificates (ranging in value from less than a league to two or more) to loyal soldiers and civilians constituted one method of solidifying support for the regime in the absence of overflowing public coffers. The fifty leagues of bounty distributed after the Desert Campaign have already been noted. By decree of December 17, 1840, all those people participating in federalist victories received similar gifts, which many recipients sold for hard cash to estancieros like the Anchorenas.[114]

Rosas also pursued a financial policy that pleased his hacendado clients. From his predecessors the governor inherited an enormous deficit, a depreciated currency, and a large public debt. Unlike Viamonte, however, Rosas did not attempt to restore the gold value of the peso. His program for financial recuperation followed the conservative tenets of strict economy in expenditures, administrative efficiency, and the consolidation of the existing distribution of national dividend.[115] The estancieros naturally approved of all philosophies of government and budgetary management that tended to preserve the economic, political, and social status quo.

To meet mounting expenses, Rosas resorted to the printing press. Paper currency circulation, beginning at 15,283,540 pesos in 1836, reached 125,264,294 pesos at the close of 1851. The advantages accruing to currency expansion seemed irresistible: it reduced public indebtedness at a rate that would have been impossible under conditions of stable money; and, perhaps more important, it enabled Rosas to maintain his administration without increasing the tax burden on the rural sector of the provincial economy.[116] The issue of paper currency did elevate prices and depress wages, thus producing a redistribution of incomes against the poorer sectors of society. The landowners obviously favored this scheme over forced loans and higher taxes.[117]

At every turn, the governor seemed poised to patronize his wealthy clientele. Estancieros obviously endeavored to monopolize commercial relations between town and countryside. Nevertheless, they encountered a considerable challenge to their claims with the *pulperías volantes* (traveling stores), which toured rural districts marketing such products as beef, hides, tallow, ostrich skins and feathers, and urban merchandise. Regarded as economically and socially subversive by the landed elite, the *pulperías* utilized carts and wagons to trade with anyone they met—sometimes in articles stolen from estancias. Rosas, hostile to the *pulperías volantes*, brought full executive pressure to bear upon them. Having forbidden them on his own estates, he extended the proscription to the whole province in 1831. The ban was never lifted while Rosas occupied the governor's seat; the law treated violators as *vagos* (vagrants) and conscripted them into the army.[118]

Saladeros (meat-salting plants) also felt the protective cloak of a friendly regime. In 1849, Rosas declared to the Assembly that "these great establishments deserve the protection of the government, because they are factories which are vital to the national wealth."[119] They constituted the largest industry in Buenos Aires by virtue of the number of people employed and the amount of capital invested. As such, the governor actively promoted the *saladeros* by providing generous tax exemptions. The customs law of 1835 exempted from export tax all jerked beef shipped in national vessels. In 1852, the total revenue of the provincial government stood at 45,195,332 pesos, only 100,000 of which were derived from duties on *saladeros*. As a result of this protection, the plants increased their output of jerked beef from 113,404 quintals (worth 1,462,042 pesos) in 1835 to 198,046.5 (2,915,796 pesos) in 1841, to finally 431,873 in 1851.[120]

Conclusion

As a populist leader, Rosas could not overtly and exclusively serve, in almost conspiratorial fashion, the interests of his own economic class. To claim that he acted as the puppet of his powerful estanciero clientele would strip this extraordinary historical personage of the charismatic dynamism that allowed him to walk the political tightrope between the upper and lower echelons of Argentine society. Nevertheless, the evidence presented necessarily leads to the conclusion that the governor sought to promote the estanciero-dominated economy and that he, in turn, received important political backing from the landowners. With such solid internal support, Rosas's ostensibly impregnable position appeared vulnerable only to external shock.

That Rosas maintained a delicate balance of all the elements of his populist coalition—gauchos, Indians, blacks, city dwellers, the Catholic Church, and estancieros—lies utterly beyond doubt. Rosas consolidated this disparate and amorphous collectivity by providing political and economic benefits to his adherents. Indeed, the most striking aspect of his political genius rested with his ability to satisfy the diverse and even contradictory claims of his followers. The Argentine people found Rosas uniquely qualified to rule a tumultuous nation. Thus, populism constituted the vehicle through which the governor executed his self-proclaimed duty to reorder society.

Examination of the causes for Rosas's demise lies beyond the scope of this work. It is worthy of note, however, that the *exogenous* hostility that precipitated the chief executive's fall emanated from Entre Ríos, Corrientes, Brazil, Uruguay, and Paraguay. The interior provinces had long resented Buenos Aires's control of customs, monopoly of federal revenue, and proscription of free commerce. Led by Entre Ríos estanciero Justo José de Urquiza, whose caudillo political profile resembled that of his vanquished victim, the combined Grand Army defeated Rosas in the famous Battle of Monte Caseros on February 3, 1852. Even as Rosas prepared to flee into exile, George Pendleton observed that the general still "exerts an irresistible [*sic*] influence on the minds of many people."[121] The fact that Rosas was ousted by outside forces confirms to a great degree the existence of a firm populist base buttressing his sovereignty.

Nevertheless, Conniff points out that the inherent weakness in such a populist state lies with the inability of its leader to delegate authority and to groom a successor. While *estancieros* comprised his social and economic peer group, the governor still found it difficult to share true authority. As early as September 14, 1835, Dorr reported that "General Rosas is little accessible to influence—only the brothers Nicolás and Tomás Anchorena are supposed to enjoy his confidence; his ministries are mere tools." On September 22, 1851, Pendleton complained to Daniel Webster that Rosas was "really assisted in his administration by no human being but his daughter." Power he retained in his own hands, and he was so sure that his command sprang from himself that he once hinted of the possibility of transferring power to Manuela.[122] Perhaps, then, the *rosista* state was destined to fall by virtue of its topheaviness.

Notes

1. Academicians have debated the definition of "populism" without achieving unanimity. Argentine sociologist Torcuato di Tella construes it as "a political movement which enjoys the support of the mass of the working class and/or peasantry but which does not result from the autonomous organizational power of either of these two sectors" (quoted in Michael Conniff, "Introduction," in *Latin American Populism in Comparative Perspective*, ed. Conniff [Albuquerque, 1982], 14–16, 25). G. Hall highlights the significance of the return to more traditional values emanating from the people, such as native culture and political and economic philosophies (quoted in ibid., 25).

2. Ibid., 21–23.

3. The historiography of the Rosas period remains enshrouded in polemic. The liberal tradition of Argentine scholarship, begun by Domingo Sarmiento, depicts Rosas as an indomitable leviathan who raised tactics of terror to unspeakable consummation and who caused his country to languish in the Dark Ages. Nationalist interpretations, exemplified by works of Ricardo Rojas and José María Rosa, contend that Rosas, boasting the support of a large segment of the population, simply represented the authoritarian product of his times. See Joseph Barager, "Historiography of the Río de la Plata Area," *Hispanic American Historical Review* 39, no. 4 (1959): 588–642; José María Rosa, *Defensa y pérdida de nuestra independencia económica* (Buenos Aires, 1954); Domingo Sarmiento, *Life in the Argentine Republic in the Days of the Tyrants* (1868; New York, 1971).

4. James Scobie, *Argentina: A City and a Nation* (New York, 1964), 88–89; John Lynch, *Argentine Dictator: Juan Manuel de Rosas, 1829–1852* (Oxford, 1981), 30–34.

5. Winthrop Wright, *British-Owned Railways in Argentina* (Austin, Tex., 1974), 8–9.

6. Ibid.

7. Ibid; Lynch, *Argentine Dictator*, 30–33.

8. Lynch, *Argentine Dictator*, 30–33.

9. Ibid., 43–44.

10. John Forbes, "Despatches to Secretary of State Henry Clay," 3 December 1828, no number, *Despatches from United States Ministries to Argentina* (Washington, D.C., 1952).

11. Forbes, "Despatches to Secretary of State Martin Van Buren," 9 De-

cember 1829, no. 87, *Despatches from United States Ministries to Argentina.*

12. Manuel Gálvez, *Vida de Don Juan Manuel de Rosas* (Buenos Aires, 1940), 14.

13. Lynch, *Argentine Dictator,* 12.

14. Ibid., 13–15.

15. Ibid., 23–25; Jonathan C. Brown, *A Socio-economic History of Argentina, 1776–1860* (New York, 1979), 110, 137, 179, 185–86.

16. Gálvez, *Vida de Don Juan Manuel de Rosas,* 15.

17. Sarmiento, *Life in the Argentine Republic,* 35–36.

18. Lynch, *Argentine Dictator,* 109–11.

19. Gálvez, *Vida de Don Juan Manuel de Rosas,* 37–38.

20. Ibid., 35–38.

21. Lynch, *Argentine Dictator,* 109.

22. Richard Slatta, *Gauchos and the Vanishing Frontier* (Lincoln, Nebr., 1983), 110–12.

23. E. Bradford Burns, *The Poverty of Progress* (Berkeley, Calif., 1980), 686–91.

24. José Luis Romero, *A History of Argentine Political Thought,* trans. Thomas McGann (Stanford, Calif., 1963), 121.

25. Juan Manuel de Rosas to Facundo Quiroga, 28 February 1832, in *Correspondencia entre Rosas, Quiroga, y López,* ed. Enrique Barba (Buenos Aires, 1950), 71–72.

26. Antonio Dellepiane, *Rosas* (Buenos Aires, 1950), 85; Tulio Halperín Donghi, *Historia argentina: De la revolución de la independencia a la confederación rosista* (Buenos Aires, 1972), 302.

27. Romero, *A History of Argentine Political Thought,* 124–25.

28. Enrique Barba, *Cómo llegó Rosas al poder* (Buenos Aires, 1972), 26.

29. Lynch, *Argentine Dictator,* 26–27; Gálvez, *Vida de Don Juan Manuel de Rosas,* 13–14.

30. Lynch, *Argentine Dictator,* 28–29.

31. Romero, *A History of Argentine Political Thought,* 116–17.

32. Lynch, *Argentine Dictator,* 42.

33. Eduardo B. Astesano, *Rosas: Bases del nacionalismo popular* (Buenos Aires, 1960), 66.

34. Gálvez, *Vida de Don Juan Manuel de Rosas,* 121.

35. Astesano, *Rosas,* 66.

36. Lynch, *Argentine Dictator,* 42–43.

37. Gálvez, *Vida de Don Juan Manuel de Rosas,* 120–23.

38. Lynch, *Argentine Dictator,* 49; Astesano, *Rosas,* 67–68.

39. Lynch, *Argentine Dictator,* 53.

40. Ibid., 54–59.

41. Estanislao López to Rosas, 12 March 1832, in *Correspondencia entre Rosas, Quiroga, y López*, 190–97.

42. Eben Ritchie Dorr, "Despatches to Secretary of State John Forsythe," 7 March 1835, in *Despatches from United States Consuls in Buenos Aires, 1811–1906* (Washington, D.C., 1948).

43. Dorr, "Despatches to Secretary of State John Forsythe," 9 March 1835, in ibid.

44. Karl Frederick Graeber, "Buenos Aires: A Social and Economic History of a Traditional Spanish American City on the Verge of Change, 1810–1855" (Ph.D. diss., University of California, Los Angeles, 1977), 245–46.

45. Jonathan Brown, "The Bondage of Old Habits in Nineteenth Century Argentina," *Latin American Research Review* 21, no. 2 (1986): 10.

46. Roberto Etchepareborda, *Rosas: Controvertida historiografía* (Buenos Aires, 1972), 48.

47. Romero, *A History of Argentine Political Thought*, 121.

48. Lynch, *Argentine Dictator*, 17–19.

49. Ibid., 25.

50. Gálvez, *Vida de Don Juan Manuel de Rosas*, 31.

51. Slatta, *Gauchos and the Vanishing Frontier*, 35, 90–98.

52. Rosas, *Diario de la expedición al desierto, 1833–1834* (Buenos Aires, 1965), 21–24.

53. Ibid., 25–42.

54. Lynch, *Argentine Dictator*, 34.

55. Rosas, *Diario*, 44–45.

56. Lynch, *Argentine Dictator*, 40.

57. Ibid., 50–52.

58. Rosas, 4 April 1833, *Diário*, 151.

59. Rosas, 15 May 1833, *Diário*, 92, 98.

60. Rosas, 27 June 1833, *Diário*, 108; 12 January 1834; Rosas to Colonel Pedro Ramos, 2 September 1833, in *El Testamento de Rosas*, ed. Antonio Dellepiane (Buenos Aires, 1950), 111–14; Rosas to Estanislao López, 5 November 1835, in *Papeles de Rosas, 1821–1850*, ed. Felix Barreto (Santa Fé, 1928), 73–75; Rosas to López, 25 April 1836, in *Papeles*, 105.

61. Lynch, *Argentine Dictator*, 55; Slatta, *Gauchos and the Vanishing Frontier*, 35, 90–98.

62. Slatta, *Gauchos and the Vanishing Frontier*, 35, 90–98.

63. Ibid.

64. George Reid Andrews, *The Afro-Argentines of Buenos Aires, 1800–1900* (Madison, Wis., 1980), 97.

65. Ibid; Dellepiane, *Rosas*, 97.

66. Lynch, *Argentine Dictator*, 111–12.

67. Andrews, *The Afro-Argentines of Buenos Aires*, 97.

68. Ibid., 158–60.

69. Ibid., 99–100.

70. Ibid.

71. Ibid., 98.

72. Halperín Donghi, *Guerra y finanzas en los orígenes del estado argentino (1791–1850)* (Buenos Aires, 1982), 15, 88.

73. Andrews, *The Afro-Argentines of Buenos Aires*, 98.

74. Ibid., 100.

75. Etchepareborda, *Rosas*, 148–49.

76. Slatta, *Gauchos and the Vanishing Frontier*, 35.

77. Halperín Donghi, *Historia argentina*, 301.

78. Dorr, "Despatches to Secretary of State John Forsythe," 5 May and 14 September 1835, in *Despatches from United States Consuls in Buenos Aires*.

79. Rosas to López, 29 August 1831, in *Correspondencia entre Rosas, Quiroga, y López*.

80. Ibid.

81. Lynch, *Argentine Dictator*, 127–28; Graeber, "Buenos Aires," 164.

82. Lynch, *Argentine Dictator*, 133–34, 188.

83. Dorr, "Despatches to Secretary of State John Forsythe," 5 May 1835, in *Despatches from United State Consuls in Buenos Aires*.

84. Dorr, "Despatches to Secretary of State John Forsythe," 5 April 1835, in ibid.

85. H. S. Ferns, *Britain and Argentina in the Nineteenth Century* (Oxford, 1960), 210–11.

86. Ibid., 213.

87. Lynch, *Argentine Dictator*, 228–44.

88. Ibid., 244–46.

89. Amory Edwards, "Despatch to Secretary of State," 3 January 1844, in *Despatches from United States Consuls in Buenos Aires*.

90. Ferns, *Britain and Argentina in the Nineteenth Century*, 212.

91. Dorr, "Despatches to Secretary of State John Forsythe," 5 May 1835, in *Despatches from United States Consuls in Buenos Aires*.

92. Lynch, *Argentine Dictator*, 178–79.

93. Ibid., 132.

94. Romero, *A History of Argentine Political Thought*, 123.

95. Ferns, *Britain and Argentina in the Nineteenth Century*, 211–12.

96. Lynch, *Argentine Dictator*, 182–86.

97. Ibid.

98. Ibid., 71–72.

99. Carlos Ibarguren, *Juan Manuel de Rosas: Su vida, su drama, su tiempo* (Buenos Aires, 1948), 155–56.

100. Barba, *Cómo llegó Rosas al poder*, 150–52.

101. Lynch, *Argentine Dictator*, 52; Vivian Trías, *Juan Manuel de Rosas* (Buenos Aires, 1969), 34–35.

102. Andrews, *The Afro-Argentines of Buenos Aires*, 15.

103. Rosas, 17 May 1833, *Diário*, 98–100.

104. Slatta, *Gauchos and the Vanishing Frontier*, 96.

105. Miron Burgin, *The Economic Aspects of Argentine Federalism, 1820–1852* (Cambridge, Mass., 1946), 199.

106. Ibid., 199–200.

107. Ibid., 200.

108. Lynch, *Argentine Dictator*, 57.

109. Burgin, *The Economic Aspects of Argentine Federalism*, 200.

110. Lynch, *Argentine Dictator*, 58.

111. Slatta, *Gauchos and the Vanishing Frontier*, 96.

112. Burgin, *The Economic Aspects of Argentine Federalism*, 200; Lynch, *Argentine Dictator*, 58.

113. Lynch, *Argentine Dictator*, 58–59.

114. Ibid., 157–64; Brown, *A Socioeconomic History of Argentina*, 179.

115. Burgin, *The Economic Aspects of Argentine Federalism*, 184–85.

116. Ibid., pp. 216–17.

117. Lynch, *Argentine Dictator*, 62.

118. Ibid., 79.

119. Ibid., 80.

120. Ibid., 80–81; Brown, *A Socioeconomic History of Argentina*, 80, 109–12.

121. George Pendleton, "Despatches to Daniel Webster," 8 February 1852, No. 7, in *Despatches from United States Ministries to Argentina*; Dorr, "Despatches to Secretary of State John Forsythe," 14 September 1835, in *Despatches from United States Consuls in Buenos Aires*.

122. Ibid.

Jonathan C. Brown

Revival of the Rural Economy and Society in Buenos Aires

No one escaped the repercussions of revolution in the Río de la Plata region. The *levas* recruited hundreds of young men in the cities and countryside. Deserters turned to banditry, preying on cattle herds and plaguing the commercial routes. Gaucho armies lay siege to Montevideo; they invaded Paraguay and Bolivia and much in between. Once the Spanish forces had retreated, armed factions turned on each other as patriot politicians sought advantage. Long subject to Hispanic incursion, the Pampas Indians took advantage of the confusion and raided rural settlements and cart trains. Merchants had to pay forced loans and extraordinary taxes; landowners lost cattle; rural women suffered kidnapping by Indians and bandits; urban women suffered their men taken into the militias. In 1825, Buenos Aires began a protracted war in the Banda Oriental with the Empire of Brazil. More *levas*, desertions, and banditry followed.

It is little wonder that the once-bustling colonial economy of the region lay in ruins. The Bolivians stopped working the rich mines of Potosí, which, during the viceregal period, had been the engine of commerce in the interior provinces and of trade at Buenos Aires. Caudillos and their personal armies of horsemen took over provincial governments. They taxed their enemies and set up customs houses on provincial borders. In the interior, overland trade came to a halt and the river trades declined dramatically.[1] Ten years of war against the Spanish royalists served as a prelude to another twenty of civil war between the provinces gathered together—without Paraguay and Bolivia of the old viceroyalty—into the misnamed United Provinces of the Río de la Plata. In 1840, one *tucumano* considered that the previous three decades had been filled with disasters and misfortunes. "After the anarchy of so many years, after the sacrifices that these peoples [of the interior provinces] were obliged to make in the wars," he wrote, "they have remained submerged in the most dreadful misery, and they need many years of peace and tranquility in order to recuperate their lives."[2] It must have seemed to many an Argentine that, in the revolutionary wars, the long-term reward of victory became economic privation.

One area of the new nation was better situated than others to recover quickly from the economic and social dislocation. The port city of Buenos Aires and its prairie hinterlands to the south and west represented a haven from the prolonged economic decay. Although the riparian provinces and even the landlocked interior of Córdoba and Tucumán eventually participated in the foreign trade of the Río de la Plata estuary, Buenos Aires province reaped most of the benefits.

Blessed with a modicum of peace, the colonial cattle ranch, called the estancia, developed into a complex business venture in the early nineteenth century. Production and marketing of pastoral products, in fact, supported the development of a diversified rural society. Farming, far from being squeezed off the land, actually expanded in relation to growth of the urban market of Buenos Aires. Commercial growth created some truly great *latifundios* in the countryside. But the large landed units, which initially pushed back the frontiers toward the south, were reduced in size and their ownership diffused. Because of improvements in Argentina's economy in the first half of the nineteenth century, rural society on the pampas surrounding Buenos Aires grew vibrant, booming, and open to economic and social opportunity.

However, opportunities were not equally shared. The frontier did not create a social democracy in which all residents enjoyed equal chances to get ahead. Economic boom went hand in hand with the effective repression that curtailed the economic opportunities of mestizos, mulattoes, and blacks. Immigrant Europeans enjoyed greater social mobility than did native-born workers of color. Why was this so? Despite the social dislocations and the mobilizations of the popular classes during the revolution and civil wars, postrevolutionary society did not shake its colonial mentalities; social discrimination once again influenced how Argentines shared the products of economic development.

Dislocation and Rebirth of Trade

Buenos Aires province remained one of those remarkable economic success stories of early nineteenth-century Latin America. Naturally, it suffered Indian raids and marauding bandits, and its rural population supplied many a soldier for the Cisplatine War, raging on the East Bank (Banda Oriental) of the Río de la Plata, today Uruguay. Like other booming areas, Spanish Cuba, Rio de Janeiro, and the Central Valley of Chile, however, the province of Buenos Aires lay within easy reach of the world's shipping lanes. British, French, and United States merchant vessels increasingly put in to the estuary of the Río de la Plata, exchanging cloth, iron goods, and wine for hides and other cattle products. Even while the fighting continued in the interior, foreign trade at Buenos Aires rose. Approximately 107 foreign ships each year put in at Buenos Aires in the 1810s. In the 1820s and 1830s, the average yearly numbers had increased to 280 vessels. Ship arrivals at Buenos Aires amounted to 452 per year in 1840s and 674 in the 1850s.[3] River shipping to and from Buenos Aires also increased up to midcentury despite the civil wars, river blockades, and foreign entanglements. During foreign naval blockades of Buenos Aires in 1825, 1838, and 1847, smaller craft simply crossed to Montevideo to exchange Argentine hides and salted meats for manufactured goods.[4] However, cheaper imports from Europe did not ruin the internal trade of the Río de la Plata. Córdoba's textiles, Tucumán's timber and sugar, and Mendoza's wines were still sold on the Buenos Aires market.[5] Overland freight hauling via mule and oxcart from the interior, in the absence of Potosí's silver, however, could not compete with the more cost-efficient shipping of consumer goods from Europe.

Markets for hides and cattle by-products flourished, as did the cattle production of Buenos Aires. To meet the growing demands, a new processing industry began to develop at the port. *Saladeros*, hide- and meat-salting plants, were established in the southern suburbs of Buenos Aires. From the countryside, cowboys drove herds of cattle to these processing factories. By 1825, more than twoscore *saladeros* were slaughtering approximately 70,000 head of cattle a year at Buenos Aires. As trade expanded throughout the 1830s and 1940s, so did the meat- and hide-salting industry. *Saladeros* at midcentury were processing more than 300,000 head of cattle and horses per year. These salting plants turned the slaughter of cattle into an efficient manufacture, but without dispensing with the traditional technology of man, horse, lasso, and *facón*, as the long knife common to Argentina was called. "The whole sight [of the *saladero*] is horrible and revolting," observed Charles Darwin in the 1830s. "The ground is almost made of bones; and the horses and riders are drenched with gore."[6] Meanwhile, the Industrial Revolution increased the output of textiles, and Argentine landowners also started to raise sheep in order to provide the cheap wool for carpet factories in New England and Great Britain. As the chief international port in the Río de la Plata estuary following the revolution, Buenos Aires also became the center of a complex of stockyards, warehouses, and slaughterhouses. Native-born traders collected the cattle and sheep products and sold them to foreign merchants, who then dispatched the cargoes by ship to the North Atlantic.

The booming shipping and processing industries during the postindependence period profoundly transformed the rural economy of Argentina. The pampas region of Buenos Aires changed from a hunting economy, as it had been for much of the colonial period, into one based on animal husbandry and the systematic production of an expanding range of pastoral and agricultural products. Grazing animals had always multiplied easily around Buenos Aires. European colonists brought sheep, cattle, and horses when they founded Buenos Aires in the late sixteenth century. Sizable herds of wild cattle soon roamed the prairies, giving rise to the *vaquería*, or commercial hunting expedition. Parties of gauchos chased the animals across the plains, capturing them with *boleadoras* and lassos. With their *facones* (long knives), the horsemen killed and skinned their prey. Besides the hides, the hunters took only the tongue for food and pieces of fat for tallow.[7] Cattle hunting clearly could not meet the demand that wider trade was to create in the eighteenth and early nineteenth centuries.

Gradually, a more systematic structure of production replaced the *vaquerías* in colonial Buenos Aires. As the city's population grew, so did its demand for fresh meat; hides also became a secondary commodity in the port's silver and slave trade. Some prominent citizens became hacendados, domesticating the cattle on lands granted to them by the city council. Landowners now hired gauchos, whose access to wild cattle, however, rendered them reluctant peons. When hacendados could not get enough wage labor, they purchased slaves to round up and brand the calves.

Soon the cattle hacienda spawned a more settled rural population. Resident peons and slaves lived in huts with their families, permanently caring for cattle, building corrals, and sowing wheat for themselves and *porteño* consumers. Many rural residents took seasonal jobs harvesting wheat and branding cattle. Incipient cattle estates began to form along the cart routes between Córdoba and Buenos Aires, and also north and south along the shores of the Río de la Plata estuary. Those haciendas laying along the Córdoba road raised mules for the interior trade and sold dried hides for export on the property. Very few cattle were sold on the hoof. On the coast south of the city, wheat, hides, and live cattle for the city's *abasto* (beef supply) were the chief money earners.[8]

In the late eighteenth century, the cattle industry developed to an even greater commercial intensity on the Banda Oriental (today Uruguay). The East Bank was well watered, more densely populated, and more protected from marauding Indians than the hinterland of Buenos Aires. Montevideo and Colonia became important late colonial emporiums for the collection of export hides. Large estates along the shoreline specialized in the domestication of cattle and produced large quantities of hides for export. The first *saladero* began processing cattle hides and salted beef for export on the Banda Oriental.[9] Paraguayan cowboys, many nearly pure-blooded Guaraní Indians and expert at handling horse and lasso, wandered through the Banda Oriental working at a succession of jobs herding cattle. They left their women and families back in Paraguay. Although there are as yet few studies on the extent of racial stratification in the countryside, aside from slavery, it is well known that Spaniards usually assumed positions of authority throughout the Río de la Plata. They predominated among the public officials, merchants, clergy, hacienda administrators, and master artisans. Persons of color found themselves in subordinate positions in the colonial social order.[10] The Banda Oriental, however, suffered the ravages of the revolution to a greater extent than Buenos Aires. The Argentine-Brazilian wars further arrested the recovery of the pastoral economy of this fertile but tragic land. Thus, in the first half of the nineteenth century, Buenos Aires province had few competitors in producing cattle.

The expanding export trade in cattle hides, sheep wool, salted meat, and tallow provided the catalyst for rural expansion. Rural population growth on the pampas even outstripped that of the city of Buenos Aires. While the number of urban residents increased yearly by 1.5 percent between 1820 and 1860, the annual population growth rate in the countryside reached 3.4 percent. In 1822, Buenos Aires had more than 55,000 inhabitants while the rest of the province had 63,000; in 1855, the city had grown to 90,000 and the countryside to nearly 184,000 persons.[11] Nothing characterized this growth and diversification more than the expanding range cattle business.

The Estancia Gains Efficiency

Prospective cattlemen initially acquired their land on the pampas from the government of Buenos Aires province. As in colonial days, quite often a simple declaration of vacant land (*tierras baldías*) sufficed for an individual to register a claim with authorities. In the 1820s, reform politicians led by Bernardino Rivadavia devised a policy in which the state rented out frontier land rather than giving it to private owners. Emphyteusis, as the program was called, allotted land in huge tracts, some thirty, sixty, and one hundred leagues square (one league equals 5.57 kilometers). The average grant varied between five to ten leagues, and foreigners as well as native-born residents received grants.[12] The collection of rents proved nearly impossible. When Juan Manuel de Rosas became governor, he sold the lands to the tenants and political friends on easy terms. Some paid in cattle and horses. Governor Rosas also made additional land grants to soldiers participating in frontier wars against the Indians. With little capital to stock the land, the soldiers sold their small grants to speculators.[13] The sheer abundance of virgin prairie, whose availability only the Indians contested, encouraged the granting of the original tracts in large chunks. Frontier estancias far to the south of Buenos Aires measured from ninety to three hundred square kilometers at mid-century.[14]

From the beginning, the commercial growth gave rise to a vigorous market in private land sales. The value of land in the province rose according to the value of its products. Land worth fifteen centavos per hectare in 1800 sold for three gold pesos in 1837 and fetched thirty gold pesos by midcentury.[15] Naturally, rising land values motivated owners to add improvements to their properties. Estancieros constructed wood corrals, *ranchos* for workers, sheds for storage and animals, ditches to protect fields of wheat and al-

falfa, orchards of fruit trees, oxcarts, residences for owners and majordomos, and perhaps a *pulpería* (country store). They also cleared
the pastures of prairie dogs and thistles. Bills of sale included all
these improvements as well as the livestock and brands.[16] Tenancy
also became a more common arrangement between owner and producer.

As land became more intensively utilized, the scarcity of labor
encouraged owners to maximize profits by renting our parcels of
their estancias to a family that would cultivate the land with their
own labor. Renting the land relieved the owner from having to raise
crops or care for milk cows with expensive hired help. Rental contracts contained additional commitments to rural property improvements, for renters typically obligated themselves to build
sheds and plant fruit trees. In the farming zone closer to Buenos
Aires, more renters than owners could be found in the 1840s and
1850s, although the absolute number of the latter was increasing.[17]
Foreigners were preferred as renters, just as they were desired as
pulperos. The owner could depend on them for stability, because the
military drafts applied only to males born in the province. As in
colonial times, Europeans moved into a middle-level social status
denied to native-born mestizos and mulattoes. Inasmuch as farming
gave the renter an income above subsistence, immigrants enjoyed
the opportunity of eventually buying their own parcels, despite the
rising cost of land.

Besides creating a market in land for rural residents, the government also provided frontier security. Clashes between settlers
and Indians were often sanguinary. When Charles Darwin passed
through the province in 1832, he noted that frontier estancias
were unusually well-fortified due to the constant danger of Indian
raids.[18] Indian depredations increased when drought threatened
the wild cattle and horses on which Indians subsisted and also
when provincial militia forces were engaged in conflicts elsewhere.
Mounted warriors armed with *bolas* and lances descended on isolated ranches. They killed the peons, stole herds of cattle and
horses, and kidnapped the women. Yet peaceful groups of Indians
always lived amongst the cattle estancias, tolerated even if not respected by the country folk. Employers wished to turn the seminomadic Indian into good peons. They were unsuccessful. Prairie
Indians were indifferent workers, and majordomos always suspected them of petty thievery. Frontier officials gave landowners

and their foremen the authority to punish peaceful Indians as if they were children.[19] For hostile Indians, the government maintained militia outposts on the expanding frontiers, and Governor Rosas regularized a colonial policy of requisitioning horses from the estancieros as a ration for the Indians.[20] By midcentury, ranches and frontier towns enjoyed relative security. But the Indian threat to the expansion of settlement would not be completely resolved until General Julio A. Roca's Conquest of the Desert in 1879. Indians were losing their ancient hunting grounds.

Natural conditions in an era before railways, barbed wire, and windmill water pumps also explain the extension of these early estancias. The coarse virgin vegetation of the pampas supported fewer numbers of livestock until extensive grazing gradually allowed the succulent, shorter strains of grass to grow through. Seasonal and cyclical water shortages also played a role. While one square league (thirty-one square kilometers) of good pasturage might support as many as fifty thousand sheep in good seasons, it was hardly sufficient to support less than one-third that number through years of water shortage.[21] During the 1830 drought, estancieros removed their herds completely from pastures having no water at all, selling cheaply to others or relying on relatives who still had fresh water lagoons on their properties.[22] Argentina's cattle business in the nineteenth century necessitated production on large landed estates because traditional ranching techniques placed a ceiling on the efficiency of land use. But as production became more intensive, when land was converted from cattle to sheep and from sheep to crops, the efficient landed unit of production decreased in size. This process continued throughout the early nineteenth century on the pampas within the province of Buenos Aires.

The boom in foreign trade made investment in cattle estancias quite profitable for Argentine businessmen. Old merchant families, eased out of export commerce by foreign traders, converted their assets to land and cattle.[23] In the 1820s, the Anchorena merchant clan shifted capital from overseas and river commerce to ranching, eventually creating the largest of all the cattle operations. By 1864, the Anchorenas owned 9,582 square kilometers (or more than 1.6 million acres) of ranch land on the rich pampas.[24] Wealthy landowners lived in Buenos Aires, leaving daily ranch management in the hands of resident managers and foremen. In the port city, they dealt directly with merchants who collected goods for export and with slaughterhouse owners, who sought timely delivery of fattened steers. Argentine estancieros were not disinterested absentee landlords but successful businessmen who linked the production of the countryside to domestic and export markets in the city.

Despite the visibility of wealthy ranchers, the family ranch and family farm was by far the most common productive unit on the pampas. A majority of the ranchers lived on comparatively modest spreads, which they worked with the aid of family members and a few hired hands. Even on the larger ranches, the foremen and *puesteros* (in charge of *puestas* or pastures) would be family men, living in separate huts with wives and children. Their sons eventually might work for their father's employer. Native-born and migrant women were found on the prairies, although in fewer numbers than men. Yet they raised families on the *puestas*, farms, ranches, and in small towns; some took over ranch management when their husbands died. Few immigrant women, however, found their way into rural society. The typical rural residential unit was a farm or small ranch with six to eight persons: a man, his wife, their children, a peon, an orphan, and perhaps a slave or a *liberto* (those born to slaves after 1813 and considered chattel until age twenty-one, when they were to become free).[25] In addition, disparate sources seem to indicate a constant turnover of land tenure. Business failures, trade recessions, the effects of drought, and increasing costs of rural production provoked the sale and rental of numerous rural properties.[26] Most estancias were held by individuals and families; only occasionally in this era did one find ownership by religious organizations and companies. Quite often, landowners rented parcels of their property for the income needed to improve production on the rest of their land. Renting rural property offered newcomers, especially Europeans, the opportunity to operate ranches and farms in this era of growing markets.

Absence of formal credit institutions enhanced the importance of family financial resources in the early nineteenth century. Pastor Obligado, who in the 1850s operated a family cattle estate with a brother and a cousin, secured investment funds from a number of relatives. Sales of cattle during slaughtering season then permitted him to repay these loans and also to pay a yearly stipend to the family matriarch, the widow Obligado, who had inherited a share of the property. Another rancher, Antonio Soler, depended upon his family for two-thirds of the capital needed to begin operations in

1848. For the remainder, he acquired a bank loan of 840 gold pesos. Soler used the capital to purchase cattle, to repair corrals and buildings, and to pay itinerant peons for rounding up and branding the livestock. Within two years, he easily paid off the bank credit in five installments—paying 2 percent monthly interest on the principal.[27]

If costs and interest rates were high, estancieros continued to gain worthwhile profits on their investments. Profitability nearly matched the reproductive rate of livestock herds, although the popular legend that ranchers of the era enjoyed profit rates of 30 percent seems exaggerated. In fact, a true calculation of profit rates for early nineteenth-century cattle ranching is difficult. We have little information about total investment in these estates. But there is evidence about the yearly expenditures and income of various ranches. Extant account books reveal that income exceeded expenditures among the larger ranches and farms by 15 to 20 percent in good years, but certainly not each year.[28] Argentine ranching appeared to have been profitable, except that Indians, droughts, and scarce labor also made it a risky venture.

In order to supply the growing demand for pastoral goods, estancias had to solve the one problem that earlier had plagued the colonial cattle industry—stock reductions. Droughts always threatened to desiccate cattle and sheep. Wholesale slaughter to capitalize on favorable export prices frequently endangered the cattle population as well.[29] *Saladeros* proved dangerously efficient, and the government suspended their slaughtering operations in 1819 in order to protect Buenos Aires urban consumers from a scarcity of meat.[30] Clearly, cattlemen would have to rationalize the grazing industry, domesticate and control the herds, compensate for the scarcity of labor in the countryside, and account for the rude technology of pastoral production. These factors largely explain the characteristics of the estancia in nineteenth-century Argentina.

Expanding foreign trade accounts for much of the profit margin in ranching, yet Argentine producers themselves streamlined and rationalized cattle production. After all, cattlemen had to contend with a gradual decline in the prices of pastoral raw materials in Buenos Aires' markets. They perfected the roundup, branding, and care of newborn livestock through diligent management of herds and flocks.[31] Selective cattle breeding by castration rather than by the introduction of blooded stock assured the maximum reproduction of domesticated animals destined for *porteño* slaughterhouses.

Sheepmen did improve the stock, importing fine merino and South-down sheep in order to increase the length and weight of the wool fleeces. Merino wool brought more than twice the price of wool from the mixed breeds and six times that of native sheep.[32] Because labor was scarce and expensive, ranchers had to make other improvements in production to remain competitive in international markets, and they succeeded.

The major cost-saving breakthroughs for the cattle industry came in the marketing of livestock and livestock products. In the 1810s as in colonial times, the estanciero butchered most of his own cattle and prepared the hides and tallow at the ranch. An account book for 1812 reveals that one rancher made only 12 percent of his revenues from the sale of live cattle—probably to the butchers who purveyed beef to the residents of Buenos Aires. By midcentury, however, the estanciero sold a major part of his herd on the hoof to the port's stockyards and slaughterhouses. Cattle drivers delivered great herds of up to eight hundred head of cattle directly to *saladeros*. Because the meat-salting plants also produced tallow and grease, the cattleman had to provide steers and cows with "fat meat."[33] Moreover, estancieros also delivered cattle and horses on the hoof to the provincial government. These animals traveled to the frontier for the supply of the military posts and Indians. In the 1830s, the Anchorenas were dispatching great herds, numbering as many as 1,300 head of cattle and horses, as far south as the fort of Bahía Blanca. There were times, however, when this arrangement created more trouble than income for landowners. The provincial government in the 1810s and 1820s did not always have enough money to pay for the requisitioned animals.[34] The estanciero now garnered 70 percent of his revenues from the sale of live animals.[35] Much of the costly processing of pastoral goods on the ranch was eliminated.

While larger estancieros in the city marketed their own products, the smaller cattlemen and farmers depended upon the development of a rural marketing system. In Buenos Aires, merchants specialized in exchanging imported goods and consumer items for the pastoral goods of the countryside.[36] Independent cartmen, cattle drivers, and country merchants (*pulperos*) in the rural areas collected the livestock, hides, wool, tallow, and grease for delivery to the stockyards and warehouses of the port city. For example, two carters named Moncada and Cuevas shared the freight traffic between Buenos Aires and Dolores on the southern frontier. In the small rural towns, which multiplied as the frontier was pushed back, blacksmiths, builders, and carpenters gathered. They constructed the capital improvements to the surrounding ranches and farmlands. Small merchants collected export products and sold imported goods, liquor, horse equipment, tobacco, yerba mate, and playing cards. Commercial and artisan shops spread onto the prairies at the same time that ranches and farms were formed. In 1854 alone, 244 new commercial concerns and 151 artisan shops were established.[37] Migrants from the interior provinces came to rural communities to seek seasonal work in shearing and branding and to work throughout the rest of the year as cattle drivers and carters. That 39 percent of the rural population at midcentury resided in the small villages of the pampas testifies to the importance of the domestic marketing system.[38] The expansion of cattle raising across the virgin prairies encouraged the growth of a sophisticated and increasingly efficient rural economy.

The Production Zones

By midcentury, the countryside of Buenos Aires province had developed into three production zones extending outward along lengthening radii from the city (see Map 3). First came the agricultural zone, then a mixed zone of farming and ranching (where most of the sheep ranches were located), and finally the cattle-ranching zone.

Each zone produced a range of goods but specialized in its own products (see Table 10.1). Inputs of manpower and foreign tools boosted agricultural production on those lands close to the domestic market of Buenos Aires. In the 1850s, at least 10 percent of all rural males either owned or rented farms—not to mention the additional number of peons and itinerant workers in agriculture.[39] Therefore, land closer to the city tended to be densely populated, intensively utilized, and more valuable. One found a more complex and diversified rural society nearer to Buenos Aires. Conversely, frontier land was sparsely populated, less intensively exploited, and cheaper.

Agriculture dominated the rural areas close to the port city. *Chacras* (farms) in this area were given over to the cultivation of perishable foodstuffs for the local market: squashes, peaches, potatoes, pumpkins, turnips, onions, and lettuce. European immigrants, such as Basques and Galicians, were prominent in cultivating foodstuffs

Table 10.1
Rural Production in Buenos Aires Province by Zone, 1854

	Zones		
	Agricultural	*Mixed*	*Ranching*
Live cattle delivered (no.)	29,161	44,992	201,530
Cattle- and horsehides (no.)	49,889	59,729	114,390
Wool (arrobas)	6,844	17,507	1,479
Wheat (fanegas)	17,176	10,048	15,801

Source: *Registro estadístico de Buenos Aires, 1854* (Buenos Aires, 1855), 55; *Registro estadístico de Buenos Aires, 1855,* 2 vols. (Buenos Aires, 1856), 2:76.

for the urban market.[40] Native-born rural residents subsisted traditionally on yerba mate, beef, salt, and tobacco. Immigrant farmers raised chickens and dairy cows in this agricultural belt, milking at dawn and delivering eggs, milk, butter, and cheese to Buenos Aires each day by horseback. Ditches, bushes, and cactus barriers generally protected the *chacras* from wandering livestock.[41] Immigrants rented at first but in time began to buy their own farms. Within this area, farmers grew wheat, barley, corn, and alfalfa. Wheat growing had declined somewhat during the 1820s, when low tariffs permitted the import of cheaper flour from the United States. Later, Governor Rosas instituted a tax on imports of wheat.[42] Argentine agriculture needed tariff protection because local farming methods were rather crude and inefficient; transport by oxcarts was costly, and labor was scarce.

Transportation to and from the Buenos Aires marketplace determined the proximity of farming to the city, because bullock carts proved too slow to market perishable foodstuffs. Moreover, ranchers discouraged cultivation on the outlying estancias, these larger estates farthest from the city specializing almost exclusively in raising cattle and horses.[43] On the frontiers, crops for local consumption were produced on land surrounding the rural towns. Still, agriculture flourished. The foundation of new farms easily outstripped—in total units if not in size—the establishment of new cattle estancias. In the last six months of 1854, for example, 381 new farms came into existence, compared to only 191 livestock ranches. Along with other products, farmers marketed nearly 325,000 bushels of wheat

Table 10.2
Place of Origin, Buenos Aires Rural Population, 1854

Origin	Men (%)	Women (%)	Total (%)
Native to Buenos Aires	39.8	34.8	74.6
Migrant from interior	9.0	5.9	14.9
Foreigner	7.6	2.9	10.5
Total	54.5	43.6	100.0

Source: *Registro estadístico de Buenos Aires, 1854* (Buenos Aires, 1855), Table 9.

in that same half-year period.[44] On the pampas, the family farm had not succumbed to the production of cattle products for export but complemented the export sector.

Cattle occupied the area between the sheep runs and the expanding frontiers, where they held sway for several reasons. Cattle could graze on the rough, tall grasses of the virgin pampas, whereas sheep thrived on the short grasses. The latter sprouted when a generation or so of cattle had eaten down the tall weeds and yearly burning had "sweetened" the rough pastures.[45] The sheep walks in Argentina's second productive belt, after all, once had been cattle country. Cattle also were wide-ranging grazers and required land on which to roam. Typically, cattlemen (and sheepmen, too) needed both lowland and highland pastures. In the summer months, grasses on the high pastures were usually parched and useless, so herds grazed on the grasses of lowlands that had been marshes during the wet, winter months.[46] Given the need for expansive pasturage, it was logical to start new herds on the cheaper ranges of the frontier areas. Finally, cattle were delivered to the market more easily on the hoof. Sheep raisers, on the other hand, sent their wool and sheepskins to Buenos Aires via oxcart or, if near the ocean, via coastal shipping.

Constant expansion of all three production belts offered much economic and social opportunity for newcomers. By midcentury, a quarter of the rural population on the pampas had been born outside Buenos Aires province. An 1854 census of the province's rural population, then numbering more than 183,000 persons, noted the breakdown given in Table 10.2. While native Creoles and migrants worked the cattle, industrious immigrants found jobs in sheepherding, construction, artisanry, and petty merchandizing. Newcomers

Table 10.3

Rural Occupation in Buenos Aires Province, 1854 (as percentage of total adult male population)

	Zones		
Occupation	*Agricultural (%)*	*Mixed (%)*	*Ranching (%)*
Ranch owner	9.4	7.1	8.5
Ranch renter	4.3	12.0	13.0
Farm owner	8.5	2.6	3.4
Farm renter	4.1	9.7	3.9
Peon	26.5	43.2	42.6
Merchant	9.1	6.2	7.3
Artisan	6.6	3.4	2.7
Military	0.9	0.4	2.8
Other	24.0	14.6	11.0
Without occupation	6.6	0.8	4.8
Total	100.00	100.00	100.00

Source: *Registro estadístico de Buenos Aires, 1854* (Buenos Aires, 1855), table 10. Ten of thirteen agricultural districts, thirteen of thirteen mixed districts, and twenty-two of twenty-five ranching districts reporting.

seemed to find greater opportunities in the agricultural zone, where the infrastructure was more highly developed (see Table 10.3).

Besides economic opportunities in the expanding marketing system, the immigrant also found advancement as a renter or land-owner. Large cattle ranches were subdivided numerous times between 1820 and 1850 as the value of the land and its products steadily rose. In order to remain competitive, owners realized they had to rent and sell parcels of their properties to reinvest in the oxcarts, wooden posts for corrals, lumber for houses and sheds, tools, furniture, kitchen utensils, supplies, and labor to run their remaining properties more efficiently. Landowners also parceled large properties among their sons and sons-in-law.[47] Older cattle estancias became numerous smaller sheep ranches, and the latter were divided further into yet smaller dairy and vegetable farms. Each step in the process intensified land use and rural production on the pampas. On the frontier, owners still held the terrain in giant tracts and worked them as huge production units. Land closer to the expanding markets of Buenos Aires underwent subdivision, and the units of production became smaller. In district after district straddling the Salado River, the larger cattle estates of the early nineteenth century gave way to smaller, more intensively worked properties producing sheep and eventually cash crops. Sons of estancieros and immigrant Europeans usually benefited from the spread of landownership; native-born peons did not.

Labor Conditions on the Pampas

The structure of the estancia followed traditional Hispanic patrimonial organization. Although the owner of large properties lived in the city, his control was more or less effective. He made all arrangements for marketing the ranch's products in the city. As a ranch administrator in the 1820s, Rosas managed the operation of his own ranches as well as those of his wealthy cousins, the Anchorenas. From his residence in Buenos Aires, he maintained the accounts and corresponded with his *mayordomos* at the ranches in letters and papers carried back and forth by messengers on horseback.[48] Studies show that the biggest estancieros in a particular sector of the countryside, especially in the sparsely settled frontier areas, effectively dominated the entire area through their monopolies of *pulperías* and the means of transportation, carriages and carts. Their control over the workers as a personal following, even as a personal militia, went a long way toward enforcing order in the rural hinterland.[49] Still, this control was never complete.

On the ranch proper, the *mayordomos* and *capataces* carried out the owner's will. *Mayordomos* managed the larger estancias, directing the work of more than twenty men, receiving and dispatching goods, keeping records, and communicating with the owner. The manager usually controlled the men through two or more *capataces*, or subordinate foremen. They were responsible for directing the labor of about ten workers each. Smaller ranches lacked the majordomo, and the *capataz* assumed the role. *Mayordomos* and *capataces* were expected to be able to read the owner's instructions, to count heads of cattle and horses, and to write down the size of herds.[50]

A few permanent workers were well dispersed throughout the estancia. Whether a cowpuncher or a shepherd, this permanent employee had the responsibility for up to 1,000 head of cattle or 1,500 sheep in a certain section of pasturage within the ranch. In his *puesta*, he maintained a rude hut and a corral. The herd assigned to this worker was the *rodeo*.[51] The *puestero* performed most of his duties on horseback, rounding up the cattle, riding the limits of his pasturage (which may have been several square kilometers) for strays. Branding and slaughtering, of course, were performed partly on foot. Shepherding, which included the washing and shearing of sheep, required more handling on foot; it did not appeal to the gaucho. Methods of paying the peons varied greatly: cowhands received wages and shepherds shared in the profits. British sheepmen gave their shepherds about one-third to one-half of the increase in his flock per year.[52] Cowhands earning a flat wage also received rations of salt, tobacco, and yerba mate from employers.[53] An ethnic division of labor evolved on the pampas. Native-born mestizos and mulattoes and migrants from the interior usually handled cattle; immigrants went into sheep raising, farming, and merchandizing. Native-born males were susceptible to the military drafts while the exempt foreign-born saved to buy land. The same kind of social process was marginalizing persons of color in the city of Buenos Aires, where immigrants also enjoyed opportunities for mobility.[54]

Manpower in the Argentine hinterland was always scarce in the nineteenth century. Estancieros especially complained of how levies of gaucho-soldiers for the militias drained the labor pool. Labor shortages also meant that landowners had to put off branding, castration, and other chores. As late as 1846, because of the lack of laborers, large numbers of cattle without brands wandered through the fenceless prairies of Chascomús. Several estancieros had to request the local military commandant to set his troops to branding the cattle. It was in the frontier area where the dearth of labor especially retarded agriculture. "The land all around here is very fertile, and ready for the plough," observed a traveler at midcentury, "but where the population is not sufficient to care for the cattle, they [*sic*] cannot be expected to attend to the labour of agriculture."[55] In times of crisis, such as the 1830 drought, cattlemen were unable to turn dying cattle into dried meat and hides or to move the herds to less desiccated pastures. Peons made themselves scarce and expensive. In fact, the ranch managers found that available peons held out for higher wages in the rancher's time of need. As the British traveler above concluded, "Resources of the country are altogether neglected for want of an industrious population."[56]

In the 1820s vagrancy laws were passed to limit the wanderings of gauchos and to curb their criminal behavior, such as cattle theft. Rural labor codes stipulated that peons were to be considered vagabonds liable to impressment into the provincial militia unless they carried certificates of satisfactory employment.[57] Some historians believe that the estanciero labor demands, together with the military levies, reduced the native worker's life of freedom on the pampas and disciplined him to become an immobile resident peon. "As the recruitments were always unjust and were applied to those who did not own property," writes Ricardo Rodríguez Molas, "the landed domain and the defense of privilege and cattle constituted the causes of the laws." Other scholars see these legal restrictions on gauchos not as a product of the developing economy but as a vestige of colonial practices against the lower orders of society or as testimony to the elite's concern about how the revolution had disrupted the traditional social order.[58]

Nonetheless, the intensification of land use on the pampas does not seem to have eliminated (indeed it enhanced) the individual's ability to move from job to job if not up the social ladder. Labor scarcity was endemic. Recruitment into the militias, the end of the slave trade, and the free birth laws had depleted the numbers of slaves in Buenos Aires province. In the 1820s, some of the larger owners sent agents to the interior to purchase slaves for their estates. Rosas accomplished this when he managed the estates of his cousins, the Anchorenas. He went to Santa Fé to buy at least forty male slaves, aged fifteen to forty-eight years, for various of his and the Anchorenas' ranches.[59] Moreover, *provincianos* also were coveted employees, because the press gangs could only recruit men born in Buenos Aires Province.

For the most part, the men in the countryside were native-born of mainly European or mixed blood. All called themselves *blancos* (whites), although many had a swarthy skin color. Some ranches also had many mulatto and black workers (*pardos* and *morenos*), descendants of African slaves. In the era of revolution, despite the voracious appetite of the militias, many estancieros still relied on the African-Argentine work force. In 1812, Juan Chacón, a Spaniard born in Andulusia and his wife, María Rosa Gómez, owned an estancia in Rincón San Pedro north of the city. Two sons and two daughters lived with him. So did three slave families, numbering nineteen persons, and three additional single male slaves.[60] African-Argentines still were contributing to the rural labor pool several

Table 10.4
Racial Distribution of Laborers in the Largest Estancias of San Antonio de Areco, 1854

Owner	Blancos	Pardos/Morenos
Isabel Carrasco	7	14
José María Sosa	4	18
Norberto Antonio Martínez	13	15

Source: *Registro Estadístico de Buenos Aires, 1854,* Table 9.

decades later. In the cattle district of San Antonio de Areco (population 1,668), the larger estates hired *pardos* and *morenos:* of those estates supporting more than twenty persons, the 1838 census listed the residents as given in Table 10.4.

Some Indians even lived in groups close to Buenos Aires. The religious estate of Chacarita de los Colegiales in San José de Flores had thirty-nine *blancos,* nine *pardos/morenos,* and thirty-eight *indios.*[61] But the elites considered these lower-class persons, the *gente de pueblo,* as fit only for wage labor. Lack of a rudimentary education prevented them from rising to the rank of majordomo, and social prejudices militated against affording them opportunities to rent land or to run a country store.

Meanwhile, the labor shortage also created opportunities for immigrant workers. They took jobs that self-respecting gauchos would not do—digging ditches to protect orchards and gardens from cattle, for instance. Irish and English immigrants worked for British sheepmen. English immigrants became adept at digging wells and constructing *bebederos,* watering holes for cattle. Often they charged, and received, more than the landowners wanted to pay. One enterprising Basque immigrant was able to purchase land and stock it with sheep after several years of traveling about the countryside in an oxcart buying wool and horsehair for resale in Buenos Aires.[62] Owners favored foreigners, especially literate Spaniards, as *pulperos,* operators of country stores. They were thought to be able to prevent the natives from running up their bills and to be immune from the latter's "weakness" for liquor and gambling. Immigrants had opportunities to save money and acquire property by first working as artisans and farmers. "I have often known poor [immigrant] men to make one hundred pounds a year each, in making ditches alone," remarked a foreign clergyman. "In a country like this, where there are no stones, a large number of labourers must find employment at work of this kind."[63]

Seasonal work harvesting grain, branding cattle, and shearing sheep existed in abundance, in part because the native-born worker refused to give his services full time. A continuous stream of men and women came to the pampas from interior provinces and as far away as Paraguay to accomplish this part-time work. During the cattle roundup and sheep-shearing time, the rancher obtained labor from the nearby rural communities. But a lack of men often forced sheepmen to hire women and children, usually native-born locals or *provincianos,* for shearing. One British sheep-raiser paid them 20 to 25 paper pesos per day plus food. When available, a male shearer commanded twice as much.[64] A native-born laborer who hired himself out with a string of his own horses could get 20 to 25 pesos per day in the cattle-branding season. The high pay encouraged some wandering peons to steal horses in order to gain this degree of independence. To attract workers, some estancieros were even willing to advance salaries and provide them ample credit at the *pulpería.*[65] Sheep and cattle raising remained profitable ventures despite the constant complaints about labor scarcity. Production efficiencies and strong external demand accounts for this profitability, for certainly labor was not cheap. Profits in agriculture, however, required the rental or sale of land to immigrants. Thereby, the big landowner shifted the problems of labor scarcity to the immigrant renter.

Despite the increasing labor demands, the militia recruitments, and the vagrancy laws of the first half of the nineteenth century, adult males working as hired hands may have been able to preserve some measure of dignity in the countryside. The perpetual labor shortage in this era of expansion favored the worker. His real wages rose from 7½ gold pesos per month in 1804 to 12 pesos in 1864.[66] Permanent labor, as opposed to seasonal workers, actually may have been quite stable, and satisfactory relationships between *peón* and *patrón* often passed from one generation to the next. Profit sharing was not unknown, especially among the foreign-born shepherds, who earned up to one-half of the sale of wool, grease, and sheepskins.[67] Furthermore, the resident peon supported his family on his employer's estate, where he had a hut, rations of beef, and a small garden plot. For instance, the Chacra San Francisco, an unusually large farm located forty kilometers southeast of Buenos Aires, supported approximately thirty persons—including the wives and children of four renters, four peons, and a *pulpero*. Itinerant laborers finding seasonal work as carpenters, brickmakers, tree planters, fencemakers, wool shearers, and harvesters numbered approximately forty persons per year.[68] Not only were actual labor conditions in the countryside more personal and satisfying to the peon than the harsh laws suggest, but estancia work supported numerous rural tradesmen and artisans as well.

Production on the estancia, of course, demanded a certain amount of diligence among the workers, and ranchers pursued worker productivity tirelessly. Rosas's detailed instructions to his *mayordomos* spells out exact procedures for everything from the care of horses to the branding of cattle and skinning of carcasses. He required that the herds be rounded up daily and counted often to prevent the straying of cattle. Dying animals were supposed to killed immediately and skinned, their carcasses being boiled down for fat and tallow. Animals killed for food were to be completely dressed and consumed. Cows in fold or with calf were separated from the herd and carefully attended. Within the first week, the calves' ears were marked for identification. Rosas was concerned that boundary markers on his estancia be maintained and that his neighbors' strays be returned immediately. No one was to sleep late. It rankled Rosas when his administrators could not keep an accurate count of the livestock. Other landowners also impressed various efficiencies onto their workers. The sheep raisers allowed their shepherds to kill some of the animals for meat but required that "the skin, tallow, and grease [be] set apart for the proprietor, and collected periodically."[69] Undoubtedly, many of these proscriptions remained unenforceable, given the dispersed nature of ranching, the shortage of workers, and the labor turnover.

In fact, much evidence exists as to the inability of the landowners to transform the native-born worker into a dependent, hardworking, and stable peon. Workers in the countryside had a long tradition of escaping labor discipline. They tended to take the day off whenever they felt like it—a day of rain was as good an occasion as any. Already, the gauchos had gained rights to leisure time on the numerous fiesta days. Employers needed permission from the police to get them to work during a festival. Moreover, the employer frequently had to put up with a lack of respect among his peons. They could and did insult the owners and their foremen.[70] The work habits of the native-born laborer apparently did not improve much with the growth of the provincial economy. Most refused to perform any work on foot—such as ploughing, ditch digging, gardening, or repair work. Apparently, native-born workers could not be left alone without strict supervision. Each estanciero had to be involved full time in the work of his ranch in order "to escape pillage" from his own workers. While the successful rancher may have lived in town, wrote one observer,

> he must still pass a considerable part of his time on his estate, to superintend personally the operations of buying and selling; for as those transactions take place generally between persons who know nothing of the arts of writing and account keeping, unless the payments come direct into the hands of the principal himself, sad mistakes are too likely to occur.[71]

Clearly, if the employer wanted diligence from his employees, he had to be there to enforce it. Otherwise, the peons took advantage of him, gaining a reputation for procrastination. Observed another foreign traveler, "a life of a procrastinator is an *everlasting tomorrow.*"[72] It was as if the *gente de pueblo* were purposely snubbing their social superiors, who already disdained the customs and skin color of the lower class.

The gaucho of colonial times had retained his freedom because of the availability of land and wild cattle, which gave him a means of subsistence other than working for a wage on the landholding of others. Nineteenth-century economic growth closed off that alternative to the country resident. Yet the rural rustic was resilient. He actually retained his personal freedoms because the growing economy not only increased the demand for his services but even multiplied his opportunities to move about and work as he pleased. Culturally, the work offered familiar social occasions steeped in the gaucho's own traditions. The cattle roundup on large estancias attracted as many as thirty itinerant peons and their strings of horses. Between lassoing, branding, and castrating the cattle, there would be beef roasts, singing and guitar playing, smoking and storytelling, horseplay, and mock or real knife fights.[73] As long as he was free to move about, the gaucho never felt out of his element.

The restrictive laws and militia recruitment, more arbitrary than systematic in their enforcement, never succeeded in reducing the workers' mobility. Short-term work contracts still seemed very much the norm. The horseman would work for three or four months and then ask for his pay so he could move on. The Anchorenas attempted to encourage a more permanent labor force by raising the wages of those who stayed six months or longer. Nevertheless, most of their workers stayed on for no more than nine to twelve months.[74] They were not called *mensuales* (monthly ones) for nothing. Peons also maintained a pernicious habit of leaving their work without notice. Formal contracts, where they existed, acknowledged the brevity of such employment and were written for short periods of time, like six months.[75] Given the scarcity of labor, the worker easily retained the privilege of leaving early. He could always find another job.

Each worker simply had numerous opportunities in this expanding rural economy. Even if he did not wish to dismount, the native-born worker could handle cattle for any number of estancieros, participate in cattle drives, sign on with a *saladero*, or work a team of oxen. No streamlining of the commercial system ever eliminated the numerous middlemen either, such as small peddlers, dealers in local goods, warehousemen, shopkeepers, and *acopiadores* [speculators]. Desperate natives could always dismount and shear sheep. Even hanging about the *pulperías* of Buenos Aires, the gaucho could get a two-week job here and there, obtaining a ration of bread and yerba in the bargain. Moreover, he could also depend on an estanciero or *pulpero* to help him in his illegal activities. He easily found buyers of a few hides taken from stolen cattle.[76] Such activity provided a time-honored alternative to wage work, which anyway was multiplying.

No doubt, the political problems and the arbitrary exercise of authority did provide some check to the complete freedom of the peon. Landowners took the passbook system seriously enough to make sure that their foremen and *provinciano* employees were registered with the local authorities. The police of Buenos Aires did apprehend some workers who lacked the proper documents, and press gangs were particularly active on the frontiers during times of political stress.[77]

But in the countryside the government only had the ability to be arbitrary, to enforce the vagrancy laws here and there. It could not be systematic for lack of resources and lack of cooperation from the powerful landowners. In 1826, the provincial government appointed two commissioners to eliminate vagrants and deserters from the countryside. One commissioner covered the north and the other the south. Just two! Already in the 1820s, the work of these men was compounded by the diversification of rural occupations, for not everyone in the countryside was a either a *peón de estancia*, with proper documents, or a vagrant. There were those who wandered about digging wells, for example.[78] Moreover, the landowners themselves sought to subvert the press gangs. Rosas the ranch administrator instructed his majordomos to mislead the militia recruiters. They were to claim that the peons of a certain frontier estancia had deserted their jobs and those who were working there actually were temporary employees from another ranch, which apparently exempted them from the draft. The claim was spurious.[79] The draft exemption for *provincianos* encouraged cattlemen to recruit workers from the interior. It also motivated otherwise respectable landowners to cheat a little. Rosas instructed his majordomos to tell militia officers that all his peons were born ouside the province. He also wanted them to claim that the only native-born persons at his ranches were, in fact, foremen and majordomos, yet another exemption.[80]

Later, when his accession to the governorship altered his perspective somewhat, Rosas's own militia recruitments seriously reduced the numbers of workers available to the rural estates. Yet his own cousin, Nicolás Anchorena, also showed himself unwilling to give up his workers to the draft. Anchorena was not about to deliver their peons for duty at the frontier military posts. He searched for loopholes in the militia recruitment regulations, resolving to notify the peons of the new regulations, then "leaving them in liberty to comply or not comply" with the law. "Neither you nor I have *obligations, power, or authority under the law* to oblige the peons to go" into the militias, Anchorena wrote to his foremen. "Take advantage of the opportunities to talk to the men so that they understand the exceptions they have by law."[81]

Therefore, the owners' efforts to rationalize the livestock business had to account for the peons' demands for personal freedom, if not for social mobility. Naturally, the landowners attempted to promote reproduction of the herds and to cut waste. Such actions represented profit to the estanciero. The problem was largely resolved by the 1830s, when capitalization and expansion of the cattle and sheep industry enabled the estancia to attain its nineteenth-century characteristics of size and profit. Although employers attempted to increase the efficiency and the rhythm of work, the peons turned the scarcity of labor—for which their preferences were partly responsible—to their advantage. They successfully demanded higher pay, moved from job to job, and flaunted the vagrancy and impressment laws. Landowners did not profit at the expense of the workers, however, but from the strong demand for pastoral products. The structure of the estancia proved flexible enough after all. It served as the chief mode of frontier expansion despite the scarcity of labor.

Conclusion

While the interior provinces stagnated or moved ahead slowly, the rural economy of Buenos Aires bounded ahead confidently, absorbing Indian raids, occasional uprisings, political divisions, and a chronic labor shortage. Admittedly, landholdings were large, a fact accounted for by the tradition-bound production methods of the day. Yet landed units were reduced in size and their ownership diffused. Stimulated by the cattle industry's need for an expanding rural infrastructure, pampas society displayed increasing complexity in its structure. Most country folk worked on the land as proprietors, renters, and hired hands. But natives, migrants, and foreigners also found opportunities in artisanry, commerce, and transportation. Much of the opportunity and diversity of rural society can be attributed directly to the development of the pampas as producer for the external market.

Meanwhile, the economic and social transformation of Buenos Aires province also further differentiated it from the provinces of the interior. By the 1830s, the trend was clear. Trade at the port of Buenos Aires was the single most important economic growth pole in the entire region. The province became the most populous and the wealthiest. Its politicians and state government became the first among provincial equals. As the so-called United Provinces restructured itself following the wars of independence, Buenos Aires province assumed the region's economic, social, and political leadership, which thereafter it would never relinquish.

Other inequities of postrevolutionary Argentina had their roots in the colonial social order. While the native-born working class salvaged a degree of autonomy and independence in the era of economic resurgence, it clearly did not enjoy social mobility. Expanding rural society tended toward the elimination of the prairie Indians. Economic growth also was shared unequally. The biggest landowners, themselves scions of colonial Spanish merchants, favored European immigrants in subordinate positions as renters and petty merchants. Native-born persons of color—be they mestizos, blacks, or mulattoes—found opportunities galore, but at the bottom of the rural social ladder. Sons and daughters of the *gente de pueblo* worked in the meat-salting plants and on ranches, doing the shearing, harvesting, and branding, driving cattle, and conducting oxcarts. They chose to exercise a measure of personal freedom in the developing but still rigidly stratified rural society. Native-born persons of color moved from job to job and searched for higher wages and leisure in defiance of the laws and contrary to the wishes of the landowners. Postrevolutionary rural society of Buenos Aires province became vibrant but hardly egalitarian.

Notes

1. Alfredo Bousquet, *Estudio sobre el sistema rentística de la Provincia de Tucumán de 1820 a 1876* (Tucumán, 1878), 25. For the economies of the interior, see Jonathan Brown, *A Socioeconomic History of Argentina, 1776–1860* (Cambridge, 1979), 201–7. Early travelers to the interior provinces noted the economic deterioration. See Joseph Andrews, *Journey from Buenos Aires through the Provinces of Cordova, Tucuman, and Salta to Potosi*, 2 vols. (London, 1927); Peter Schmidtmeyer, *Travels into Chile, over the Andes, in the Years 1820 and 1821* (London, 1824); Edward Hibbert, *Narrative of a Journey from Santiago de Chile to Buenos Ayres* (London, 1824); Francis Bond Head, *Rough Notes Taken During Some Rapid Journeys Across the Pampas and Among the Andes* (London, 1826); Luis Alberto Romero, *La feliz experiencia* (Buenos Aires, 1976), 46, 62.

2. "Después de una anarquía de tantos años, después de los sacrificios, que se obligó hacer á estos pueblos en las guerras han quedado ellos handidos en la mas espantosa miseria, y necesitan de algunos años de tranquilidad y de paz para establecer y recuperar sus perdidas" ("Copia de un acapite de carta escrita de Tucumán" [letter 184], Archivo General de la Nación, Buenos Aires, [hereafter cited as AGN], Colección Biblioteca Nacional [hereafter cited as BN] 679 [9939]).

3. See Clifton B. Kroeber, *The Growth of the Shipping Industry in the Río de la Plata Region, 1794–1860* (Madison, Wis., 1957), 73, 127; Brown, "Dynamics and Autonomy of a Traditional Marketing System: Buenos Aires, 1810–1860," *Hispanic American Historical Review* 56, no. 4 (1976): 607–8.

4. *Diplomatic Correspondence of the United States: Inter-American Affairs, 1831–1860*, ed. William R. Manning vol. 1, *Argentina* (Washington, D.C., 1932), 442–43; Kroeber, *The Growth of the Shipping Industry*, 108,

110; Vera Blinn Reber, *British Mercantile Houses in Buenos Aires, 1810–1880* (Cambridge, 1979), 16–19.

5. Miron Burgin, *The Economic Aspects of Argentine Federalism, 1820–1852* (Cambridge, Mass., 1945), 14–15.

6. Charles R. Darwin, *The Voyage of the Beagle* (New York, 1958), 104; Alfredo Montoya, *Historia de los saladeros argentinos* (Buenos Aires, 1956), 33–36; Brown, *A Socioeconomic History of Argentina*, 109–12.

7. For a description of the *vaquería*, see Horacio C. E. Gilberti, *Historia económica de la ganadería argentina* (Buenos Aires, 1961), 29–32, and Emilio A. Coni, *Historia de las vaquerías del Río de la Plata (1555–1750)* (Madrid, 1930).

8. Tulio Halperín Donghi, "Una estancia en la campaña de Buenos Aires: Fontezuela, 1753–1809," in *Haciendas, latifundios y plantaciones en América Latina*, coord. Enrique Florescano (México, 1975), 447–63; Samuel Amaral, "Rural Production and Labour in Late Colonial Buenos Aires," *Journal of Latin American Studies* 19, no. 2 (1987): 235–78; Carlos A. Mayo, "Landed but not Powerful: The Colonial Estancieros of Buenos Aires (1750–1810)," *Hispanic American Historical Review* 71, no. 4 (1991): 761–80.

9. See "Estancia del Rey. Cuentas de varias estancias encargadas a distintos capataces," 1800, AGN, Sala 9, 34-2-6 (2526); John Mawe, *Travels in the Interior of Brazil*, 2d ed. (London, 1823), 28–30, 34; Mayo, "Estancia y peonaje en la región pampeana en la segunda mitad del siglo XVIII," *Desarrollo Económico* 23, no. 92 (1984): 609–16; Brown, *A Socioeconomic History of Argentina*, 39–46; Juan Carlos Nicolau, *Antecedentes para la historia de la industria argentina* (Buenos Aires, 1968), 38–39; Ricardo D. Salvatore and Brown, "Trade and Proletarianization in Late Colonial Banda Oriental: Evidence from the Estancia de las Vacas, 1791–1805," *Hispanic American Historical Review* 67, no. 3 (1987): 431–60; Jorge Gelman, "New Perspectives on an Old Problem and the Same Souce: The Gaucho and the Rural History of the Colonial Río de la Plata," *Hispanic American Historical Review* 69, no. 4 (1989): 715–32.

10. Lyman Johnson, "The Impact of Racial Discrimination on Black Artisans in Colonial Buenos Aires," *Social History* 6, no. 3 (1980): 301–16; Susan Migden Socolow, *The Merchants of Buenos Aires, 1778–1810: Family and Commerce* (Cambridge, 1978), 18; George Reid Andrews, *The Afro-Argentines of Buenos Aires, 1800–1900* (Madison, Wis., 1980).

11. Ernesto J. A. Maeder, *Evolución demográfica argentina de 1810 a 1869* (Buenos Aires, 1969), 33–35; Mark D. Szuchman, *Order, Family, and Community in Buenos Aires, 1810–1860* (Stanford, Calif., 1988), 188–89.

12. See Jacinto Oddone, *La burguesía terrateniente argentina*, 3d ed. (Buenos Aires, 1956), 76ff, and Burgin, *The Economic Aspects of Argentine Federalism*, 96ff.

13. In 1833, for example, Nicolás Anchorena made cash purchases of the

land credits from nine army veterans. J. M. de Rosas to Anchorena, Río Colorado, 14 June 1833, AGN, Sala 7, 16-4-8; Horacio Juan Cuccorese and José Panettieri, *Argentina, manual de historia económica y social*, vol. 1, *Argentina criolla* (Buenos Aires, 1971), 384; Miguel Angel Cárcano, *Evolución histórica del regimén de la tierra pública, 1810–1916* (Buenos Aires, 1972), 44–46; Andrés Carretero, *La propiedad de la tierra en la época de Rosas* (Buenos Aires, 1972), 30; Halperín Donghi, *Guerra y finanzas en las orígenes del estado argentino (1790–1850)* (Buenos Aires, 1982), 219.

14. "Registro gráfico de los terrenos de propiedad pública y particular de la Provincia de Buenos Aires," 1864, AGN, Sección Mapoteca.

15. Pedro M. López Godoy, *Historia de la propiedad y primeros pobladores del Partido de Pergamino*, 2 vols. (Pergamino, 1973), 2:713–14.

16. "Testimonio de la escritura de venta," Buenos Aires, 21 January 1851, AGN, Sala 7, 16-4-11 (1736); Diana Hernando, "Casa y Familia: Spatial Biographies in Nineteenth Century Buenos Aires" (Ph.D. diss., University of California, Los Angeles, 1973), 262, 469–70.

17. Contract, n.p., 28 September 1821, AGN, Sala 7, 4-4-1; D. Vélez Sarsfield to Juez de Paz, Arrecifes, 21 November 1855, AGN, Sala 7, 16-4-11 (1770); Carretero, *Orígenes de la dependencia económica argentina* (Buenos Aires, 1974), 131–32.

18. Darwin, *The Voyage of the Beagle*, 88.

19. Report, n.p., 1825, AGN, Sala 7, 17-4-7 (1321); Juan Arista J. Anchorena, Averías, 7 August 1830, AGN, Sala 7, 4-4-3; Prudencio de Rosas to Manuel Morillo, Buenos Aires, 31 July 1831, AGN, Sala 7, 16-4-8 (1423).

20. Receipt, Ignacio Ibarra, Guardia de Ranchos, 14 November 1827, AGN, Sala 7, 4-4-2; William MacCann, *Two-Thousand Miles' Ride through the Argentine Provinces*, 2 vols. (London, 1853), 1:234; Hugo Edgardo Biagini, *Como fue la generación del 80* (Buenos Aires, 1980), 60.

21. See the descriptions of the pampas in Darwin, *The Voyage of the Beagle*, 101, and MacCann, *Two-Thousand Miles' Ride*, 1:198–99, 273.

22. N. Anchorena to José Manuel Saavedra, Buenos Aires, 20 August 1830, AGN, Sala 7, 4-4-2.

23. Hernando, "Casa y Familia," 22, 69–70; Luis Alberto Romero, "Buenos Aires: La sociedad criolla, 1810–1850," *Revista de Indias* 41, nos. 163–64 (1981): 143. For an appreciation of how many sons of colonial merchants went into ranching in the 1820s, compare the list of colonial merchants in Susan Migden Socolow, "The Merchants of Viceregal Buenos Aires" (Ph.D. diss., Columbia University, 1973), appendix D, to the list of emphyteusis titleholders in Oddone, *La burguesía terrateniente argentina*.

24. Brown, "An American Cattle Empire in Nineteenth Century Argentina," *Agricultural History* 52, no. 1 (1976): 605–29.

25. "Censo de habitantes: Capital y provincia de Buenos Aires, 1938," AGN, Sala 10, 25-6-2.

26. "Registro gráfico, 1836," "Registro gráfico, 1852," courtesy of Eduardo Saguier; E. Costa to Rosas, Montevideo, 5 September 1849, AGN, Sala 7, 16-4-10 (1722).

27. "Libros de cuenta corriente de Pastor Obligado," AGN, BN 800–801.

28. Halperín Donghi, "La expansión ganadera en la campaña de Buenos Aires (1810–1852)," *Desarrollo Económico* 1–2 (April–September 1963), 69–70; Cuccorese and Panettieri, *Argentina criolla,* 211, 218–19. Also see the ranch account books in AGN, BN 800, 801; "Libros de cuenta de Juan José de Anchorena," AGN, Sala 7, 4-1-7; "Papeles referentes a la administración de la Estancia Las Palmas perteneciente a Doña Ana María Otarola, 1844–1852," Museo Mitre, Buenos Aires, A1-C44-C71-no. 11.

29. As in 1822, when the arrival of a number of British commercial agents sparked the wholesale slaughter of cattle for their hides. See Alexander Caldcleugh, *Travels in South America During the Years 1819–20–21,* 2 vols. (London, 1825), 1:160.

30. Alfredo J. Montoya, *Historia de los saladeros argentinos* (Buenos Aires, 1956), 48–54.

31. Julio Broide, *La evolución de los precios agropecuarios argentinos en el período 1830–1850* (Buenos Aires, 1951). Juan Manuel de Rosas, the cattleman-turned-politician, wrote a comprehensive manual for the care and management of livestock. See Rosas, *Instrucciones a los mayordomos de estancia* (Buenos Aires, 1951).

32. Herbert Gibson, *The History and Present State of the Sheep-Breeding Industry in the Argentine Republic* (Buenos Aires, 1893), 24–26, 269–79; Wilfred Latham, *The States of the River Plate: Their Industries and Commerce* (London, 1866), 23–26; Hilda Sábato, "Wool Trade and Commercial Networks in Buenos Aires, 1840s to 1880s," *Journal of Latin American Studies* 15, no. 1 (1983): 49–81.

33. See Contract, Medrano y Soler and N. Anchoreana, Buenos Aires, 20 January 1949, and Contract, N. Anchorena and Mariano Haedo, n.p., 22 January 1849, AGN, Sala 7, 16-4-10 (1714), (1715).

34. Contract, N. Anchorena and Minister of Hacienda, Buenos Aires, 27 August 1835, AGN, Sala 7, 16-4-9 (1549): "Protesta de Rosas por saca de hacienda," n.p., 14 July 1824, AGN, Sala 7, 16-4-7, (1302). On the political favoritism involved in these contracts, see Halperín Donghi, *Guerra y finanzas,* 172.

35. "Estancia San Miguel del Monte de la Familia Roca, 1809–1812," AGN, Sala 7, 15-4-3 (libro 3); "Papeles referentes a la administración de la Estancia Las Palmas," Museo Mitre, A1-C44-C71-no. 11.

36. Larrea to Letamendi, 1 December 1848, AGN, BN 371.

37. *Registro Estadístico de Buenos Aires, 1854* (Buenos Aires, 1855), 50.

38. Contract, N. Anchorena and Vicente Letamendi, Buenos Aires, 17 August 1839, AGN, Sala 7, 16-4-9 (1630); Larrea to Letamendi, 26 May 1948,

AGN, BN 381; *Registro Estadístico de Buenos Aires, 1858* (Buenos Aires, 1859) 1:135. On the cart trade, see BN 226 (3270/118), and Contract, Jan Martínez and Manuel López, n.d., AGN, Registro Gómez, 1840.

39. *Registro Estadístico de Buenos Aires, 1854,* table 10. For trade in agricultural tools to Argentina, see United States Treasury, "Annual Reports of Commerce and Navigation of the United States," in *Executive Documents of the U.S. Senate and House of Representatives* (Washington, D.C., 1822–62).

40. Avelino Lerena to Mariano Lozano, Chacra, 23 May 1842, AGN, BN 300 (5435/285); D. V. Morete to Felipe Senillosa, Lomos, 18 May 1826, AGN, Sala 7, 4-4-3; J. A. B. Beaumont, *Travels in Buenos Ayres, and the Adjacent Provinces of the Rio de la Plata* (London, 1828), 31; Caldcleugh, *Travels in South America,* 152.

41. Head, *Rough Notes,* 23; Latham, *The States of the River Plate,* 34; John Miers, *Travels in Chile and La Plata,* 2 vols. (London, 1826), 1:11.

42. Burgin, *The Economic Aspects of Argentine Federalism,* 239–40.

43. Rosas forbade planting of any kind and enjoined his foremen to remove squatters. See Rosas, *Instrucciones a los mayordomos de estancia,* 16–17.

44. *Registro estadístico de Buenos Aires, 1854,* 50.

45. Latham, *The States of the River Plate,* 14, 17.

46. MacCann, *Two-Thousand Miles' Ride,* 1:273.

47. Cuccorese and Panettieri, *Argentina criolla,* 218–19; López Godoy, *Historia de la propiedad,* 1:217.

48. Rosas, *Instrucciones a los mayordomos de estancia,* 54; Rosas to Morillo, n.p., 6 November 1826, AGN, Sala 7, 16-4-7 (1320).

49. Halperín Donghi, "La expansión ganadera en la campaña de Buenos Aires," 91, 108–9.

50. Rosas, *Instrucciones a los mayordomos de estancia,* 54.

51. MacCann, *Two-Thousand Miles' Ride,* 1:279; Beaumont, *Travels in Buenos Ayres,* 64; Gibson, *The History and Present State of the Sheep-Breeding Industry,* 276; Latham, *The States of the River Plate,* 28; López Godoy, *Historia de la propiedad,* 1:37.

52. Gibson, *The History and Present State of the Sheep-Breeding Industry,* 276–77, Latham, *The States of the River Plate,* 1:177; Sábato, *Agrarian Capitalism and the World Market: Buenos Aires in the Pastoral Age, 1840–1890* (Albuquerque, 1990), 84, 92, 112.

53. Rosas, *Instrucciones a los mayordomos de estancia,* 54–55.

54. Karl Frederick Graeber, "Buenos Aires: A Social and Economic History of a Traditional Spanish American City on the Verge of Change, 1810–1855" (Ph.D. diss., University of California, Los Angeles, 1977), 101–4, 110–11; Romero, "Buenos Aires," 149, 153; José M. Mariluz Urquijo, "La mano de obra en la industria porteña (1810–1835)," *Boletín de la Academia Nacional de la Historia* 33 (1962): 607, 614.

55. Gibson, *The History and Present State of the Sheep-Breeding Industry*, 258; MacCann, *Two-Thousand Miles' Ride*, 1:62, 144–45.

56. N. Anchorena to José Manuel Saavedra, Buenos Aires, 26 June 1830, AGN, Sala 7, 4-4-2; Juan Décima to J. J. C. Anchorena, Camarones, 26 April 1830, AGN, Sala 7, 4-4-3; Woodbine Parish, *Buenos Ayres and the Rio de la Plata: Their Present State, Trade, and Debt* (London, 1839), 256.

57. See Halperín Donghi, "La expansión ganadera en la campaña de Buenos Aires," 99–100; Andrés M. Carretero, *Orígenes de la dependencia económica argentina* (Buenos Aires, 1974), 78; Ricardo Rodríguez Molas, *Historia social del gaucho* (Buenos Aires, 1968), 197–99.

58. "Como siempre las levas son injustas y las realizan con aquellos que no poseen bienes: la tierra impera, la defensa del feudo y del ganado constituyen las causas de las leyes" (Rodríguez Molas, *Historia social del gaucho*, 139). David Bushnell, *Reform and Reaction in the Platine Provinces, 1810–1852* (Gainesville, Fla., 1983), 23–24; Mark D. Szuchman, *Order, Family, and Community in Buenos Aires, 1810–1860* (Stanford, Calif., 1988), 20–21; Richard W. Slatta, *Gauchos and the Vanishing Frontier* (Lincoln, Nebr., 1983); Ricardo D. Salvatore, "Class Struggle and International Trade: Rio de la Plata's Commerce and the Atlantic Proletariat, 1790–1850" (Ph.D. diss., University of Texas, 1987), chap. 13.

59. "Filiación de los esclavos," 24 February 1825, 4 April 1825, AGN, Sala 7, 16-4-7 (1312), (1317); Receipt, José Manuel López la Rosa, Santa Fé, 14 April 1823, AGN, Sala 7, 4-4-3.

60. "Padrones de Buenos Aires: ciudad y campaña," 1812–17, AGN, Sala 10, 10-7-2. On the underenumeration of blacks in Argentine censuses, see Andrews, *The Afro-Argentines of Buenos Aires*, 87–89; Marta B. Goldberg, "La población negra y mulata de la ciudad de Buenos Aires, 1810–1840," *Desarrollo Económico* 61 (1976): 81; Socolow, "Buenos Aires at the Time of Independence," in *Buenos Aires: 400 Years*, ed. Stanley R. Ross and Thomas F. McGann (Austin, Tex., 1982), 22; Graeber, "Buenos Aires: A Social and Economic History," 180, 231–33; Luis Alberto Romero, *Buenos Aires criolla, 1820–1850* (Buenos Aires, 1983), 60.

61. "Censo de habitantes; capital y provincia de Buenos Aires," 1838, AGN, Sala 10, 25-6-2.

62. Morillo to J. J. C. Anchorena, Camarones, 24 November 1830, AGN, Sala 7, 4-4-3; Charles B. Mansfield, *Paraguay, Brazil and the Plate: Letters Written in 1852–1853* (Cambridge, 1861), 164; MacCann, *Two Thousand Miles' Ride*, 1:25, 99.

63. MacCann, *Two Thousand Miles' Ride*, 1:227–28.

64. Gibson, *The History and Present State of the Sheep-Breeding Industry*, 270; Latham, *The States of the River Plate*, 1:25.

65. MacCann, *Two-Thousand Miles' Ride*, 1:25, 58; Halperín Donghi, "La expansión ganadera en la campaña de Buenos Aires," 99–100.

66. Wages are quoted in constant "gold pesos" in order to compensate for the inflation of the circulating paper pesos. Juan Alvarez, *Las guerras civiles argentinas* (Buenos Aires, 1972), 67–68; "Libro diario de la Chacra San Francisco, 1860–1870," AGN, BN 739; Halperín Donghi, *Guerra y finanzas,* 228–29; Slatta, *Gauchos and the Vanishing Frontier,* 30, 35.

67. Latham, *The States of the River Plate,* 24–26, and Agustín Isaías de Elía, "Los Ramos Mexía: Historia y tradiciones de viejas estancias argentinas," unpub. ms., 95–97. I have read this manuscript through the courtesy of Eduardo Saguier.

68. "Libro diario de la Chacra San Francisco, 1860–1870."

69. Rosas, *Instrucciones a los mayordomos de estancia;* Rosas to Morillo, Cerrillos, 8 January 1826, AGN, Sala 7, 16-4-7 (1324).

70. Enrique Ochoa to Juan Moreno, Recoleta, n.d.; Pedro L. Echagüe to Moreno, Barracas, 7 February 1848; Ochoa to Moreno, Buenos Aires, 11 January 1851, AGN, BN 226 (3270/5), (3270/57), (3270/242); Anon., *A Five Years' Residence in Buenos Ayres, During the Years 1820 to 1825* (London, 1825), 69.

71. Beaumont, *Travels in Buenos Ayres,* 63–64.

72. MacCann, *Two-Thousand Miles' Ride,* 1:156; Caldcleugh, *Travels in South America,* 1:179–82.

73. Latham, *The States of the River Plate,* 32.

74. See the pay records in Morillo to J. J. C. de Anchorena, 22 and 24 October 1830, AGN, Sala 7, 4-4-2; Morillo to Saavedra, Camarones, 25 July 1827, AGN, Sala 7, 16-4-7 (1354).

75. Contract, Jorge Sanders and Pedro Lazala, Lobería, 25 June 1949, AGN, Sala 7, 16-15-4 (2236).

76. "Cuenta de gastos en la obra," Buenos Aires, 28 July 1827, Sala 7, 4-4-2; Sábato, "Wool Trade and Commercial Networks in Buenos Aires," 79; Slatta, *Gauchos and the Vanishing Frontier,* 120–21; César A. García Belsunce, *Buenos Aires, 1800–1830: su gente* (Buenos Aires, 1976), 93; Salvatore, "Class Struggle and International Trade," 820–22.

77. Rosas to Morillo, 24 October 1826, Rosas to Salvadores, San Martín, 12 November 1926, AGN, Sala 7, 16-4-7 (1335), (1338); Simón Pereyra to Moreno, Casa de V., 11 December 1846, AGN, BN 116 (3270/31).

78. Rosas to Moreno, Cerrillos, 18 January 1827, AGN, Sala 7, 16-4-7 (1345). On the lack of police in the rural areas, see García Belsunce *Buenos Aires, 1800–1830: salud y delito,* (Buenos Aires, 1977), 276–80.

79. Rosas to Morillo, n.p, 24 October 1826, AGN, Sala 7, 16-4-7 (1335); Cuccorese and Panettieri, *Argentina criolla,* 190.

80. Rosas to Angel Salvadores, San Martín, 12 November 1826, AGN, Sala 7, 16-4-7 (1338); Slatta, *The Gaucho and the Vanishing Frontier,* 128. Ricardo Salvatore has evidence that, later as governor, Rosas eliminated these

exemptions for *provincianos* and that in the 1840s a large percentage of the militia recruits were from the provinces.

81. "Dejando a los peones en libertad, para que cumplan ó no cumplan, por que *Usted, ni yo tenemos obligaciones, poder, ni autoridad por la lei,* para obligar a los peones, á que vayan. . . . Aprovechará si las oportunidades para hablar, de modo que la gente deja las excepciones, que tiene por la lei" (N. Anchorena to Morillo, Buenos Aires, 28 December 1834, AGN, Sala 7, 16-4-7 [1542]).

The Contributors

Mark Szuchman, who teaches at Florida International University, has written extensively on nineteenth-century Argentine social history, including books on immigration and mobility in Córdoba and on family and community in Buenos Aires. He has also edited a volume of essays on Latin American values and attitudes from the seventeenth through the nineteenth centuries. At present, Szuchman is managing editor of the *Hispanic American Historical Review.*

Jonathan Brown is professor of Latin American history at the University of Texas at Austin. In 1980, he won the Bolton Prize for a book on nineteenth-century Argentina, and his subsequent articles on Argentine history have appeared in the *Hispanic American Historical Review*, the *Latin American Research Review*, and *Ciclos.* Brown's current research focuses on Latin American labor history.

Samuel Amaral, having taught at the Universidad de La Plata in Argentina, is now an associate professor of history at Northern Illinois University. His published work concentrates on late colonial–early national Argentina as well as on Juan Perón. He has had a research appointment at the Hoover Institute at Stanford University, where he edited a collection of Perón's letters from exile. At present, Amaral is completing a book on the nineteenth-century economic history of Argentina.

Lyman Johnson, who teaches at the University of North Carolina at Charlotte, has written a textbook on colonial Latin America with Mark Burkholder. He has also published numerous articles and edited books on colonial economic history, on crime and the police in Argentina, and on the Spanish American political economy during the Independence period. Presently, Johnson is completing a book on the working class of colonial Buenos Aires.

Ricardo Salvatore is professor at the Universidad Torcuato di Tella. Presently, he is working on a book about markets, coercion, and workers' identity in early nineteenth-century Buenos Aires province. His articles on economic and labor history have appeared in numerous journals in the United States and Argentina. Salvatore has taught at the National University of Córdoba and the University of Minnesota and held research appointments at the Instituto Di Tella, the Institute for Advanced Studies at Princeton, and the Program of Agrarian Studies at Yale University.

Tulio Halperín Donghi teaches at the University of California, Berkeley, where he holds the chair in Latin American history. His book on politics, economics, and society in early nineteenth-century Argentina was awarded the Clarence Haring prize. His many other publications include influential articles published in Europe and the Americas as well as numerous books on Latin American and Argentine history. He is currently writing a comprehensive history of Argentina.

María Pilar González Bernaldo, a native of Argentina, earned her doctorate in history at the Université de Paris I. She has published numerous articles in France and Argentina, and her first book, *La création d'une nation: Histoire politique des nouvelles appartenances culturelles dans la ville de Buenos Aires entre 1829 et 1862,* is now at press in France. González Bernaldo has a teaching and research position at the Université de Paris VII-Jussieu.

Kristine Jones obtained her doctorate at the University of Chicago, where she wrote a dissertation on the indigenous peoples of eighteenth- and nineteenth-century Argentina. Several of her articles on that subject have appeared in Argentina and the United States. Recently, on a Fulbright fellowship, Jones extended her research interests to Chile. She has taught at the University of Illinois and Bowdoin College and is now resident director for the Council on International Educational Exchanges at the Pontifica Universidad Católica of the Dominican Republic.

Kevin Kelly earned a master's degree in Latin American Studies at the University of Texas in 1988. He then obtained a juris doctorate degree at the Georgetown University Law Center and is now associated with the Brown & Wood law firm in Washington, D.C., specializing in corporate securities work. The article in this volume is the outgrowth of Kelly's master's thesis.

Thomas Whigham associate professor of history at the University of Georgia, is author of *The Politics of River Trade: Tradition and Development in the upper Plata: 1780–1870* and *La yerba mate del Paraguay, 1780–1870.* Educated at Stanford University, he received his doctorate degree in 1986. Whigham is currently working on a history of the 1864–1870 Paraguayan War.

Index